GOETHE

A CRITICAL INTRODUCTION

GOETHE

A CRITICAL INTRODUCTION

BY

RONALD GRAY

*Fellow of Emmanuel College and
Lecturer in German in the
University of Cambridge*

CAMBRIDGE
AT THE UNIVERSITY PRESS
1967

Published by the Syndics of the Cambridge University Press
Bentley House, 200 Euston Road, London N.W. 1
American Branch: 32 East 57th Street, New York, N.Y. 10022

© Cambridge University Press 1967

Library of Congress Catalogue Card Number: 67–10256

Printed in Great Britain
at the University Printing House, Cambridge
(Brooke Crutchley, University Printer)

CONTENTS

Preface   *page* vii

PART I

1 Life and Works   3

PART II.   1749 TO 1786

2 Poems before 1786   27
3 *Die Leiden des jungen Werther*   48
4 Dramatic Works   56

PART III.   THE TURNING-POINT AND THE WHOLE

5 Autobiographies and Diaries   97
6 Science   114
7 *Faust Part I*   126
8 *Faust Part II*   160
9 *Wilhelm Meister*   186

PART IV.   1786 TO 1832

10 Poems of the Classical Period   203
11 *Die Wahlverwandtschaften*   216
12 *Der West-Östliche Divan*   226
13 Poems of his old age   240
14 Conclusion   253

Notes   260
Select Bibliography   271
Chronological Table of Goethe's life and works   274
Index   283

PREFACE

This book was written to provide a concise account of Goethe's works, including not only information about their sources, their relation to Goethe's life, position in German literature, influences, dates and so on, but also a critical account of how they have struck me after long acquaintance with them and some of the books written about them. I have been particularly concerned to distinguish as definitely as I can between those works which have meant a great deal to me and those which have impressed me much less. But I have not wanted to carp at Goethe's stupendous range of efforts, rather to bring into the forefront that way of reading works of literature which is being driven out by great quantities of the academic writing which appears these days. Of course information is required, especially about foreign literatures, if we are to gain a fuller understanding, and I have supplied as much of it as I could. But we get nowhere by merely registering this, comparing themes and topics, analysing characters, observing features of language, unless we have in our minds the basic questions—was Goethe what T. S. Eliot called him, 'one of the wisest of men', is he still what Matthew Arnold called him, 'the clearest, the largest, the most helpful thinker of modern times'? Do the words of Goethe's foremost admirer today, Emil Staiger, still stand—should we be asking not what Goethe means to us, but how we look in comparison with him, as a part of that standard of humanity, 'das Maß des Menschen', which he represents?

'That praises are without reason lavished on the dead', wrote Dr. Johnson, 'and that the honours due only to excellence are paid to antiquity, is a complaint likely to be always continued by those, who, being able to add nothing to truth, hope for eminence from the heresies of paradox.' As usual, the critic does well to listen here too to Johnson's admonition, especially if he proposes to question an established reputation.

But after all, if that reputation is securely based, its firmness will be seen and felt in the works themselves, or so at least we may hope. It is only from Goethe's works that we can answer the questions already proposed, and the answers will come only from the attempt at close involvement with them, feeling what they mean to us when we have got rid of as much insincerity as we can.

One essential part of any such study of Goethe must be a concern with his poetry, yet his productions were so varied and numerous that to give a reasonable account of them in an introductory work, while still keeping proportion with the whole, seemed impossible. This book was therefore written alongside a separate volume of selected poems, now published, in which information and criticism are offered in the 'occasional' way which seemed more suited to them. The chapters on Goethe's poetry in the present volume, amounting to a quarter of it, are meant to relate the poetic achievement to that in the drama and the novel, and so give comparatively little space to detailed observations on individual poems.

In the two volumes together, though, I hope to have made available a companion to the reading of Goethe which will spur readers to finding an answer to the questions proposed. If we cannot get from Goethe's plays what Johnson said we could get from Shakespeare, 'the highest pleasure that the drama can give'—and nobody is likely to make that particular claim—can we get a similar pleasure from some other part of his works? Or if not from his works, from his life and his works taken as a whole? My apology for writing this book at all, when so many thousands have already been published, is that (as a glance at Pyritz's bibliography will confirm) the amount of critical appreciation of Goethe, as distinct from biography, commentary, cultural history, and works of the 'Goethe and...' variety, is very small indeed. It plays a smaller part in this book than I would have liked, since a large part of my task was to inform. All the same, I should be glad to think it might arouse, even after initial opposition, at least a measure of general agreement. To quote Johnson, with a small adaptation, one last time: 'because human judgment, though it be gradually gaining upon certainty, never becomes infallible; and approbation, though long continued, may yet be only the approbation of prejudice or fashion; it is proper to inquire, by what peculiarities of excellence [Goethe] has gained and kept the favour of his countrymen'.

As on several former occasions, I am deeply indebted to members of the staff of the Cambridge University Press for help both in the composition and in the presentation of this study.

Cambridge   R.D.G.
March 1966

Faust conjures up the Earth-Spirit: Goethe's own drawing of the scene.
By courtesy of the Goethe National Museum, Weimar.

I

LIFE AND WORKS

> Where wast thou when I laid the foundations of the
> earth?...When the morning stars sang together, and all
> the sons of God shouted for joy?   Job, xxxviii

There is no writer so paradoxical as Goethe. His name is
mentioned in company with those of Homer and Dante,
Cervantes and Shakespeare and Tolstoy. He is not only the
German in the world pantheon, but also the one whom Carlyle
called 'the universal Man': a lyric poet, a draughtsman, a
playwright, a novelist, a translator, an actor, a theatre manager,
a minister of state, an administrator, a geologist, a meteorolo-
gist, a botanist, an anatomist, a student of chromatics, a
philosopher, a critic, a mystic, and a lover; and again, as a
writer, so large in his outlook that he could welcome influences
upon himself so various as Spinoza and Shakespeare, the botanist Linnaeus and the theosophist Swedenborg, the Bible along
with Propertius, Catullus, Tibullus and the Koran, Chinese
poetry and Voltaire, German legend and Euripides, Persian
poetry and Greek epics. He could send home-grown asparagus
to his mistress Charlotte von Stein, and meet Napoleon and
Beethoven on an equal footing. And with all this, he is known
to the world today by his *Faust*, which for all its profundity
remains for many people inaccessible, and by his poetry, which
in some of its best aspects is untranslatable. His plays are
scarcely ever performed outside Germany; his novels will not
bear comparison with those of the nineteenth-century masters,
the value of his scientific work is questionable, yet his genius is
beyond dispute. In Germany itself, although it is still sacri-
legious for any critic to doubt his professorially guarded
reputation, his eminence is the subject of satirical amuse-
ment too, largely because well-educated families are expected
to devote at least a yard of book-shelving to him. He has
been inflated so hard as a superior cultural asset that there are

3

sure to be some who will look so much the harder for a fatal flaw.

It would be an astonishing thing in any human being if no such flaw were to be found. What matters in the case of Goethe is not so much that a flaw is there, as the reason why it is there. He is one of the first of those who, in the wake of Rousseau (1712–78), saw their lives as demanding no other justification than that they had been lived, and lived intensely. That is what he meant when he wrote 'Der Zweck des Lebens ist das Leben selbst', 'the aim of living is Life itself'—not Life in any merely material sense, of course, but in the fullest sense imaginable. Goethe did not see Life as a testing ground, a race to be run, a pilgrimage, a battle, or as a bed of roses, but as something to be rejoiced in, whatever it brought:

> Du danke Gott, wenn er dich preßt,
> Und dank' ihm, wenn er dich wieder entläßt.*

He was, as he said himself, a born Pelagian, incapable of believing that God could have wanted the world to be anything else than what He had made it, and therefore incapable of opposing any one part of himself against another, at least for any long time. 'Hätte Gott mich anders gewollt, so hätt er mich anders gemacht' is a saying of Goethe's old age that reflects his mind at most stages of his life: if God had wanted him otherwise He would have created him otherwise. God must have wanted his faults too.

Although he expresses himself in a religious vocabulary, Goethe is thus the precursor of twentieth century existentialists, many of whom are, through Nietzsche, his direct descendants, however little the family likeness may in some cases show. Existing out of some central intensity, experiencing pleasure and pain at their fullest, while not making a cult of either: this is the 'modern' attitude which brings him nearest to André Gide and James Joyce, Rilke and Sartre and Hemingway. He did not see himself so much as a precursor, but rather

---

* Thank God when he oppresses you, and again when he releases you.

—at least on occasion—as the expression of his times, almost a personification of the 'Will' at work in the universe, riding the crest of an advancing wave. And at times you might almost be persuaded that some such being as a 'Zeitgeist' exists, so much does Goethe resemble his own Faust, stretching out his own self to cover the selves of all humanity. It is often as though he were what Thomas Mann was later to call himself —a seismograph recording the tremors and earthquakes of his age, or, as Goethe put it in *Egmont*, the almost helpless driver of a chariot that is hurtled forwards irresistibly by the horses of Time.

Looking at Goethe's principal works, you can see something of the mood which inspired that feeling. As a young man of twenty-one, he came into contact with the philosopher and critic Herder (1744–1803), from whom he learned both of the new insistence on German national literature, which was to shape his work for a while, and of the belief in the genius of the poet as a microcosmic form of the deity. Partly as a result, it entered his head to take the old legend of Faust, which at that time had about as lofty a reputation as a Punch and Judy show, and make of it a play which came to be accepted as symbolizing the striving of the whole German nation for two hundred years to come. More than this, Goethe sensed the social movements of his day, and incorporated these too in his work. Wilhelm Meister, the hero of the novel which occupied him all his life, ends his long apprenticeship to life as a surgeon, doing practical good to his fellow-men. Wilhelm thus comes a long way from the actor and dramatist he originally was, and perhaps on the whole modern civilization has gone a similar path: it too has paid more and more attention to social, rather than artistic or religious formulations of life. Faust, in the play which was equally long in the writing, ends as the ruler of something that looks not unlike the Welfare State: again, a stranger end could scarcely be envisaged for the Romantic challenger of the heavens. But Goethe's ear for the 'Zeitgeist' was alert. If he did not know that the Communist Manifesto would appear sixteen years after his death, he knew of the so-called socialistic reforms of the Austrian Emperor Joseph II while he himself was in his thirties, and he knew what the French Revolution meant, in social terms, much though he abhorred it. Both Wilhelm Meister and Faust begin as questers; they end their lives as social beings, all thought of heaven obliterated from their minds.

Yet Goethe was not the 'Socialist realist' writer one might suppose from this, for all that Lenin took a copy of *Faust* with him into exile. It is true that the pattern of his ideas is dialectical enough for modern Communists to see in him an ancestor of dialectical materialism and of the Marxist State. But Goethe was too much of a quietist and a chamaeleon to call strenuously for change, and the very adaptability that makes him resemble Marx also precludes real resemblance. Besides, there was always the unsociable, inward-turning Goethe alongside the man with a social concern.

One of the distinguishing features of Romanticism, and thus of intellectual life in the nineteenth century, was the determination to face the worst that might be experienced, without recourse to any saviour from a transcendental world. It was part of the determination to face experience as a whole and unflinchingly, in pleasure or pain, and this in turn was part of the conviction that a man who could do all this, as it were, globally, would himself achieve almost divinity. This determination might take the form of welcoming depraved, perverted experience, as it did with the Marquis de Sade, or Rimbaud, or it might be a deliberate conjuring up of horrors, as with E. T. A. Hoffmann, or Poe, or Gogol, or, in different ways, Baudelaire, Rilke and Kafka. Again Goethe had his finger on the pulse of the times. Not only does Faust encounter horrors and perversions in his ascent of the Brocken mountain on Walpurgis Night, he does so in the belief that by climbing to the very summit to confront Satan himself he will succeed in solving Life's riddle. The suicide of Werther in Goethe's early novel is also perversely motivated—one has the sense that Werther kills himself not merely in desperation but in the belief that it is the only true way to perfection, seeing himself as a kind of Christ, called upon to die for the sufferings of the world, albeit by his own hand.

On the whole, however, the plumbing of such depths was far from Goethe's ideal: neither Faust nor Werther is to be confused with the man who wrote about them. It may be true that in some respects Goethe anticipates Freud, and it is certainly true that Freud thought highly of him. But the phantasmagoria of the unconscious mind have little place in his work. When they reappear in *Faust*, in the second, 'classical' Walpurgis Night scene, they are well under control; in *Wilhelm Meister* they are confined almost entirely to the insane Harper, who disappears in the sequel to the first novel. Despite his openness to experience Goethe chose here to shun the aspects of his personality that might become too painfully dominant: we see his Orestes in *Iphigenie* and the poet in *Torquato Tasso* come very close to madness, but each of them escapes, at least within the play, into a world of practicalities. There were things that Goethe declined to encourage, and his condemnation of Romantic depravity was of a piece with this. The kind of world he wanted to live in was the one he constructed for himself in the house on the Frauenplan in Weimar: cool and white, noble yet not extravagant, domestic, spacious, classically simple, and watched over in one of the rooms by the gigantic gleaming head of a marble Juno: a place of order and symmetry from which he could retire at need to the 'Gartenhaus', the cottage amid trees which he himself had planted, with its steep tiled roof and lattice for climbing plants, a place of green shade and quiet walks. It was scarcely a Romantic world in any sense; as George Eliot remarked, in contrast with the study of Sir Walter Scott, with its elegant gothic fittings, its delicious easy chair and its oratory of painted glass, Goethe's private quarters with their common deal bookshelves and the two small study windows, the dark little bedroom and the absence of any object chosen for the sake of luxury or beauty, had rather a hardy simplicity.

Goethe could not escape from what he was, and what his ancestors had been. Brought up in the patrician house at

Frankfurt, with its three rows of windows and broad win-
dowed gable above, and dormers rising steeply higher still, he
could scarcely help sharing in that massive, good-tempered,
broad-cheeked spirit that had gone to the making of it, and
which seems especially German when it is met in Bach's music
or Dürer's portraits or even, less distinctly, in the well-
proportioned largeness of modern German suburban houses.
His father enjoyed a position of some esteem in the Free City,
and might have chosen more extravagance, yet the house had
a serene simplicity rather than elegance, the lace curtains gave
a cool light, the broad staircase and the chequerboarded stone
floors on the landings and the realistic 'Dutch' landscapes by
Frankfurt artists made a sober dignity. This was really where
Goethe belonged, from his birth in 1749 onwards, and he did
not essentially leave it when in 1775 he abandoned Frankfurt to
settle for the remainder of his life in the court of Duke Carl
August (1757–1828) at Weimar, just over a hundred miles
away.

Goethe did thus make the attempt at breaking away from
the world of his ancestors. Though his earliest verse is in the
rigid tradition of rationalistic Enlightenment, or deliciously
erotic after the manner of some pieces of Dresden china, the
works which first brought him fame are rebellious in theme or
content. In his historical drama *Götz von Berlichingen* (1773),
a Shakespearean treatment of the life of a sixteenth-century
robber-baron, he had made an impassioned demand for a
return to the vigorous, manly virtues, in contrast to the over-
refined 'rococo' civilization of his own day (a civilization
which was, however, already at that time giving rise to the
music of Haydn (1732–1809) and Mozart (1756–91)). In *Werther*, the novel which, after 1774, made him known all over
Europe, he drew a portrait of a man who found life in that
civilization intolerable. In *Faust*, published in 1808 but already
begun in the 1770s, he had projected a work which was to be
wholly German, full of mystery and magic, far from the
French clarity which was the ruling passion of architects,
landscape gardeners, city planners, and of many established

8

poets and dramatists. And in his poems, he had written in a great variety of tones, spirited, tender, earthy, vulgar, frank, majestical, wild and peaceful. He became known as the most talented of all the 'Stürmer und Dränger', as the poets of his generation came to be called, a 'Genie' to whom the whole world stood open and for whom no experience was impossible.

In suggesting that Goethe should come for a visit to Weimar, the Duke had no intention of interrupting the kind of life that Goethe was leading; on the contrary, he joined in it himself. Skating on the 'Schwansee' became all the rage, Carl August and the poet stood in the market place for hours together, cracking sledge-whips for a wager, they shared the same bedroom, and were known to play unpleasant pranks on some of the Duke's subjects. At the same time, the Duke was not merely a 'hearty', but genuinely glad to have so distinguished a poet at his court, which was the more remarkable in that Weimar was no city like Mannheim or Berlin, but scarcely more than a walled village of thatched cottages surrounding the ducal residence, while the whole duchy would not have made a large English county. Carl August's generosity and warm welcome led to a close friendship, with the result that Goethe stayed not only a few months but for the best part of sixty years, and that Weimar became a place of pilgrimage for visitors from all over Europe. Goethe also showed very soon that he was not interested only in hunting, dicing, and drinking wine out of skulls. Not long after his arrival he met the Baroness von Stein, wife of the Duke's Master of Horse, and fell deeply in love with her sweet, soft earnestness and her remarkable openness of mind and character. Goethe had been in love many times before this, with Friederike Brion (1752–1813) at Strasbourg, with Lotte Buff (1753–1828) at Wetzlar, with Lili Schönemann (1758–1817) at Frankfurt, and had flirted with many more. He had never forgiven himself for abandoning Friederike; he had made Werther commit suicide in despair of ever enjoying the love of a woman who, like Lotte, was already engaged; he had never quite explained to himself how he could have come so close to marrying a

9

society beauty like Lili, whose whole world was utterly remote from his. In Charlotte von Stein (1742–1827), seven years his senior and the mother of seven children, he found a mature woman who appreciated his poetry, calmed his spirit, and gave him the chance of regaining the balance of his mind, for he felt later on that 'Sturm und Drang' had brought him to the brink of insanity.

The relationship with Charlotte was a marriage of minds. It sometimes had to be clandestine (to avoid having his name taken at the town-gate in accordance with the regular practice, Goethe would leave on foot, joining Charlotte in her carriage at an appointed spot outside), but general sympathy was accorded to a woman whose husband was seldom at his own home more than once a week, and those who knew of the affair never found cause for offence. Goethe's verses to 'Lida', as he called Charlotte in the published poems, are concerned with the peace, certainty, harmony and serenity she brings to him, and in the idealized women of his plays, the heroine of *Iphigenie auf Tauris* (begun 1778) and the Princess of *Torquato Tasso* (begun 1780), we see the expectations Goethe cherished. Within a few years of his arrival at Weimar, the 'Stürmer und Dränger' had vanished and his place had been taken by a poet whose regard for classical models, both Graeco-Roman and French, was as high as that of any earlier German poet of the eighteenth century. One can see the transition quite clearly in his play *Egmont* (begun 1775), with its Shakespearean opening scene, written before Weimar, and its classicizing stichomythia, its formal exchanges between pairs of characters, its almost total lack of stage-action in the later acts. With *Iphigenie* and *Tasso*, both products of the early years at Weimar, the form is that of the French classical tragedies which Goethe had spiritedly rejected only a decade before.

Together with this greater regard for classical form, marked also in Goethe's poetry by the occasional introduction of the French-inspired alexandrine line, and by experiments in the Italian 'ottava rima' stanza, there went an interest in science and in practical affairs: it was as though the discipline demanded by the one (in contrast to the free rhythms in his poetry and the loosely constructed plays of before 1775) were reflected also in the objectivity required for the other. In the early 1780s Goethe began the investigations into anatomy, botany and geology which were to be one of his chief interests for the remainder of his life (optics and meteorology were added later). He also began to serve as an administrator of the ducal domains, concerning himself with the forests, the silver-mines, the roads, and thereby acquiring the title of Privy Counsellor.

Yet for all his real gratitude to Weimar, Goethe remained discontented. For several years after 1780 his duties and his scientific studies allowed comparatively little time for creative work, and although he was writing the first draft of his novel *Wilhelm Meisters Lehrjahre* at this time, as well as some of his best-known poems, a certain pedantry enters some of his lyrics, he becomes a little pontifical, and the flood of ideas of earlier years seems to have dried up. During these years he wrote occasional plays, 'Singspiele' for the entertainment of the court, in which the chief attraction was the sight, perhaps, of bonfires lit along the river Ilm (though this particular entertainment also happens to contain his celebrated 'Erlkönig' poem), a piece in celebration of the Duke's birthday, and another, rather touchingly, in mourning for the stage-carpenter—there was no snobbery about these official offerings. The patent of nobility was conferred on him and he became not only Herr Doktor and Herr Geheimrat but also *von* Goethe.

All in all, it was more than he could stand. Goethe's nature was very adaptable: he could live in harmony with a great variety of people and fall in love with many different women, but the experience of ten years at the court, with only rare absences, was beginning to stifle him. Just why it was that, in 1786, while holidaying at Karlsbad in Bohemia, he suddenly packed his bags without a word to anyone and went off to Italy, to remain there for nearly two years, will never be known for sure. He had always wanted to go to Rome since he first saw the Piranesi engravings in his father's house, and Italy had come to represent for him almost heavenly perfection, the

home of the heroes of antiquity and a place as near to Greece
and the memories of Homer as he might easily reach in those
days (Greece being then in the hands of Turkey, still constantly
at war with Austria). In the classical South he could look for
those ideal forms of men conceived by the Greeks and handed
down by them in their statuary; he could seek that 'primal
plant' of whose existence he was convinced, the plant which
was almost the Platonic idea of a plant, from which all other
plants derived. The 'Ur-Mensch', the 'Ur-Pflanze', the 'Ur-
Landschaft'—these were the names he used for the real em-
bodiments of the perfect shapes set down by the gods in
Mediterranean fields, and there were moments of excitement
when he was convinced he had found them, when he wrote
back to Charlotte that he had discovered a key with which he
could unlock all the secrets of Nature. What really impressed
him was the feeling that things were essentially as they were
meant to be—'What a splendid thing a living creature is!',
he writes—'how adapted to its situation, how true, how
existent!' 'Wie wahr, wie seiend!'—this was the clue he had
been looking for. Things that were really themselves—it
happened to be crabs that Goethe was observing at the moment—were fulfilments of themselves, and thereby, in a
special sense of the word, 'true'. With this realization, Goethe
felt himself as though reborn, as he wrote home in letter after
letter. 'Though still the same as ever, I feel transformed to the
innermost marrow.' True enough, he still was the same Goethe,
with his past unchanged, and all the conflicts he had gone
through indelibly implanted in his mind, and yet he felt a kind
of clarity and grace of movement which transfigured everything, showing him the ideal forms, not hidden behind the
real ones as though the real were merely a mask, but illuminating them, or catching the eye like a new configuration of the
same shape, not noticed before. Together with this went a new
feeling of liberty, especially in sexual love. Except in the erotic
poems of his undergraduate days, Goethe had scarcely touched
on such matters before; in *Faust*, partly inspired by his own
feelings of guilt, the enjoyment of sexual pleasure brings harsh

punishment to both woman and man; in *Iphigenie* and *Tasso* the women seem hardly conscious of any sexual attractiveness and certainly are provided with none by the author. In Italy, as Goethe records in the *Römische Elegien* (begun in 1788 after his return), all this was changed. In these imitations of Catullus, Tibullus and Propertius he celebrates love simply as a means of bodily delight, without thought of the high ideals inspired by Charlotte von Stein. The ecstasy of a naked embrace becomes as true for him, in its way, as the encounter of two minds: it is 'seiend', and needs no other justification.

Yet, as the contemporary critic Friedrich Schlegel (1772–1829) said, there is a note of irony in the Elegies. Although they are not 'naughty', as his early anacreontic verse sometimes was, they betray a certain self-consciousness, an awareness that an antique relationship with women is being relived. Goethe was, one may say, pioneering an attitude which for good or ill has become far more widely accepted since his day, and he knows this sometimes more than he knows or deeply cares for the woman who shares his bed. Indeed the whole Italian experience, immensely liberating as it was for Goethe as a man, was less of a liberation for his creative writing. He completed or versified *Iphigenie*, *Tasso* and *Egmont*, and added scenes to *Faust* while he was there, and he amassed a variety of experiences. But the work he was to conceive and publish during the next fifteen years or so, from his return to Germany in 1788 onwards, did not have the quality one might expect from so transfiguring an experience as the Italian Journey. The classical forms he adopted in his verse, the Homeric hexameter and the elegiac couplet, were difficult to manage in German without stiffness. Apart from that, Goethe's chameleon nature seemed to undergo yet another surprising change on his return home. The relationship with Charlotte von Stein had been strained when he abandoned her so abruptly in order to make for Rome; it broke completely when he settled down in Weimar, not four weeks after his return, with a girl of humble rank and no intellectual pretensions whatsoever. Goethe was more faithful to Christiane Vulpius

(1765–1816) than many husbands are to their wives, even though he did not officially marry her until 1806, after she had borne him several children. Frau von Stein might call her his 'Hausmamsell', and there might be malicious gossip about her vulgarity and secret drinking, but there was a deep affection on both sides, and when Christiane died Goethe recorded in his diary the 'emptiness and deathly silence within me and without'. And yet this ordinary marriage (ordinary in the sense that it was 'gutbürgerlich' in almost all but the possession of marriage lines) was not what one might have expected from the Italian experience.

The surprising quality in Goethe both as a man and as a poet after 1788 was partly due to events of which he had no inkling before that date. Within barely a year of his return home came the fall of the Bastille, and the ensuing years filled him with increasing aversion as the revolutionaries in France established the Reign of Terror. The serenity he had gained in Italy might have been shattered by these happenings: if human nature could be like this, where could its justification lie? Did it not contain some deep-seated depravity, and was it enough to be 'seiend'? The position Goethe took was that all violent upheaval was unnatural, that ideally human nature should grow steadily, unfolding itself as a tree unfolds its leaves, smoothly progressing towards its full flowering. But the literary works written in the years of the Revolution rarely convince. The plays of this period are either trivial, like *Der Bürgergeneral* (1793) and *Die Aufgeregten* (1794), or obscure like *Die natürliche Tochter* (begun 1799). Goethe seeks to put forward the virtues of his countrymen, loyalty, industriousness, conscientiousness and obedience, in contrast to the contemporary French example of vengeful intolerance and heady fanaticism, but the impression he creates is more comfortable than inspiring, even in so ambitious a work as his epic poem *Hermann und Dorothea* (1796). Nowhere in these works do we have any sense of what the Reign of Terror really meant to Goethe: the experience of those hideous years is blotted out, as though the eulogizing of admirable qualities were sufficient in itself. There is nothing daring or exhilarating or tenacious about the characters Goethe created at this time, and the total effect of his defence of the 'Bürger' as opposed to the revolutionary strikes one now as humdrum.

For several years after his return to Weimar, Goethe was oppressed more than he usually cared to admit. It needed the friendship of the dramatist Friedrich Schiller (1759–1805), ten years his junior and one of his keenest admirers, to restore the confidence and zest he had experienced on first arriving in Italy. His despondency ('Dunkelheit und Zaudern' were his words for it to Schiller) was dispelled by the younger man's analysis of their two characters, and with this encouragement Goethe's creative powers returned in greater strength. He revised and completed the novel *Wilhelm Meisters Lehrjahre* (published 1795–6 but begun during his first years in Weimar), a work which Friedrich Schlegel compared in importance with the French Revolution itself, and which had considerable influence not only on the German Romantic movement but also on the main stream of the German novel (the so-called 'Bildungsroman' or 'novel of character-formation') right through into the twentieth century. He composed the epic poem *Hermann und Dorothea*, since described as 'the Song of Songs of the German burgher' (although here again a note of irony is sometimes detected). He collaborated with Schiller in writing a collection of ballads, with the purpose of raising the general level of popular taste. Most important of all, he revised, and completed by 1806 (publishing it in 1808), the work by which he is most widely known and which is always associated with his name, the First Part of the Tragedy of *Faust*.

Such was Goethe's longevity, it comes as a shock to recollect that by 1808 he had reached the age of fifty-nine, and that to most readers he was still known primarily as the author of *Götz* and *Werther*, both having been published more than thirty years before. The appearance of *Faust* and of his novel *Die Wahlverwandtschaften* in 1809, followed by his *Theory of Colours* in 1810, together with the works revivified or inspired by Schiller, did much to re-establish Goethe's reputation with the German public, although, even so, it was not until about 1875 that he exceeded Schiller in the popular estimation. At the same time, Goethe was consciously moving towards that supreme position in German letters which has since then been accorded to him: he had begun to feel himself as the representative figure which he later became. Above all (so far as the external world was concerned) he was impressed by the personality of Napoleon (1769–1821), who had so asserted himself against the chaos of the Revolution that ultimately France had begun to move with him almost as one man. True, this had meant humiliation for Germany, as Goethe well knew when the Prussian armies were defeated at Jena, only a few miles from his home; but he was never inspired to join the patriotic poets who called on their countrymen to throw out the invader. He owed too much to French culture, he confessed, ever to feel hatred for the French. What really concerned him deeply was the 'daemonic' nature of Napoleon, the ability to carry out his own will against all opposition, qualities which made the Emperor appear like Fate itself, or, as Goethe said on another occasion, like a 'compendium of the world'. Napoleon was what the philosopher Hegel (1770–1831) was shortly to call a 'world-historical man', one of those who both embody and create the movement of their age and thereby bring about their own justification. He was thus, within the world of politics and war, a figure corresponding to the ideal poet as Schiller had conceived of him: one who was in touch with the very heart of things, whose will was almost a divine Will, and whose actions had an instinctive rightness or propriety.

At no time did Goethe ever publicly claim rightness or propriety for himself, and if the temptation to do so arose, he was not without good sense to deal with it. All the same, these ideas coloured his thought to some extent. His autobiography, *Dichtung und Wahrheit*, begun in 1809 and continued for more than twenty years, was a deliberate attempt at portraying not merely his own life but also the circumstances of his time, and the interaction of one upon the other. Its con-

cluding book (still treating of his early manhood) refers directly
to the 'daemon' as he felt it to have been within him, and the
thought of representativeness at least hovers in the background.
By 1814, shortly before Napoleon's final defeat, this thought
had taken yet a further development.

It had been Faust's wish to experience all that human kind
ever had to suffer or enjoy:

> Und was der ganzen Menschheit zugeteilt ist,
> Will ich in meinem innern Selbst genießen,
> Mit meinem Geist das Höchst' und Tiefste greifen,
> Ihr Wohl und Weh auf meinen Busen häufen
> Und so mein eigen Selbst zu ihrem Selbst erweitern,
> Und, wie sie selbst, am End' auch ich zerscheitern!* [1]

This wish had been Goethe's too, in so far as Faust was his
alter ego. He had been inspired by Herder's vision of Shakespeare to think of the poet as a man who contained all humanity
within his single self. In Italy, as he had been encouraged by
Schiller to believe, he had reached out beyond his merely
German personality to a Mediterranean one quite contrary to
it, and had successfully fused the two. Now, in his early sixties,
he began to think of a still more ambitious project. The
translations by Hammer of the Persian medieval poet Hafiz
caught Goethe's imagination and induced him to take up once
again the interest in Islam which he had had in his twenties.
The result, from the middle of 1814 onwards, was a new flow
of poetry such as he had not known for years past, partly in
imitation of the Persian, partly in 'conversation' with him,
partly written in praise of a Persian mistress, 'Suleika', who
was in reality a friend's newly married wife, Marianne von
Willemer (1784–1860), with whom Goethe had fallen deeply
in love shortly after the new inspiration came to him. The
collection of poems which emerged over the next five years,
the *West-Östlicher Divan*, contains some of the most delicate

---

* And all that all mankind has to endure, I will enjoy within my inner self,
the highest and the lowest will I grasp in my spirit, heap on my bosom all
their weal and woe, and thus extend myself to all their selves and then,
like them, be wrecked.

and tender, as well as the most ironically subtle, the most trivial, and the most boisterous poetry Goethe ever wrote. Its significance here, however, lies chiefly in its title, and the aim it reflects, for Goethe's purpose this time was to effect a fusion of East and West, Islam and Christianity; it was a further development of the idea which had driven him to Italy, and which was to tempt him, a decade later, to experimenting in the moods of poetry from China.

All this time, Goethe's interests in other fields did not slacken. He continued to make scientific studies on such things as the spiral tendency in plants, the formation of clouds, the comparison of animal skeletons, and Sanskrit literature; he became First Minister of the Duchy of Weimar, collected majolica-ware, gems, and geological specimens, directed the State-theatre and instructed its actors, set up a botanical museum and a veterinary school, spent much time amalgamating the libraries of Jena, and continued to work at his autobiography and at short stories. His home became internationally known; he was visited by Prince Metternich, Heine, Thackeray (and many other Englishmen), Field-Marshal Blücher, Beethoven, Weber and Mendelssohn, the dramatist Grillparzer, the explorer von Humboldt, the kings of Holland and Bavaria. He was interested in the project for a Panama Canal, and is said to have foreseen the need for one at Suez. He read, and was often in personal correspondence with the younger generation in many countries: Stendhal, Victor Hugo, Fenimore Cooper, Carlyle, Scott, Byron, Pushkin, Mieckiewicz; Mendelssohn and Berlioz sent him their compositions based on *Faust*, Gérard de Nerval his translation and Delacroix his illustrations to the play.

'If you would step into the infinite', Goethe wrote in a rhymed epigram at about this time, 'follow the finite in all directions.' That is precisely what he seemed to be doing. But with all these far-flung enterprises Goethe was also insistent on an attitude which often seems quite the reverse of all he stood for, the attitude of 'Entsagung', or renunciation. With all his compendiousness, Goethe was aware of the sheer infinity even of finite directions and purposes: you had in the end to be content with the small area it was possible to cover in a single lifetime, and to renounce the highest ambitions. You might feel as Cherubino did in Mozart's *Figaro*, 'Ogni donna mi fa palpitar'—and Goethe was never more deeply in love than he was at the age of seventy-four, with Ulrike von Levetzow (1804–99)—but you had to give up one love after another as you came to realize that no one mistress was ever more than a foreground to an immensity of love beyond. You might try various professions as Wilhelm Meister had done: in the end, as in the sequel to the novel, the *Wanderjahre*, you had to see the need for settling to a less all-embracing, but socially useful life. Similarly in *Faust* (of which Goethe wrote the Second Part, published in 1832, in his late seventies), the man who had striven for all experience—and who was now declared to be saved from the devil's clutches precisely because he had striven—found prospective contentment in the thought of performing one single, useful task for mankind.

The contradiction between this 'renunciation' and Goethe's all-embracingness should not be diminished. It was one of the many paradoxes which he quite deliberately announced, especially in his later years, and had to do with that daemonic spirit of which he wrote, in the final pages of his autobiography, that 'it manifested itself only in contradictions'. He would counsel both intense self-assertion and self-abnegation, sometimes in a rational spirit, as necessary alternations in any human life, sometimes less rationally, as aspects of a simultaneous fusion. He would say of such men as Napoleon and Tamburlaine, whose colossal determination was so impressive, that they could be conquered by nothing less than the universe itself. Human power was useless (*pace* Nelson, Blücher, and Wellington): only the elements themselves, as in the Russian winter which in 1812 had driven Napoleon back from Moscow and shattered the Grande Armée, were of comparable force. 'Nemo contra deum nisi deus ipse', Goethe concluded in the autobiography, with mysterious words which can, perhaps, be elucidated a little. None could be against God unless it were

God himself (or unless he himself were also a god—the Latin allows of ambiguity here). His meaning may have been something like this: that at the heart of everything there was a strange contradictoriness—'polarity' was the word Goethe commonly used for it, with the idea of the twin poles of a magnet in mind—an attractiveness and a repellence, creation and destruction, a pulsating expansion and contraction, assertion and counter-assertion, which men often saw as good and evil, heaven and hell, whereas moral concepts were in reality only one facet of the whole in which immorality and even amorality were at least equally representative. The essential thing in all this dynamic whirl was activity. As Faust had said, translating after his own fashion the first chapter of St John's Gospel, 'In the beginning was the Deed.' To be in activity, sheerly, naïvely, without reflection, was to be beyond the sphere of morality; it was to enjoy 'des Handelns ew'ge Unschuld', the eternal innocence of action, as Goethe put it in the *Divan*. You might rise or sink on the ebb and flow of this primal rhythm, you might be brought to the top of Fortune's wheel as Napoleon was, and still find the inexorable downward pressure compelling you to sink to the very bottom again: all this was the surge of life of which you might approve or disapprove, in which you might or might not decide to share, but which would go on regardless of any individual fate. If, however, you reached the stature of a world-figure, then certainly some power equally great would compel you to your knees. The creative god brought forth the destructive one, and both were simultaneous aspects of God the Whole.

This aged wisdom of Goethe's was nothing new to him. It was a development of the insight he had had when he made the Earth-Spirit speak, in one of the earliest scenes in *Faust*, of the whole creation as 'birth and the grave, all one vast sea'. Faust, it is true, had not been able to endure the sight of so immense an alternation, and Werther too, in Goethe's youth, had despaired of Nature as a prolific, life-creating monster that constantly devoured itself. Now, in his old age, Goethe was able to witness it all with more equanimity. There was, it was true, only one everlasting repetition of the same basic pattern of growth and decay, never progressing, never moving towards the triumph of good over evil, but the whole was in any case one triumphant jet of delight in living, all contained within the even greater peace of God:

> Wenn im Unendlichen dasselbe
> Sich wiederholend ewig fließt,
> Das tausendfältige Gewölbe
> Sich kräftig ineinander schließt,
> Strömt Lebenslust aus allen Dingen,
> Dem kleinsten wie dem größten Stern,
> Und alles Drängen, alles Ringen
> Ist ewige Ruh in Gott dem Herrn.*

Or to use another metaphor, this one from *Faust*, life was a torrent of water which, as its spray passed through the divine sunlight, gave off the splendidly coloured rainbow. The torrent was always the same, the rainbow would never alter, there was everlasting sameness in the sequence, and yet there was everlasting celebration, and peace.[1]

Since Friedrich Gundolf published his book, *Goethe*, in 1916, this image of the poet has come to be very widely established. That is to say, it is generally speaking not only accepted as true that Goethe's wisdom was expressed in something like the terms just set forth (clearly, so elusive a thing will not lend itself to summary statement without loss), it is also widely held that Goethe's own life and work was of just the same paradoxical nature. To use Gundolf's own imagery, Goethe is like a circle or sphere, a unity which can be comprehended at a glance, and which is always the same, always complete and 'rounded off', as we say, and yet whose surface offers never-ending possibilities of movement. Goethe's work and life are themselves a great unity, on a microcosmic scale, in which we as his readers may move as he moved within the world that

---

* When in the infinite the same flow of events is eternally repeated, and the vault of a myriad of forms knits solidly together, then joy in life streams out from all creation, from the smallest as from the greatest star, and all stress, all conflict, is eternal peace in God the Lord.

contained him. We may admire here, or censure there, as we do in life anyway, but the essential is that we should recognize the splendour and the peace of the whole. Thus one of the most perceptive critics ever to have written on Goethe, Professor Staiger, from whom the flaws in the works are seldom hidden, although he is also quick to see other qualities, offers this comfort to readers for whom, as he confesses, he has torn one of the masterpieces of German literature into innumerable shreds. Within the whole Goethean *œuvre*, such criticisms are of no ultimate consequence. 'If we shut our eyes a little', he writes, 'and the contours of the individual parts begin to fade into a hazy mist, the humanity of Goethe, the Goethean spirit in the most general and most indefinable sense becomes so powerful, so irresistibly great, that one gladly rests content and reads on without the least offence.'

This is something like the language a lover might use, and, if it disturbs us at all, we shall need to put our point delicately as well as clearly. What is there to be said against Goethe's work that really matters? Is not the vast array of his achievements dazzling in itself, so that any defects are about as significant as cracks in the wall of the Sistine Chapel? It has been alleged by some of his critics that he was incapable of writing a tragedy, that his delight in living and his faith in the innocence of Nature were shallow, not deeply aware of suffering. But we come on to treacherous ground if we start examining who has suffered how much, and denying the right to rejoice to some while conceding it to others. In any case, one can always find at least a certain number of passages in Goethe—the 'Parzenlied' in *Iphigenie*, the bitter insights of Tasso, the despair and remorse of Faust, the sense of utter loss in the 'Marienbader Elegie'—to quote on the other side, and the whole argument soon becomes distasteful. It has been said that Goethe was lacking in warmth of humanity, that he was too intent on cultivating his own ego ever to make real contact with anyone, that he owes a large part of his reputation to the need of the united German nation, after 1871, to add a great national poet to its military glories; it has been said that his works have an immoral influence (*Werther* was banned in Catholic Italy during his lifetime) and that they are dull (which afforded George Eliot the opportunity to defend him against the charge of immorality, seeing that a dull author could scarcely also seduce). He has been accused of heathenism, lack of patriotism, lack of concern with the democratic and liberal movements of his day, of authoritarianism, and even of writing bad poetry. There is something to be said in favour of every single one of these charges. The question remains, are they of any consequence in a life so multiple in its interests and achievements? More important, are they of any consequence in trying to form a view of his literary work as a whole?

There are two ways of answering these questions. We can point to the undeniable facts of Goethe's great range and reputation, matters of history which nothing can ever controvert. These are important in themselves, like other historical matters: they tell us what the past was like and so give us a perspective to the present. We can, however, also try to find out what Goethe's work means in this present—trying for the whole sense of a poem or a novel or a play, so far as it will communicate itself to us in our circumstances. This personal response from the reader is never cultivated enough, least of all in reading works in foreign languages, where everyone feels modesty about his ability to comprehend, let alone criticize. And yet if there is any point in reading in foreign languages at all, rather than in translations, it must be that with time it is possible to learn not only the literal meanings of words but their overtones and associations, as in our native language. If this cannot be done, there is nothing to be gained from reading a foreign work in the original. If it can be done, then it should begin to be done as soon as possible in the learning of the language; it should not be postponed, as it is postponed now, to some supposedly absolute stage when complete knowledge is achieved. The choice appears to lie between accepting either the authority of the past or the native critic, on the one hand, or the witness of the present moment, guided by the past and by native tradition, on the other. What follows now chooses

PART II

1749 TO 1786

POEMS BEFORE 1786

The achievement of Goethe in poetry is so staggeringly un-precedented as to provoke the inquiry, how the German language could suddenly become so expressive. His earliest extant poem, written with remarkable facility at the age of seven, shows how the small boy conceived of poetry from his browsing in his father's library.

> Erhabner Großpapa! Ein neues Jahr erscheint,
> Drum muß ich meine Pflicht und Schuldigkeit entrichten.*

The naïvety of its alexandrines is not merely that of a child; there was something inherent in the classicizing lines which tended to make them sound, in German, less than mature. The twelve syllables which in French could be made the vehicle of most noble passions became heavily marked iambic trimeters, divided off from one another by weighty caesuras and line-endings, once they were transferred to the more accented language of German speakers. Thus the poets who copied the French—and they were still in the majority when Goethe was a boy—tended to sound like country parsons in silk breeches and flowered waistcoats. An occasional poet of genius, like Andreas Gryphius in the previous century, might overcome the difficulties of adapting an accented language to a verse-form which treated all syllables as equal. The writer perhaps most widely read in Goethe's childhood, Gellert, makes a flatter impression. In the lines from 'Der Menschenfreund' which follow, the kindly good-nature Gellert commends, in a way so characteristic of his times, appears a little wide-eyed just because of the verse-form, its caesura halting every line with a thud at the mid-point:

> Wie selig lebt ein Mann, der seine Pflichten kennt,
> Und, seine Pflicht zu tun, aus Menschenliebe brennt,

---

* Respected grandpapa, a new year now appears, and therefore must I do my duty and obligation.

Der, wenn ihn auch kein Eid zum Dienst der Welt verbindet,
Beruf, und Eid und Amt schon in sich selber findet!
Ihm wird des Andern Wohl sein eignes Himmelreich;
Er fühlet meine Not, als träf ihn selbst der Streich;
Und das, was ihn beherrscht, ist ein gerecht Bestreben,
So treu, als er sich lebt, der ganzen Welt zu leben.*

The regular rise and fall, and the neat rounding off of thoughts in end-stopped lines and rhymed couplets suggest a certain commonplaceness in virtue, which is perhaps why, despite their admirable intention, the lines fail to strike home. Like many other literary works of the mid-eighteenth century, they convey a sense of complacency, contentment with one's lot, and satisfaction with one's own endeavours, which even the youthful Goethe did not escape. In the *Poetical Thoughts on the Descent into Hell of Jesus Christ*, 'written by request', Goethe can still, at the age of fourteen, begin writing on so grandiose a theme with the words 'Welch ungewöhnliches Getümmel!'†—the cataclysmic event is still seen with a comfortable and almost condescending assurance of personal safety.

It was through Gellert and others like him that German middle-class society became acquainted with the religion of Reason, the Enlightenment whose greatest representative had been Leibniz, in the late seventeenth century. Reason was not, however, the sole guiding force in those times. Just as in England the age of Pope and Johnson was also that of William Law and Wesley, so in Germany there flourished alongside rationalism various irrational, emotional forms of religion and philosophy, chiefly known by the name of Pietism. Here there was the very reverse of calm assurance, as may be seen from the 'autobiography' of Anton Reiser (by Karl Philipp Moritz,

---

* How happy lives the man who knows his duties, and who from brotherly love is afire to do his duty, who, though no oath binds him to serve the world, finds vocation, oath and [priestly] office in himself. Another's wellbeing becomes his own heaven; he feels my distress as though the blow had struck him himself, and what rules him is a just endeavour to live as faithfully towards the world as to himself.

† What an unusual clamour!

1757–93), in which the fearful effects of a sermon are described: 'the destructive power of the elements, the crash of the universe, the trembling and shaking of the sinner, and the joyous awakening of the righteous were represented in a contrast which excited Anton's imagination in the highest degree', while in another sermon the preacher was 'interrupted from beginning to end by tears and sobs, so much beloved was he by his congregation'. Such scenes as these were not uncommon either in Germany or in England at that time, and the spirit which produced them was familiar to Goethe at least in so far as his mother associated with Pietist circles and introduced him, in his late 'teens, to one of its most mystically inclined representatives, the Fräulein Susanna von Klettenberg (1723–1774).

The introduction of a more irrational element in poetry, prepared by the Swiss critics Bodmer (1698–1783) and Breitinger (1701–76) in the 'thirties and 'forties, was spurred on by the poet Klopstock (1724–1803), the first canto of whose epic *Der Messias* appeared in 1748, a year before Goethe's birth, and whose influence on Goethe's verse becomes plain after 1770. In Klopstock the alexandrine disappears—to be replaced very often, it is true, by other classicizing forms, the hexameter and the elegiac couplet—and in at least a portion of his work there emerges a quite untrammelled kind of writing in 'free rhythms': rhythms, that is, dictated only by the poet's feeling for what is proper at a given moment. Here the poet is unconstrained by the need to rhyme or to adhere to a metre. His feeling pours out as the Pietist's feeling pours out at the sermon, he allows himself the majestic sweep and the contrite withdrawal just as the mood takes him, and a heartfelt utterance is, so to speak, his creed. In one of his best-known poems, the 'Frühlingsfeier' of 1759, Klopstock allows his emotion to overcome any sense of bathos that might occur as he fervently declares that he will not soar like the angels through the universal oceans, but will worship and soar only around the 'drop in the bucket', namely the earth, or again as he weeps to think that perhaps the caterpillar has no immortal soul and comforts himself with the thought that after death he will find out whether it has or not. The criteria of good sense mean little to him as he lets himself go, but he can also write verses that are already beginning to look Goethean:

> Mit tiefer Ehrfurcht schau' ich die Schöpfung an,
> Denn du,
> Namenloser, du
> Schufest sie!*

It is this veneration for all created things that carries Klopstock along, and it is his complete disregard of reason and taste that, despite absurdities, prepares a mood that will later liberate Goethe.

For the most striking thing about Goethe's first really original poetry (that is, after the anacreontic and erotic poetry of his undergraduate days at Leipzig, from the 'Sesenheimer Lyrik' addressed to Friederike Brion onwards) is not only its frankness and freshness but also its carefree naturalness. As a citizen of Frankfurt, he was accustomed to pronouncing his 'g's' soft: he wrote 'Mädgen' and 'Gretgen' where others would write 'Mädchen' and 'Gretchen', and thus it seemed perfectly natural, in what has become one of his most famous pieces, to rhyme 'Ach *neige* / Du Schmerzens*reiche* / Dein Antlitz gnädig meiner Not'. Another poem begins with a similar change of consonant—'Spude dich, Kronos'—(where the verb, already a dialect form, is elsewhere spelt 'spute dich'); it is at the same time literally a cheerful command to Father Time to 'get cracking'. Where the familiarity in the rhyme of the first quotation brings the Virgin Mary ('die Schmerzens-reiche') endearingly close, a similar mood in the second makes Time appear an ordinary mortal companion. The Goethe who wrote these two phrases, in his early twenties, had an easy negligence which could write without inhibitions, unashamed of dialect or of personal idiosyncrasies. Occasionally, this might lead to incoherence as it did later in the 'Kronos' poem,

---

* With deep reverence I regard the Creation, for Thou, nameless one, Thou didst create it.

where the words tumble out in disregard of all syntax and grammar ('Frisch den holpernden / Stock Wurzeln Steine den Trott / Rasch in's Leben hinein!'),* or as in the dithyrambic 'Wandrers Sturmlied', where the literal meaning is hard to find. More important, this negligence was also a confidence in his own ability, and a trust in his own language. Goethe was 'walking on water' and not caring if he seemed at times to be drowning.

The extraordinary thing is that he never did drown, never fell into the self-consciousness and bathos to which Klopstock was prone—at least not in his early verse. There might be a Klopstockian note about Goethe's 'Mailied', but there was no overwrought solemnity. Where Klopstock had written in 'Frühlingsfeier', lines like these, ecstatically vibrant—

> Ergeuß von neuem du, mein Auge,
> Freudentränen!
> Du, meine Harfe,
> Preise dem Herrn!
>
> Umwunden wieder, mit Palmen
> Ist meine Harf' umwunden; ich singe dem Herrn.
> Hier steh' ich. Rund um mich
> Ist alles Allmacht und Wunder alles†—

Goethe was writing in 'Mailied' lines that are strictly unquotable out of context, since the rising emotion swells on from verse to verse in a way that fends off interruption: one simply has to read through the whole poem. By comparison Klopstock limps, and one can well believe that his harp is, as he says, wrapped round with deadening palm-leaves. Goethe's leaping excitement, disciplined to the extent that he retains two stresses to the line, not only maintains itself through to the end, it is also more personal, in the sense that Goethe is more concerned with what is happening to *him*. There is an in-

---

* Fresh the stumbling / Stick roots stones the trot / Quick, into life!
† Pour out again, O my eye, tears of joy; and thou, my harp, praise the Lord. Wound round again, with palms is my harp wound round; I sing unto the Lord. Here I stand. Round about me is all almighty power, all marvel.

credulous zest in 'Mailied', in the very idea that all this splendour could possibly be there for the poet to exult in:

> Wie herrlich leuchtet
> Mir die Natur!

('Mir' receives an unusually strong stress within this line);

> O Mädchen, Mädchen,
> Wie lieb ich dich!
> Wie blickt dein Auge!
> Wie liebst du mich!

(the girl is being asked to join in his own wonderment at her love for him); and

> Sei ewig glücklich,
> Wie du mich liebst!*

a line which is not very clear, but which seems to say something like 'seeing that you love me', or 'so long as you love me', or 'since it makes you so happy to love me, be happy for ever'. All through, there is this sense of being ministered to, both by the blossoms and the pollen and by the loving girl.

There can be no doubt that it was this feeling of being glad to be Goethe, glad to be a German and a native of Frankfurt, glad to be loved by Friederike, that enabled him to sustain his flow of poetry in such profusion. There are scores and scores of poems from his early twenties, on party-games, brigands, swimming, riding on horseback, wading through a downpour of rain; there are folksongs, ballads, fables, dialogues, as well as love-lyrics and attacks on hostile critics. At the same time, there are also signs of a curious detachment, which was perhaps the means whereby Goethe avoided the excesses into which unbridled spontaneity might have led him. It is not a very marked detachment, at first, sometimes no more than a

---

* How gloriously does Nature gleam on me!
    O maiden, maiden, how I love thee! How thine eye glances at me, how thou lovest me!
    Be happy for ever, as thou lovest me!

surprising remark, as when he begins a poem with the thought that he is glad to leave the cottage where his sweetheart lives in order to walk through a forest of dead trees. Or there is the poem 'Glück der Entfernung' in which he writes of the strange sense that he is happier away from his sweetheart than with her, and concludes:

> Aufgezogen durch die Sonne
> Schwimmt im Hauch ätherscher Wonne
> So das leichtste Wölkchen nie,
> Wie mein Herz in Ruh und Freude.
> Frei von Furcht, zu groß zum Neide,
> Lieb ich, ewig lieb ich sie!*

The comparison of himself with a cloud, and the affirmation that he feels neither fear (of losing the girl's love) nor envy (of any other suitor) reveals Goethe's distance from the feelings to which, as the last line paradoxically brings out, he is eternally committed. Thus the strange combination of self-affirmation and self-detachment, which was to become more explicit in Goethe's later life, already begins to make itself felt.

The paradox runs through even Goethe's love-poetry. The candour of his lines to Rickchen, as he often called Friederike, did not commit him wholly to the simple artlessness one imagines to have been in her, and within only a few years he was just as deeply committed—to his own astonishment—to the fashionable young lady of Frankfurt society, Lili Schöne-mann. The constancy that seems to be implied in 'ewig lieb ich sie!' is not constancy to a single woman, but rather to a woman whom he loves in and through the individual women he meets and loves from time to time. This explains why we so seldom 'see' the women whom Goethe loved through his lyric poetry; what we are aware of, rather, is the kind of emotion they arouse in him, which seems to reflect their character. There is an excitedness and a confidential humour

---

* Not the lightest cloud, drawn on high by the sun, floats in the breath of etherial bliss as does my heart in peace and joy. Free from fear, too great to feel envy, I love her, love her eternally.

in Goethe's poems to Friederike which is never again repeated: the easy, friendly tone of 'Erwache, Friederike', with its mock use of conventional forms of address (she is asked to awaken from early morning sleep and drive away the darkness since one look from her eyes brings daylight), followed by a series of gentle jokes both at his own and at her expense, and ending with an apology for the badness of his verse (which does have some pretty poor rhymes) on the grounds that his Muse, namely herself, was asleep—all this has a fresh frankness that must correspond to something which Friederike encouraged in him. By contrast, the poem about 'Christiane R.', whoever she may have been, though still humorous, has a rollicking tone which suggests a quite different personality:

> Ich seh sie dort, ich seh sie hier
> Und weiß nicht auf der Welt,
> Und wie und wo und wann sie mir
> Warum sie mir gefällt.*

The 'wie' and the 'wo' and the 'wann' and the 'warum' are like a zestful laugh, echoing somewhat the feeling of the nursery rhyme, 'Es kommt ein Bi-ba-Butzemann / Um unser Haus herum-di-dum'; the poet is blithely enjoying the looks of what must have been a buxom and full-lipped young woman, and 'und weidlich eins geküßt'†, a phrase which occurs later on in the same poem, continues the sense of a rumbustious courtship. There is still humour in the poems to Lili Schönemann, especially in 'Lilis Park', though perhaps we see less of her through Goethe than of some others. In the poems to Charlotte von Stein, however, a completely new note enters, one of recollected, serene, steady-paced, unexcited contemplation. He has complete confidence in her ability to understand, and perhaps for this very reason no longer needs the humorous note which sometimes sounds like an implicit apology for exaggeration: Goethe was aware, perhaps, in the

---

* I see her here, I see her there, and can't for the life of me say how and where and when I like or why I like her so.
† and a thumping good kiss I give her.

excitement of his earlier loves, that he was more conscious of his own emotion than of them, and laughed genially at his own rapture. With Charlotte, although there is surprisingly little of special value among the poems written to her ('An den Mond' and 'Warum gabst du uns die tiefen Blicke' are completely outstanding), the need for this laughter had gone: Goethe believed in her in a different way.

Yet at all times, throughout Goethe's life, there is something of the mood of the poem 'Liebhaber in allen Gestalten': he will take on any shape that his lover desires, and yet remain the unchangeable self which he knows himself to be:

> Doch bin ich, wie ich bin,
> Und nimm mich nur hin!
> Willst du Beßre besitzen,
> So laß sie dir schnitzen,
> Ich bin nun wie ich bin;
> So nimm mich nur hin!*

He is not the puppet-doll which a woman can have carved to suit her tastes, and he never yields completely. Hence, perhaps, the special quality of Goethe's poetic language, which always has a hard edge, in these early years at least. He does not go in for alliteration very much, certainly not revelling in it as Rilke was later to do, sensually bathing in the repeated sounds (compare 'Stiller Freund der vielen Fernen, fühle...'—a typically Rilkean run, and contrast the alliteration in the 'Christiane' poem just quoted). This is as much as to say that Goethe does not surrender completely, there is nothing Keatsian about his verse either in a good or a bad sense. With Keats one is often aware of the temptation to yield to the sheer luxury of sounds, a temptation turned to splendid account in the 'Ode to Autumn'. There is nothing rich in that sense any-where in Goethe. Where there is ecstasy in his poetry it comes rather through repetition, nowhere better illustrated than in 'Ganymed' or in 'Wandrers Sturmlied', with its refrain on

---

* But I am what I am, so take me as I am; if you want to have better, get them to carve you some; I am what I am, so take me as I am.

'Wen du nicht verlässest, Genius', 'Den du nicht verlässest, Genius', and its frequent reiterations throughout. Again, there is not very much in the way of imagery. Some striking lines of course come to mind, the darkness looking out of the bushes with a thousand eyes in 'Willkommen und Abschied', the gaunt flanks of winter in 'Ein zärtlich jugendlicher Kummer', the soul-soothing effect of the valley filled with moonlight in 'An den Mond'. But Goethe's mind does not see Nature habitually as a means of making his thoughts more vivid, possibly again because of a certain ultimate detachment. He says what he has to say much more straightforwardly, without ornamentation, and some of the chief features that stay in the memory are his use of quite simple words like 'offen', 'rund', 'liebe' (a favourite adjective in early poems, often whittled away in rewritings), 'heilig', 'Freude', 'Mut', 'selig', 'herrlich', 'gut', and his prolific invention of new compounds, 'silberprangend', 'freudehell', 'sturmatmend', 'neugierge-sellig'—all of these latter with the sudden impact of a new insight which goes towards the making of poetry, while the former seem sometimes to stand on the page, ordinary as they are, with what has been called 'the illumination of the usual'. Particularly significant is the number of compounds which Goethe makes with 'um-' and 'all-': 'umsausten', 'umfangend', 'allliebend', 'warmumhüllen', 'umschwebet', 'allheilend', 'allgegenwärtig', and his use of 'tausend' in one form or another: 'tausend-schlangenzüngig', 'tausend Flaggen', 'tausend Stimmen', 'tausend Ungeheuer'. All these convey in one way or another the sense of prodigality and all-inclusiveness which is an instinctive part of Goethe's mode of writing —these words are used out of his continual sense of being surrounded and identified with the great profusion of creation; he does not use imagery much, perhaps because he feels so much at one with the world outside (or so much that the world outside is himself) that he does not look for comparisons between one part and another; it is all one organic whole in which distinctions almost disappear. The fact that he does use the adjectives just referred to is also part of the same frame of mind: this world which 'is' himself is good and holy and splendid and joyful, and these words spring naturally to his mind.

Equally memorable are Goethe's rhythms. In his earlier verse he scarcely ever adheres to a particular verse-form. At most he adopts the simple quatrain or octet rhyming abab, or a sestet rhyming aabbcc. Just as often he writes in free rhythms after the model of Klopstock or Pindar, or in the four-stressed 'Knittelvers' of Hans Sachs, almost equivalent to doggerel. But whether or not he adheres to a form, Goethe's melodiousness, and his rhythmical inventiveness, show great variety. 'Mailied' and 'Willkommen und Abschied' are well enough known examples, but there are also such passages of intensity as

> Weh! Weh! Innre Wärme,
> Seelenwärme,
> Mittelpunkt!
> Glüh entgegen
> Phöb Apollen;*

and

> Wie im Morgenglanze
> Du rings mich anglühst,
> Frühling, Geliebter!
> Mit tausendfacher Liebeswonne
> Sich an mein Herz drängt
> Deiner ewigen Wärme
> Heilig Gefühl,
> Unendliche Schöne!†

---

*
> Woe! Woe! Inward warmth,
> Warmth of soul,
> Central point!
> Glow out against
> Phoebus Apollo!

The sense here is that some centre of his being must glow out in rivalry against the sun.

† How, in the gleam of morning, you glow at me from all around, Spring, my darling! How there presses against my heart, with the bliss of love a thousandfold, the holy sense of thy eternal warmth, thou never-ending beauty!

to set against the lighter movement of:

> Auf der Welle blinken
> Tausend schwebende Sterne,
> Weiche Nebel trinken
> Rings die türmende Ferne*

or the long drawn-out sigh of 'Der du von dem Himmel bist', or the pretty, tripping measure of 'Das Veilchen', and the conversational, rough humour of 'Zwischen Lavater und Basedow'. The activity of the verse is often one of the most striking things about it, accounting a little for the large number of composers who have been attracted to set Goethe's lyrics to music. And this fact is not unimportant in trying to come to some total view of Goethe's verse, for he himself came increasingly to see action, deeds, activity, movement as the prime justification of life.[1]

Despite the comparative disregard of form in Goethe's earlier poems, certain lines begin fairly soon to re-establish themselves. The alexandrine which we have already seen him using as a child disappears almost completely during his most 'Sturm und Drang' days; the associations with French classicism which it had were enough to repel a champion of national and natural self-expression. Yet already in 'Lilis Park', written in 1775, it reappears, with some justification it is true, since the whole point of the poem is humorously to lament Goethe's enslavement to the Francophile world in which Lili Schönemann lived and to which her charms enticed him. It recurs even sooner in 'Adler und Taube', written in 1774 or earlier, if we regard as one line the two lines 'O Freund, das wahre Glück / Ist die Genügsamkeit';† but then again these words, so much in the spirit of Gellert, are spoken by a prissy dove who is being contrasted with a wounded eagle, and we need have no doubt about where Goethe's sympathies lay in that case. (That the alexandrine had this kind of association for

---

* On the wave glitter a thousand floating stars, soft clouds swallow up all around the towering distance.

† O friend, true happiness is in contentedness.

Goethe cannot be doubted. In the same poem the first words spoken by the dove are presented in the same rhythm, though again in a 'divided' line: 'Du trauerst, liebelt er; / Sei gutes Mutes, Freund!'* Similarly, in 'Katechisation' (1773) an alexandrine is awarded by Goethe to a pedant who is neatly mocked by one of his pupils.)

It is disconcerting, then, to find, after Goethe had spent some years adapting himself to the ways of the court at Weimar, that he used the alexandrine more frequently for serious purposes, with no purpose of satire in mind. This is particularly notice-able in 'Ilmenau' (1783), in which not only does Goethe relate and expound his reconcilement with a life far removed from that of the 'Genie', but also the alexandrine is used more and more frequently as the poem proceeds, until in the rather conventional ending it is the dominant feature among lines, none of which has any other precise form. The metrical change coincides with a change in Goethe's whole attitude.[1]

'I know', writes T. S. Eliot in 'The Music of Poetry', 'that a poem, or a passage of a poem, may tend to realise itself first as a particular rhythm before it reaches expression in words, and that this rhythm may bring to birth the idea and the image; and I do not believe that this is an experience peculiar to myself.' Certainly it seems to be an experience which Goethe would have confessed to sharing. Much in the same way as the alexandrine insinuates itself into his consciousness, so the trochaic tetrameter gradually increases in frequency through 'Mahomets-Gesang', and ends up in a triumphant march-rhythm which completely occupies the final lines—and very appropriately so, for the whole theme of the poem is the triumphant progress of the river, and, allegorically, of the poet-genius.[2] And again in the 'große Hymnen' of the first Weimar period either the dactyl-cum-trochee line, or the five-syllable line with two stresses emerges in much the same way, not always dominating, and not always gathering frequency, but nevertheless making its presence felt in an irregular way.[3]

In these poems Goethe is surely feeling his way towards

---

* 'You grieve', he lovingly coos; 'be of good cheer, my friend.'

form out of a barely conscious sense that it is essential to him, and that the simple forms of his early poems will no longer serve his purpose, which is becoming more authoritative and representational. The folksong and ballad which he practised under Herder's guidance had their value, he may have felt (and with good cause, if he thought of 'Der König in Thule'), but as time went on he had things to say which could not be expressed in such media, and he looked for grander, statelier measures. In 'Ilmenau' one has the impression that he is toying for a while with the 'ottava rima' or Italian stanza, although none of the verses are actually in that form. In 'Zueignung', however, written in the following year, the Italian stanza is used faithfully throughout, and this is a fact of some significance to which we will return.

Alongside Goethe's love-poems and his nature-lyrics there is always the type of poem represented by 'Mahomets-Gesang', declaring the might and quasi-divine power of the poet himself, or his *alter ego*. 'Prometheus' is one such, so are 'Wandrers Sturmlied', 'An Schwager Kronos' and 'Harzreise im Winter'. Apart from the Mahomet poem, none of these has any noticeable pattern in its rhythms, and indeed for the most part they are the expression of an extreme individualism, scorning form along with all other forms of organization. At the same time, these Titanic outbursts were not meant as pure expressions of Goethe's own beliefs. To some extent they were like masks which Goethe donned for the moment—both the Prometheus and the Mahomet poems were originally connected with dramatic projects—and he could equally well put on another mask if the thought occurred to him. A particularly good instance of this are the poems 'Prometheus' and 'Ganymed', the one written in defiance of the gods, the other written in loving submission, and both written in the same year. Already in 1774, then, Goethe was allowing his thoughts to be influenced by the idea of 'polarity', the belief that the nature of Man and of the universe (of which man was, for him, a microcosmic image) is formed of two 'polar' opposites, and that the task of wisdom is to bring these opposites into unity and harmony.

More of the same kind of thought is found, though obscurely expressed, in 'Harzreise im Winter'[1]—at the back of Goethe's mind is the idea, to become more explicit later, that defiance and adoration, good and evil, and all forms of opposed contrasts whatsoever can be fused in one, and that in the deity they are so fused, or are subsumed in such a way that, although within the world of phenomena each appears separate, in him they are indistinguishable. This is the sense, both literally and physically, of the opening lines of 'Harzreise im Winter':

> Dem Geier gleich,
> Der auf schweren Morgenwolken
> Auf sanftem Fittich ruhend
> Nach Beute schaut,
> Schwebe mein Lied.*

for the savage feeling of the 'Geier gleich', setting the teeth apart in a predatory slit, is set rhythmically against the gentle 'Auf sanftem Fittich ruhend', so that the last line comes ambiguously with its '*Schwebe* mein Lied': the hovering is both fiercely possessive and yet in a way loving, since the prey referred to is in reality a man whom Goethe is trying to help. Seeing himself as a bird of prey, yet also as a kind of saviour, Goethe was foreshadowing some of the developments in his later thought.

For the time being, however, all this is merely sketched in; the first implications of the doctrine of polarity are only beginning to be realized. They will come out much more explicitly in the aphorisms of his old age and in his scientific studies. The thought of the 'Hymnen', written between 1779 and 1783, is not so much paradoxical, in the sense that some of the poems of his old age are, as self-contradictory or confused. Perhaps they were never meant to be taken together as the common expression of a unified philosophy, though it has been claimed that they were. Perhaps something of the dramatic mask adopted for 'Prometheus' and 'Mahomets-Gesang' was

---

* Like the bird of prey that, resting above the heavy clouds of morning on gentle wing, looks for its victim, let my song hover.

still intended; certainly the rhythmically splendid 'Gesang der Geister' was originally divided into parts spoken by different speakers, just as 'Mahomets-Gesang' was. But what disturbs is not the fact that in the 'Gesang der Geister' Nature is seen as beneficent, whereas in 'Das Göttliche' she is unfeeling, or that in 'Das Göttliche' the gods are to be honoured as though they were helpful and good, whereas in 'Grenzen der Menschheit' they are mere onlookers at the spectacle of the river of life, in which men rise for a moment and are drowned eternally. What is disturbing is the inconsequential way in which one verse of 'Das Göttliche' affirms that we live our lives in accordance with great, bronze, eternal laws of destiny, while the next goes on, as though it were a matter of course, to declare that we are all victims of blind chance. If paradox is intended here, in some sense of wisdom, it is thrust at us without comment and so far as we can see without even any awareness of contradiction. Did Goethe intend here another fusion of opposites such as he hinted at in the 'Harzreise im Winter'? He may have done; yet it is just as disturbing to find in 'Grenzen der Menschheit' an argument which begins by saying that the poet feels childlike devotion to the Almighty and that men should not dare to compare themselves with the gods, but then goes on to show how men are inferior to the gods in physical size, and in being mortal rather than immortal. These seem trivial points to make, in comparison with the spiritual or moral ones that might have been made on either side, with the result that the majestic rhythms sound a little hollow;

> Ein kleiner Ring
> Begrenzt unser Leben,
> Und viele Geschlechter
> Reihen sich dauernd
> An ihres Daseins
> Unendliche Kette.*

This final verse of 'Grenzen der Menschheit' is disappointing, if all that it affirms is that each man's life is another link added

---

* A little ring encircles our life, and many generations continually link themselves to the endless chain of their existence.

to the chain which makes up the existence of the gods: what cause for 'kindliche Schauer treu in der Brust'* is there in such mere prolongation? Others of the 'weltanschaulich' poems have a similar lack of impetus to carry them through to a conclusion related to their beginnings, perhaps because the doctrine of polarity, leading Goethe to expect contradictions as an inherent part of life, was beginning to make him negligent of logical sequence. There is quite often a hiatus in the thought: there is one in the very beautiful 'An den Mond' ('Füllest wieder...') between the last two verses and those preceding them, and there is one in 'Ilmenau', where the difficulties which the poet remembers, difficulties of Goethe's own which were almost driving him to his own damnation, as he felt, are suddenly dismissed as though they had never existed, with an imperious 'Verschwinde, Traum!'.† Goethe is moving into a period of his life when the connection between one moment and the next will seem decreasingly important, when the sheer existence of a single moment will be sufficient in itself, and he will be able to forget the past as Orestes does in *Iphigenie*[1] or Faust in *Faust Part II.*

The decision to stay in Weimar also played a part in this development of Goethe's poetry. 'Ilmenau' is the poem in which Goethe declares his full allegiance to the Duke Carl August; it is also the poem in which the alexandrine comes to play an increasingly important role. That it also contains such a hiatus as has just been indicated shows how deleterious an effect the society of Weimar had on Goethe, in some ways. Even the quantity of memorable poems written between 1780 and the journey to Italy in 1786 is small in comparison with those of earlier years. And some further insight into what was happening can be gained from the poem 'Zueignung', written in 1784, two years before the escape which, Goethe felt, was necessary to his whole poetic existence. 'Zueignung' is one of the best-known of all Goethe's poems; the novelist and poet Wieland said of it that he knew of 'nothing finer, nothing more perfect in any language'. It is the first of Goethe's poems

---

* Childlike awe loyally felt in my breast.   † Vanish, dream!

43

ever to adhere strictly to the regular metre and rhyme scheme of the 'Italian stanza'. It also marks, or seems to mark, a turning-point in his career, in that he declares his intention of no longer burying his talent or concealing the light of truth which has been revealed to him as a poet. In a sense, it is his declaration of loyalty to Weimar and to society in general: the 'Torquato Tasso' in Goethe[1] here becomes reconciled to the 'Antonio' in him. Yet the poem is ponderous in movement, periphrastic, full of clichés, heavily symbolical and inflatedly solemn, ending on the flattest of notes:

> So kommt denn, Freunde, wenn auf euren Wegen
> Des Lebens Bürde schwer und schwerer drückt,
> Wenn eure Bahn ein frisch erneuter Segen
> Mit Blumen ziert, mit goldnen Früchten schmückt,
> Wir gehen vereint dem nächsten Tag entgegen!
> So leben wir, so wandeln wir beglückt.
> Und dann auch soll, wenn Enkel um uns trauern,
> Zu ihrer Lust noch unsre Liebe dauern.*

This is not the realization in language of any great event in a poet's life, such as it seems meant to portray. What is worse, the female figure of Truth who appears to the poet as though in a vision seems intent on giving him a magic veil which will conceal the truth from himself and others, whenever the truth begins to become oppressive. He has only to cast the veil into the air, and 'the grave will become a bed of clouds', sweet odours will surround him, and cool breezes play. It is all rather naïvely stated, despite the noble form, and could scarcely be more lame in its avowal that Goethe intends to serve men in future by offering them spurious comfort.[2]

The adaptation from 'Stürmer und Dränger' to courtier, administrator, scientist, and man of affairs, difficult enough in all conscience, was proving after ten years to be damaging to

---

* So come then, friends, whether upon your way the burden of life presses heavily and yet more heavily, or whether a freshly renewed blessing adorns your path with flowers, decorates it with golden fruits—let us go forward united to meet the ensuing day! And then when our grandchildren mourn for us, to their delight our love will still endure.

Goethe's poetry. The man most gifted with the music of words since the days of the Minnesinger Walther von der Vogelweide was being stunted in his growth, and he was aware of it. True, he could still achieve the miraculous with such a poem as this:

Über allen Gipfeln
Ist Ruh;
In allen Wipfeln
Spürest du
Kaum einen Hauch;
Die Vögelein schweigen im Walde.
Warte nur, balde
Ruhest du auch.*

He could still write such poems as 'Erlkönig', 'An den Mond', and the intensely evocative lines that follow:

Nur wer die Sehnsucht kennt,
Weiß, was ich leide!
Allein und abgetrennt
Von aller Freude,
Seh ich ans Firmament
Nach jener Seite.
Ach! der mich liebt und kennt,
Ist in der Weite.
Es schwindelt mir, es brennt
Mein Eingeweide.
Nur wer die Sehnsucht kennt,
Weiß, was ich leide!†

But the part of himself which he projected in the novel *Wilhelm Meister* as the youthful Mignon, an instinctive, intuitive figure of strange yearnings and promptings, knew how crippling and stifling life at Weimar had become, and it was in

---

* Over all the summits is peace. In all the treetops you will sense scarcely a breath. The birds are silent in the wood. Wait, friend, soon you will rest too.

† Only he who knows what longing is knows what I suffer. Alone and separated from all joy I look into the firmament to what lies beyond. Alas, he who loves and knows me is afar off. My senses reel, my bowels are burned with fire. Only he who knows what longing is knows what I suffer.

her mouth that Goethe set one of the finest poems he ever
wrote:

Kennst du das Land, wo die Zitronen blühn,
Im dunkeln Laub die Gold-Orangen glühn,
Ein sanfter Wind vom blauen Himmel weht,
Die Myrte still und hoch der Lorbeer steht,
Kennst du es wohl?
Dahin! Dahin
Möcht ich mit dir, o mein Geliebter, ziehn.*

This has a rhythmic life, as well as a fervour, of which 'Zueignung' knows nothing. In each of the first four lines, the
slight pause after the fourth syllable gives a lilting hesitation
expressing in a way otherwise ineffable the nature of Mignon's
longing. The serenity of the scene owes nothing to imagery:
it is Goethe at his best because he is not using images, he is
drawing a picture meaningful in itself. These oranges and tall
laurels and unmoving myrtles have a significance which does
not invite further investigation. The next verse continues to
strike home with picture after picture of real things in real
places:

Kennst du has Haus? Auf Säulen ruht sein Dach,
Es glänzt der Saal, es schimmert das Gemach,
Und Marmorbilder stehn und sehn mich an:
Was hat man dir, du armes Kind, getan?
Kennst du es wohl?
Dahin! Dahin
Möcht ich mit dir, o mein Beschützer, ziehn.†

What, indeed, had they done to the intuitive Goethe who had
known how to write 'Fetter grüne, du Laub' and 'Meine Ruh
ist hin'? Could he regain that wholeness of purpose which was

---

* Knowest thou the land, where the citrons bloom, where in dark foliage the
  golden oranges glow, a gentle wind blows from the azure sky, the myrtle
  stands unmoved, and the laurel grows on high—knowest thou it, then?
  'Tis there, 'tis there, that I would go with thee, o my beloved.
† Knowest thou the house? On pillars rests its roof, the hall gleams, the
  chamber shines, and marble images stand and look at me: 'What have they
  done to thee, thou poor child?'—Knowest thou it, then? 'Tis there, 'tis
  there, that I would go with thee, O my protector'.

46

the whole aim of his doctrine of polarity, with its stress on fusion and unity, but which he seemed to be losing as he became increasingly self-conscious, increasingly aware of what he wanted to do, so that he could seldom do it without a divided mind? There were difficulties, even dangers on the way:

> Kennst du den Berg und seinen Wolkensteg?
> Das Maultier sucht im Nebel seinen Weg,
> In Höhlen wohnt der Drachen alte Brut,
> Es stürzt der Fels, und über ihn die Flut;
> Kennst du ihn wohl?
> >   Dahin! Dahin
> Geht unser Weg! o Vater, laß uns ziehn!*

Goethe moved into allegory to express it, but there were, as he here admits, still dragons to be encountered, such as could not be dismissed with the blithe 'Verschwinde, Traum!' of 'Ilmenau'. They would have to be met, and he had in a sense seen them already (since for him an external reality was an event in his own inward world): he had been to Switzerland and had seen Italy from the top of the St Gotthard pass. That was where the path lay, and he would have to take it. The course he adopted, and the only partly satisfactory unity which he found, mistaking it for a better one, must be traced later. But it was a good many years before he really found his way back to poetry after his decline from the heights he had already climbed.

---

* Knowest thou the mountain and its clouded path? The mule seeks there in mist its track; in caverns dwell the ancient brood of dragons, the rock hurtles down, and over it dashes the torrent; knowest thou it, then? 'Tis there, 'tis there that our path leads. O father, let us go.

3

'DIE LEIDEN DES JUNGEN WERTHER'

The Sorrows, or perhaps better *The Sufferings of Young Werther*, was Goethe's first and startling European success. (In China, Werther was modelled in porcelain, so far had his fame spread.) Not only Werther's blue coat and yellow breeches were imitated, but also his suicide, and despite his pleasure Goethe was later to grow weary of the popular acclaim which met him even in Italy, where he travelled incognito, as though after twelve years and more he were the author of no other work. For him, it had been an episode based on his own experiences—his unrequited love for Lotte Buff, betrothed to his friend Kestner, and his quarrel with the husband of Maximiliane Brentano—and on the reports of the self-inflicted death of a man scarcely known to him, the young Karl Jerusalem. He had been deeply involved in a tragic renunciation akin to Werther's, but had scarcely intended Werther to be taken as a model in all his deeds and moods. He had meant to write a novel, not a tract, a portrayal of a possible fate, not a desirable way of life; so, at least, he felt afterwards—his precise attitude at the time of writing is probably impossible to define.

Seeing the disastrous consequences for so many readers, Goethe was inclined, when speaking in his old age, to agree with the Roman Catholic authorities who had banned the book in Italy. Despite the words counselling the reader who felt as Werther did to 'draw comfort' from his sorrows, the book remained dangerous, as indeed Goethe's opponents had predicted; it continued to have the words printed at the beginning, in the address to the reader: 'Whatever I have been able to glean of the story of poor Werther I have eagerly gathered together, and present it to you here, knowing you will thank me for it. You cannot deny his spirit and character your admiration and love, or his destiny your tears...' So long as

Werther continued to be thought worthy of admiration, the effects Goethe deplored were likely to continue too.

For us, today, the question is not so much of the book's dangerousness, as of its qualities as a novel. It is clear now, if it was not then, that Goethe had no firmly conceived intention of justifying and thereby encouraging suicide, however close he may have been at times to taking his own life. He had rather intended to move his readers with the story of a young man so irrevocably and hopelessly in love, as any one of them might have been, that no other course but suicide seemed open to him. At the same time, he had drawn a picture of a youth of his day, overjoyed at the emotions aroused in him by the scenes of Nature, wide open to every impression, living from moment to moment at an intensity almost unbearable.

Some critics see the value of *Werther* rather in this expression of a new irrationalism, than in the story itself. 'The important thing, about *Werther* from an artistic point of view', writes Ernst Merian-Genast, 'is not the subject-matter, however sensational it may have been in its day; not the suicide from unhappy love of a talented and noble youth, but the human content, the new relationship to nature and art, to passion and reason, death and eternity, and its fashioning by the poet.' Yet it may be questioned whether the subject-matter can be so divided from the themes: Werther's 'relationship to death and eternity' may be new, but that says nothing about its value. The 'new relationship' is after all Werther's relationship, and will hold our attention and sympathy to the degree that he does.

Here lies the difficulty, for it has been recognized for a long time now[1] that Werther's feelings are those of an extreme sentimentalist. His way of weeping floods of tears at most of his meetings with Lotte, of throwing himself on the floor at her feet, trembling and shuddering when he kisses her hand, even grinding his teeth, could seem insane if we did not have the feeling that it is merely melodramatic. Yet a certain real imbalance is there, as the prose style sometimes shows. As Emil Staiger says, many readers would agree with Albert when he accuses Werther of often talking random nonsense ('Radotage').

It is of course possible to suppose, as does Goethe's most prominent champion in England today, Philip Toynbee, that Goethe was unaware of his hero's apparent insanity, and to conclude that *Werther* is 'one of the most preposterous books ever written by a great writer'. The very name, suggesting 'worthy one', and the invitation to the reader to admire Werther, suggest a large measure of sympathy, and the *mores* of the day may well have influenced Goethe more than we would readily suppose. In the times of 'Anton Reiser', already referred to, extremes of emotion were common enough. When a certain Doctor Zimmermann returned to Hanover after an operation he was received by his son and friends, he says, 'with a thousand tears of joy. Some were speechless with happiness, others swooned away, others fell into convulsions.' Herder's fiancée wrote to him that she had fallen on her knees in the woods one evening and placed glow-worms in her hair, taking care to place them in couples so as not to disturb their love-making. As Walter Bruford says, 'there was a strong sentimental strain in evidence, not peculiar of course to Germany at this time, but particularly pronounced there'. In such a society Werther could well appear more normal than he does now.

But if there is to be any lasting interest in this novel it must be because of the artist's handling of his matter, rather than as a document of an age of sentimentalism. We must suppose that Goethe is detached from Werther at least to some extent, and that he is as concerned as we are to fathom the strange nature which unfolds itself in these letters. Werther's malady does emerge very clearly from his letters. He sways violently from extreme self-depreciation to extreme self-assertion, and is never able to call a halt, despite his awareness of this condition. At the same time, he has a tenacity in believing himself in the right which accepts both extremes in his character as equally proper. Thus, when an acquaintance to whose sweetheart Werther has been too openly attentive offers a protest, Werther delivers a long homily on the need to avoid 'bad humour'. One should rejoice with one's friends, prosper their happiness, not display resentment which can only diminish another's pleasure: in short, the acquaintance should not have tried to spoil Werther's innocent enjoyment. On another occasion, shortly after, Werther is reproved by Albert, the betrothed of Lotte, for thinking of suicide even so far as to put an empty pistol-barrel to his forehead. To this Werther retorts, with many implied snubs to Albert, that those who really know the misery of being alive will never fail to see the greatness rather than the weakness of those who choose to die by their own hand: in short, Albert should not intervene in Werther's misery. On each occasion, Werther is convinced of the pharisaism of the man who opposes him: the course of his argument, however, depends entirely on his mood and needs of the moment. All-important for him is 'pleasure in oneself', 'a true feeling of oneself'. 'Taking what one wants is the most natural impulse in man!' he writes to his friend Wilhelm. 'Do not children grasp at whatever they have a mind to?—And I?' Again, 'I treat my heart like a sick child, and grant it every wish.' Being in love is one further way, perhaps the most valuable of all, towards strengthening his self-esteem: 'how I worship myself, since she loves me'; and even self-knowledge is no hindrance: 'I laugh at my heart—and do whatever it wants.'

Werther does not quite live up to his intentions here. He is always careful, until his last meeting with Lotte, to refrain from any open declaration of love despite his heartfelt desires. But he admires the young man who, in similar circumstances, offers even violent love to an unwilling mistress-employer. Again, he stifles the temptation to murder Albert, but takes what seems a masochistic delight in procuring from him the pistols with which he shoots himself, a delight which is heightened by the knowledge that the pistols were given with a trembling hand by Lotte herself. He denies any erotic feeling, but thrills at the touch of her foot beneath the table and revels in the thought of the canary which touched his lips after touching hers. Almost always his yielding to the promptings

51

of his heart are passive rather than active, negative rather than positive. He would like to woo Lotte but does not, would like to oppose Albert but does not; instead he puts himself passively between them, making society intolerable for all three, and finally kills himself in a manner which might have been calculated to cause them the most pain.

All this must harm the reception of the serious themes of the novel, the sense in Werther that Nature, to which he is so passionately devoted, is both a creator and a destroyer:

Mighty mountains surrounded me, abysses lay at my feet, and cloudburst-torrents hurtled downward, the rivers flooded past beneath me, and woods and mountain-chains resounded; and I saw them interweaving and intermoving in the depths of the earth, all those unfathomable forces; and now above the earth and under the heavens throng the families of countless creatures, all, all peopled with a thousand shapes; and mankind makes itself secure in its huts and builds its nests, and rules according to its own lights over all the wide world!...Ah, then, how often have I longed to fly with the wings of the crane that passed over my head, to the shores of the unmeasured ocean, to drink that swelling bliss of life from the foaming goblet of the infinite and to feel, though only for a moment and in the limited power of my bosom one drop of the blissfulness of the Being which produces all this in itself and through itself.

...And now it is as though a curtain had parted before my soul, and the scene of infinite life transforms itself before me into the image of the eternally open grave. How can you say 'This is!' when all this passes by, when all rolls past with the speed of a thunderstorm, when the whole power of its existence so seldom endures, alas, and is swept away by the stream, plunged beneath the waves and smashed against the rocks? Not a moment passes without consuming you and those about you, not a moment when you are not, when you cannot help being, a destroyer. The most innocent walk costs the life of a thousand poor insects, one step shatters the laborious buildings of the ant, and stamps down a little cosmos into a shameful grave. Ah, it is not the great, rare disasters of the world that move me, not the floods which sweep away your villages, or the earthquakes that swallow up your cities; what tunnels beneath my heart is the consuming power that lies hidden in the whole of Nature, that has fashioned nothing that does not destroy its neighbour and itself. And thus I stagger, trembling, the heavens and earth and all their weaving forces about me, and see nothing but an eternally devouring, eternally redevouring monster.[1]

This is the really important issue which Goethe might have treated with more effect. Despite the headiness of the emotion (which may be contrasted with Hamlet's on 'this goodly frame the earth' in Act II, scene ii—a speech which may well have inspired Goethe) here is a theme which was close to his deepest concerns, as we see from the repetition of it in Faust's encounter with the Earth-Spirit. But it is not realized at its deepest, even here. There is something grandiose and vague about this passage, a sense that the writer is very conscious of the effect he is creating—there is no 'throwaway' self-critical humour in it, as there is at the end of Hamlet's speech.

The sentimentality and egoism of the central character affect even the picture of Werther in his happier moments, playing with children, refusing to admit class distinctions between himself and the peasantry or the nobility, sending alms to the poor, attempting to be just to his enemies and his rival. There is always the sense that Werther is over-conscious of himself at such times, that, as in the consciousness of Lotte's love, he is really worshipping himself when he writes to his friend of these events.

However, this is a novel almost entirely in the form of letters written by Werther, and it is a feature of such novels, unlike novels told by a narrator, that the reader's view is restricted to the standpoint of the main character. In adopting such a form, Goethe was able to give more immediate expression to thoughts and feelings which must at least have passed through his mind, while he still remained, as author of the novel rather than as writer of the letters, uncommitted to them in their entirety. In a sense, he was trying them out, seeing how they might develop if he were not himself, but a man more closely identified with Werther. That he does stand outside the events though not as a judge or critic, is clear from the re-introduction of a narrator, in the final pages, who has collected together all the remaining letters of the hero and who pieces the story together at a time when no letters could possibly have been written. Yet this narrator is not a really satisfying novelistic device. While he does, at times, retain a matter-of-fact tone, he imagines himself so vividly in Werther's situation that many of the scenes he relates might have been related by Werther himself.[1] The narrator appears to know far more of the most intimate feelings both of Werther and of Lotte than he could possibly have discovered by inquiry, and his implicit purpose seems rather to be that of persuading his readers of the just necessity for Werther's suicide than of giving a full picture of the events from a point of view other than Werther's.

It is this merely apparent objectivity of the narrator which makes the final catastrophe difficult to accept as a moving conclusion. When Werther himself speaks of his floods of tears, it is one thing; when the narrator imagines them, it is something different. He, the narrator, becomes bathetic in a passage such as that immediately following Werther's reading of Ossian to Lotte, when the emotion becomes purely melodramatic and 'stagey'. The mood is disturbed in other ways. There is not only the long passage from Ossian, which the narrator quotes near the climax, and which is, today, so difficult even to read through that a serious break in our sympathy must occur. There is also the extremely unfavourable light cast on Lotte and Albert by the events just before Werther's death. Werther himself could not, of course, be present during the scene when his messenger called at Lotte's house for the pistols, on the pretext that they were needed for a journey. Had he imagined at all vividly what emotions his request might arouse in Lotte, who had often heard him speak of his intention to kill himself, he might have desisted. But the reader is given no insight into Werther's mind at this vital moment in the novel. Instead, he has the narrator's account of how Lotte, fearing to tell her husband of Werther's recent passionate embrace, did not dare even to oppose the lending of the pistols, which Albert offers so brusquely as almost to make it appear that he is willing for Werther to use them against himself. Indeed, when Lotte slowly goes towards them, takes them down from the wall with a trembling hand, and delays so long that Albert has to urge her on with a questioning glance, we can only suppose that Albert does mean them to be so used—he could not possibly fail to see what Lotte's slowness meant. In all this, it is not Werther's mind into which we gain insight, but that of the narrator, who, despite his apparent neutrality, is evidently bent on arousing every possible sympathy with Werther, rather than allowing the tragic consequences for all parties to emerge more clearly.

This is ultimately the weakness of the novel; not that it presents a sentimental character or an ending liable to encourage melancholia, but that it is too closely an outpouring of self-expression on Werther's part: there is not enough of the moulding hand of the novelist in it, and where such a hand appears to be present, it is deceptive, for it serves only to support Werther's view, not to place it in a true perspective. Yet, like almost everything that Goethe wrote, the importance of *Werther* in European history, as a novel in the tradition of Rousseau's *Nouvelle Héloïse*, cannot be denied. From the Jacopo Ortis of Ugo Foscolo to André Gide's André Walter and Rilke's Malte Laurids Brigge, works of a similar nature have continued to be written, as a rule with as much self-indulgence as Werther himself showed. By all accounts, Napoleon admired it sufficiently to read the novel seven times, though he criticized the mixture of injured ambition with passionate love, and 'did not like' the ending. Yet the judgement of Napoleon's fellow-countryman Scherer, that the book is 'the poem of the German middle-class sentimentality of that day' also deserves consideration.

4

DRAMATIC WORKS

In the first twenty years of his life as a writer, ending in 1788, Goethe had written or begun over twenty plays. In the next thirty-eight years he completed *Faust Part I* (already near completion) but apart from that wrote or began only half a dozen, none of them among his best. Only in the last seven years of his life, when he wrote most of *Faust Part II*, can the drama be said to have become again a major interest.

The indications may be that the Italian Journey marked a turning-point in Goethe's concern with the theatre, as it did in so much else. Wilhelm Meister the actor, in the early version of the novel, is last seen at the climax of his career in the theatre, whereas in the later rewriting, after Italy, this becomes merely an episode and no very important one in his life. It may be that Italy, with the peace of mind Goethe found there, tended to drive him away from dramatic conflicts and tensions.

Yet even in the dramas of before 1786, conflict is seldom present. Goethe's principal plays are more concerned with reconciliation than with struggle. This is not true, or not relevant, in the case of such early imitations of French models as *Die Laune des Verliebten* (1767) and *Die Mitschuldigen* (1768), of panoramic works like *Das Jahrmarktsfest zu Plundersweilern* (1773), a pasquinade like *Götter, Helden und Wieland* (1773), or an occasional trifle like *Erwin und Elmire* (1775) or *Die Fischerin* (1781). It is not true either of the more seriously intended, but melodramatic and exaggeratedly drawn *Clavigo* (1774), in which Goethe vicariously punished his own faithlessness to Friederike Brion. It is more applicable to the short play *Die Geschwister* (1776), in which Goethe seems to have looked for some sublimation of his more than normally tender feeling for his sister Cornelia, and of *Stella* (1776), in the first version of which he portrayed a man in love with two women at once, and ended by allowing him to marry both. *Pandora* (begun

1806) and *Die natürliche Tochter* (begun 1799), the only two of the post-Italian plays of serious interest, also tended in the direction of reconciliation, although since both remained only partly finished the nature of this reconciliation can only be guessed.

But of all the plays, almost equal in number to those of Shakespeare, only four, apart from *Faust*, still retain any regular place in the repertory of the German theatre (five, if we include *Clavigo*), and all four have in common a certain Rousseau-like trust in the goodness not only of human nature but of the process of history, provided that it is not obstructed or opposed. In *Götz* (1771–3), the first of them, the hero advances a view of society based on 'freedom', in which all men are to live in accordance with their station in life, without ambition or envy (this finds an unexpected echo in Nietzsche's *Antichrist*); Götz's tragedy is that in the circumstances of his time he cannot realize this freedom. In *Egmont*, begun not long after, the hero attempts to live freely in the sense that he takes no thought either for the morrow or for moral issues, if these cause him any care or anxiety: he tries to live in an absolute trust that the present moment is good in itself and that the future will be rewarding. *Iphigenie auf Tauris* (1778–86) puts the case even more emphatically, for whereas the earlier two plays end catastrophically (though with hope), this ends with the triumph of a woman who has staked her life on the assurance that truthfulness must convert the barbarian from his barbarity. And even *Torquato Tasso* (1780–8), though it is the one play of the four whose interpretation causes much controversy, has been widely held to imply that the neurotic 'outsider' can be brought within the fold of a loving society which is prepared to offer him his rightful place. Widely as the plays differ, all have in common the belief that everything is working for good, and surely have their roots not only in Rousseau but also in the Pietist circles of Goethe's youth.

Götz von Berlichingen, originally entitled *Geschichte Gottfriedens von Berlichingen mit der eisernen Hand*, is a chronicle play based, as to facts, on the autobiography of a notorious robber-baron of the sixteenth century, and as to form and treatment on Shakespeare's history-plays. It differs from both in that Götz's villainies are on the whole played down, and that it is less organized than even such a pure chronicle as *Henry VI*. For this, Herder is partly responsible, for although he told Goethe, on reading the first version, that Shakespeare had completely spoiled him ('Shakespeare hat Euch ganz verdorben'), Herder himself had declared, in his *Shakespeare* essay, that all Shakespeare's plays were essentially neither tragical, comical nor pastoral, but historical, by which he meant that they were episodic, a series of astounding events ('Begebenheiten') rather than an organized whole. This foreshadowing of the Brechtian 'epic' theatre, equally episodic in intention, had the effect on Goethe that he introduced a multitude of scenes, many of them striking and original: the secret 'Vehme', a forerunner of the Ku Klux Klan, which condemns Adelheid to death; the pomp of the Imperial Court of Maximilian I; the besieged castle in the woods; the pillaging and burning of villages—all of them quite new to the German stage. At the same time, he introduced so many changes of scene as to make the staging of the play in his own day difficult. Like his contemporaries, Goethe was not conscious of the construction of the Shakespearean stage, with its lack of proscenium curtains, and the consequent need to insert a small scene in the gallery above so that the forestage could be cleared for the next important piece of the main action. And so, although Goethe never fashioned out of Shakespeare anything like the phantasmagoria of Ossianic gloom which Ducis made of him in France, he did see him as a great forerunner in anarchy, untrammelled by rules, careless of form. Shakespeare to him was like a Gothic cathedral (he wrote on both in Herder's manifesto *Von deutscher Art und Kunst*): a great profusion of detail, overwhelming in its proliferations, but 'alles zweckend zum Ganzen', all aiming at the whole.

Apart from structure and choice of a national subject, however, Goethe's debt to Shakespeare in *Götz* was not great. Liebetraut is very much the Shakespearean courtier, in the tradition of Osric, and the rough speech of the soldiers in the inn of the opening scene also shows a possible Shakespearean influence. Not that the soldiers speak consistently in character: they may say 'Schlag den Hund tot',* or 'Hänsel, noch ein Glas Branntwein, und meß christlich,'† but they have no dialect forms, nothing so forceful as has, say, the seventeenth-century 'Die gelibte Dornrose' by Gryphius. It is not exactly literary speech that they use, but rather more like the language one would expect Goethe's student friends to have spoken, vulgar, clipped, boisterous, but grammatical and basically in High German. Yet a phrase such as 'Sie sollen zu ihren Händen rufen, multipliziert euch!' ‡ has a Shakespearean ring, and the melo-dramatic remorse of the villain Weislingen was surely written in reminiscence of Richard III in his tent on the night before Bosworth field. The play is in prose, perhaps because Goethe had first read Shakespeare in Wieland's prose translation, and there is a complete absence both of such grimly realistic scenes of cruelty as the death of the boy Rutland or the taunting of Warwick by Margaret of Anjou, and of any figure like the helpless Henry VI, aghast at these monstrosities and too weak to prevent them.

Goethe seeks above all to present in Götz a man in complete contrast to the effete civilization of his own day; we can guess at something of the mood which inspired him from reading part of a letter sent a few years later[1] to the Duke of Weimar, a letter in which he gives vent to the feelings that must have been with him in his student days.

Well my lord [it begins (Goethe's affectionately respectful 'Lieber Herre' is impossible to render exactly)] here I am. In Leipzig—felt a bit strange when I was getting near the place, more of that when I see you, and I simply can't say how the smell and feel of the good earth contrasts with all these black-coated, grey-coated, starch-coated, bandy-legged, wig-beplastered, sword-swaggering Magistri, the lanky highfalutin student rascals all very à la mode, and the

---

* Strike the dog dead.

† Johnny, another glass of brandy, and pour like a good Christian.

‡ They shall cry to their hands 'be multiplied!'.

dithering, simpering, cooing, swooning young women and the lecherous, hoity-toity, tail-waggling, finicky servant girls, all of which horrors greeted me today at the city gates, it being Lady Day.

Against this Goethe could have set the self-portrait by the original Götz in his 'Lebens-Beschreibung', which concludes:

And finally I cannot nor I will not deny that the Almighty GOD hath granted me many times, by his Divine Grace to a poor man, victory and good fortune against all my foes from my youth upward, and my misfortune in which I have now long time dwelt comes only from this, that when I have parleyed with my foes and opponents I have trusted them, and supposed that Yea was Yea and Nay was Nay and that what had been promised by one to another, so much should be fairly kept, and that other folk would do as I have done my life long (and if GOD will, shall continue so to do), for by such causes and over-much trust have I come, as I say, to all my misfortune, but when as a foe I have not trusted my foes, as may from time to time come to pass, I have with GOD's grace and help succeeded well, else could I not say GOD be praised, for I knew how I should conduct myself towards mine enemies; GOD the Almighty help me still.

Such a sturdy character Goethe presented in his play: the warrior knight, chivalrous and charitable, brave, devout and honest, and such he was, in part. Goethe's aim was to re-establish such qualities as ideals to be striven after, and by delving back into specifically German history he hoped, we may assume, to imitate what Shakespeare had done with such figures as King Henry V.

The difficulty which was bound to face him was that the original Götz, for all his pious conclusion, was a freebooting marauder who, like many other knights of his day, maintained the ancient 'Faustrecht' or 'right of the mailed fist', plundering and if necessary torturing merchants who passed through his domain, stealing cattle and ravaging and pillaging for years in war against Nuremberg and other cities. Something of the original Götz's spirit may be judged from this further extract from his autobiography:

One day [he writes] as I was on the point of making an attack, I saw a pack of wolves descending on a flock of sheep. This seemed to me a good omen. We were going to begin the fight. A shepherd was near us, guarding his sheep, when, as if to give us the signal, five wolves threw themselves all together on the flock. I saw it and noted it gladly. I wished them success and ourselves too, saying, 'Good luck, dear comrades, success to you everywhere!' I took it as a very good augury that we had begun the attack together.

Such a man's life offers good material for a play; it offers less good material for an appeal for the revival of Götz's qualities, and that is to some extent what Goethe tries to do.

This is not to say that Goethe was unaware of the case against Götz's individualism, which he puts quite strongly into the mouth of Weislingen,[1] who says to Götz, in a line which is very likely based on the passage just quoted, 'You regard the princes as the wolf regards the shepherd'. Yet Weislingen is the villain, and Götz's reply, to the effect that the princes are bent on their own profit anyway, though it does not justify him, remains unanswered. As John Arden says in the introduction to his adaptation, *Ironhand*, Götz is so strong a character that he needs more serious opposition than Weislingen can provide: 'the hero is seen almost entirely from his own point of view' (a remark that might be made of several Goethean heroes).

Goethe's Götz is introduced to us in the words of Brother Martin (Luther is distantly suggested): 'It is a pleasure to see such a great man'; he dies with the words 'Freedom! Freedom!' on his lips, and his epitaph, spoken by his comrade-in-arms in the last line of the play, runs 'Woe to posterity if it mistakes your worth!' Thus it becomes clear that Götz is going to incorporate some heroic quality which we shall be asked to admire especially. Yet as Ronald Peacock observes, 'there is a discrepancy between the character we actually see and the one we feel we are being asked to believe we see'.[2] The whole setting is too trivial to arouse the political interest that the word 'freedom' suggests, and Götz himself is uncertain what it means, speaking at one moment of the princes, as he does to Weislingen, as rogues who deserve to be warred against, at another time (to Georg) as noble, generous neighbours who can be trusted not to use their liberty extravagantly.[1] In either case, freedom is restricted to those in power: it does not apply to the subject.

Moreover, in the latter part of the play Götz is seen as being far from the upright soldier he claims to be. In consenting to lead the pillaging soldiers he breaks his word to the emperor, the one liege lord to whom he has always acknowledged a duty, although it is true that, ostensibly at least, he intends to prevent the soldiers' barbarity and use them in the fight for feudal privileges. Indeed he makes an explicit proviso that he will lead them for a month and decide afterwards whether they have justified his trust in them. Almost at once, however, the soldiers continue with arson and pillage, as was to be expected. (The situation is curiously like that of Faust and the barbaric handling of Philemon and Baucis in Act v of *Faust Part II*.)[2] And, although Götz is angry at this conduct, he never makes a clear stand, but is swept away by events[3] without ever having confronted the result of his action in the name of freedom; this vital issue of the play is never properly faced. Indeed the doubts as to Götz's loyalty and honesty, voiced by his wife,[4] are hushed up with what can only be called unsatisfactory arguments. Before the Imperial commission[5] Götz behaves like an old ruffian, and in general his argument is to knock his opponent down rather than give any account of his actions.

All this is of course quite true to life: the original Götz was even more of a contradictory mixture of pious devotion, blindness, generosity and brutality. It is only in so far as Goethe may be thought either to idealize Götz or to see him as the victim of a tragic conflict that any opposition need be expressed. Thus, for at least one critic, the tragedy of Götz is that he has given his word to the Emperor not to engage in further robberies, but is obliged by his very nature to go on fighting. 'Thus, true to the law governing his life, he places himself at the head of the rebellious peasants, and so becomes disloyal to the Emperor, a tragic conflict which inwardly destroys him.' In fact there is no trace of any conflict in Götz after his word has been broken: this question of loyalty is not an issue of the play at all, and his final moments are sentimental rather than deeply concerned with fundamental issues.

The man who could speak in something not unlike the language of his prototype in real life at the beginning of the play has changed considerably by the end, when we hear him speaking words such as these:

My love, if you could persuade the guard to let me go into his little garden for half an hour to enjoy the dear sun and the azure sky and the pure air...

Or, on hearing that his son has entered a monastery:

Let him be, he is holier than I; he does not need my blessing.—On our wedding day, Elisabeth, I never foresaw that I should die like this. My old father blessed us, and a whole generation of noble, valiant sons gushed forth from his prayer.—You did not heed it, and now I am the last of them all. Lerse, your face rejoices me in the hour of my death more than in the boldest affray. Then my spirit would lead yours; now it is you who hold me erect. Ah, that I might see Georg again, and warm myself at his look.—You all look down and weep—He is dead—Georg is dead. Then die, Götz...

The melodrama and self-consciousness of Götz, coupled with a 'literary' quality in his speech, give just that note to the end of the play which seems meant to make one feel that his way of living is actually preferable to that of the cunning ne'er-do-wells who will succeed him, while at the same time it makes him so 'pious' and falsely rhetorical that we cease to believe in his reality. Götz is after all, in the earlier parts of the play, a lively man: one would rather be in his company than with one of the Magistri Goethe remembered from Leipzig, and yet the real situation in which Götz finds himself is not envisaged: weaknesses are glossed over, and the issues of government which the play raises remain superficial, compared, say, with Henry's argument on the night before Agincourt. The play remains an excellent basis for a pageant-like performance, above all at some such castle as Jagsthausen, Götz's own residence, now restored. But it is the work of a brilliant young man, several years younger than Shakespeare was at the time of writing his earliest plays. *Götz* is an astonishing play to come out of a literature which had had nothing of the kind to show before: as a sheer manifesto it was of great importance. But Goethe had not only no tradition to back him, he had no audience demanding more histories, more chronicles of the German past. The national consciousness to which Shakespeare appealed had yet to be created, and Goethe's single-handed task was beyond any man. Not until Schiller's *Wallenstein* was published in 1797 did another play of note about German history appear, and a quarter of a century was too long a gap. (Contrast the dozens of histories by Peele, Greene and others, supplied to Elizabeth's London.) Goethe could not create both supply and demand, he could not make a sense of nationality out of next to nothing.

Still, in his next play of importance, *Egmont*, Goethe did attempt at first to continue in the direction he had begun. It was not about Germany, but about the closely related Netherlands at the time of their revolt against Spanish tyranny in the late sixteenth century, and thus remained close to *Götz* in some ways. It also owed a debt to Shakespeare, especially in the 'build-up' for Egmont in the opening scenes, reminiscent of *Julius Caesar*, and in the scenes of the artisans. But by the time Egmont was written Goethe was already moving away from Shakespearean influence back to the models of French and classical drama. After the opening scenes, the thronged 'Elizabethan' stage gave way to 'classical' scenes in which there were scarcely ever more than two speaking persons on stage together—and there were also passages of dialogue in which single lines were rapidly exchanged in a way recalling the classical device of stichomythia.[1] Goethe spent almost ten years between beginning to write *Egmont* and ending it, and the style shows his change of preference.

A further new development concerns the structure. *Götz* was episodic in the sense that it told a fairly long life-story in which there was no complicated plot, of the kind often found in eighteenth-century plays, but rather a series of loosely connected events, with a quite important sub-plot not directly concerned with Götz himself at all. *Egmont* is episodic in a different way, in that the scenes often advance not so much the action as our knowledge of the central character. There is first the 'build-up' for Egmont, in which the crowd praise his valour in fighting against the French, and his generosity and magnanimity. Then come scenes in which we see Egmont with his secretary, revealing his tolerance, if it is not his sovereign whimsicality, in the awarding of punishments to his subjects; Egmont with William of Orange, discussing state affairs, Egmont in love with Klärchen, Egmont as seen by Margaret of Parma the Regent of the Netherlands, Egmont with the tyrant Alba and later with Alba's son Ferdinand. These other characters have next to no connection with one another; unlike Schiller, who would surely have involved Egmont's secretary with Klärchen instead of introducing a separate lover for her, and developed the affection for Egmont shown by Margaret into something stronger, Goethe leaves each of the secondary figures in a box by itself, existing only in relation to the central figure.

This structural quality corresponds to the episodic nature of Egmont's whole philosophy, which it is the main purpose of the play to expound and explore. Egmont himself does not look for connections between one action and another. He takes each moment as it comes, almost as though foreseeing the time when Brecht would demand a theatre in which every separate scene existed for itself, in its own right. In his famous speeches to his secretary,[1] Egmont declares that he will not concern himself with what is to come:

Do I live only in order to think about living? Am I not to enjoy the present moment, that I may be sure of the next? And then consume that with cares and crotchets?...Does the sun shine on me today in order that I may reflect on yesterday, and guess at connections where there is nothing to be guessed at, no connections to be made, namely the destiny of the day that is to come?

And from this he goes on to the simile of the charioteer, helplessly carried forward by horses over which he has barely the slightest control, and which Goethe was later to describe[1] as a symbol of the Daemon driving his own life. So far as Egmont is concerned, in these speeches, there is no sequence of cause and effect, but only the passing moment which (in contrast to Faust) he is determined to relish to the uttermost. That the play itself is equally 'discrete' in structure is an indication of Goethe's sympathy, at the time of writing, with this point of view, which he presents in the best possible light.

There is next to no plot. Egmont, as a leader of the Netherlands, debates with William of Orange whether it is right to oppose the tyranny of the Duke of Alba by violence; he tries to persuade the Duke by fair argument but is thrown into prison and executed. The criticisms which must inevitably be made of so undramatic a story were made by Schiller in the *Jena Review*, almost as soon as the play first appeared. They were that Egmont's heroic merits (like those of Götz) are talked about but never seen, whereas his faults are presented very clearly. Having refused to join William of Orange, Schiller points out, Egmont takes no more thought of the impending danger than to 'bathe away the wrinkles of care from my forehead' by spending the night with his sweetheart. 'No, Count Egmont', Schiller retorted, 'if it is too much trouble for you to see to your own safety, you have nothing to complain of when the noose tightens round you.' It would have been better, he went on, had Goethe remained true to history by making Egmont a married man with several children, instead of reducing his age by some twenty years and making him a bachelor: the fact that the real Egmont had his family to think of was one reason why he did not make a firmer stand: he hoped by conciliation to find some escape from the prospect that they too might suffer, as hostages. And indeed, in so far as Schiller's comment amounts to saying that Egmont's motives for inaction on Alba's arrival sound trivial, every reader must agree with him. The fact, however, that Egmont deliberately, from a settled philosophy, chooses not to think of the morrow, does alter the case. He is not presented by Goethe as a merely thoughtless dallier: 'the whole free value of life' is—in his own words—what is at stake, and this is what the remainder of the play purports to examine: can a man live as Egmont does and succeed, or at any rate command our respect?

Freedom is not for Egmont, however, as it was for Götz, something to be fought for. It is rather something which will come with the slow processes of time; he is a pacifist in his discussions with William of Orange, protesting that open revolt will bring down on the heads of the Dutch people the wrath of Alba, and justify every conceivable cruelty. They should trust the King of Spain, he argues, and reckon on his reluctance to provoke conflict. And in consequence he takes no action at all until Alba arrives to take over from Margaret of Parma, when Egmont goes to him to plead as a reasonable man for peace and friendship. Alba is not reasonable, and, as Orange predicted, Egmont is simply arrested. The issue thus becomes, for the remainder of the play, whether Egmont's inactivity can in some other sense be justified, perhaps in terms of his philosophy of living for the moment. As he said to his secretary,[1] 'I have not yet reached the summit of my growth, and when I stand there, let me stand firmly, not fearfully'. Can he now continue to stand without fear, enduring the consequences of his creed? If he can, we may well feel the tragedy of his persistence in what is, after all, not an evil course, though it may be a mistaken one.

But inevitably Schiller's criticism of the final scene must come to mind here. For a moment, in his prison cell, Egmont had wavered;[2] care ('Sorge') assaulted him, and he almost regretted the path he had taken, only to recover his confidence again. Yet in the final scene all the seriousness of purpose in Goethe is brushed aside. As Egmont lies asleep, still in prison, an allegorical figure of Freedom appears on a cloud, in the form of Klärchen, now dead by her own hand, who 'bids him be happy, and indicates to him that his death will procure for the Provinces their liberty; she recognises him as victor and hands him a laurel wreath'. Schiller's observation on this ending was that it was operatic: no doubt he had in mind the way in which, in operas of his time, the *deus ex machina* would descend from the flies in a cut-out heaven on wires. We may also feel, however, that, although Egmont is about to suffer execution, he has by no means helped to bring about the liberation of his country since he deliberately refused to take action on its behalf. His refusal may not in itself have been bad or wrong (however much we may feel that it was ill-advised), but the fact remains, his policy of inaction has had no success, and it will take years of hard fighting to achieve the freedom which Klärchen represents.

This much of the ending is surprising enough. Even more surprising, though, is Egmont's own volte-face in the last twenty or thirty lines after the vision has faded. All along, Egmont has held that it would be wrong to cause bloodshed among civilians:

you will see the corpses of burghers, children, young maids, floating down the river towards you [he has said to Orange] and you will stand there horror-struck, not knowing whose cause you are defending, since those very people are being destroyed for whose liberty you took up arms. And how will you feel, when you find yourself compelled to confess that you took them up for your own safety?[1]

Now that he sees where his own policy has led, he reverses all that, yet without acknowledging that he has been in error or that he has in any way weakened the cause by allowing himself to be captured:

Stride on, brave people! The goddess of Victory leads you forward! And as the sea breaks through your dykes, break down and smash the walls of tyranny and hurl them from the ground they dare enclose!

Not only is this the policy which Orange counselled long before, Egmont also speaks as though he had argued for it himself:

(Drums in the distance) Hark! Hark! How oft this sound has summoned me to march freely on the field of battle and of victory! How gaily did my comrades step out on the dangerous path of glory! And I too step out from this prison to an honourable death; I die for liberty, for which I have lived and fought, and for which I now sacrifice myself in suffering.

Of course, since Egmont is in prison, the Netherlanders are not there to hear these words, which become a mere rhetorical flourish to the audience in the theatre. Besides, the people have just been seen in a cowardly light refusing to rise and liberate their leader. But apart from that, Egmont has not lived and fought for liberty, and Beethoven's inspiring music in the 'Egmont' overture should not persuade us that he has. Fighting in the cause of liberty is precisely what Egmont has refused to do, though like his historical namesake he fought in battles against the French with great distinction, as we are told in Act I. All his final speech is in contradiction to what he has stood for throughout the action of the play, both in that he is now prepared to shed blood after all, and in that he acts in order to achieve a future object, or sees his suffering as part of a pattern of events which will lead to eventual success—yet not a word of realization crosses his lips, and one may well finish reading or seeing the play with a vague impression that he is vindicated.

For a second time, Goethe shows some inconsequentiality in the construction of a play: he promises what he does not perform, and, despite anything that may be said about the excellence of the crowd-scenes, the lively temper of Klärchen, or the seriousness of Goethe's purpose, this consideration is overruling; it is not mitigated either by the extreme length of many of the speeches. A further puzzling, though not strictly relevant feature is that Egmont sets out, apparently with Goethe's approval, to do what in *Faust* is regarded as a mark of damnation—namely to live entirely for the present moment, not striving beyond it.[1] Similarly, where Götz's conception of freedom involves almost anarchical independence, defiance of practically all authority, Egmont's ideal is to work with the authorities wherever possible, to trust them even against appearances. There is no reason why such different notions should not have been tried out in this play or that; it is only because Goethe seems to uphold them and then, within the same work, to contradict or oppose them, that some doubt on the reality of his concern must be cast. Ultimately, perhaps, it is only through his doctrine of polarity[1] that such oscillations can be properly understood.

With *Iphigenie auf Tauris*, a work conceived after Goethe's decision to remain in Weimar, the trend towards classicism already noticeable in *Egmont* is completed. Not only does Goethe choose a classical subject, he treats it in the manner of the French classicists with a division into five acts, complete adherence to the unities of action, time and place, a confidant, a recognition scene such as Aristotle describes (although as 'the least artistic form', used 'from poverty of wit') in the *Poetics*,[2] and a peripeteia, or change of fortune at the end, though not in a tragic but rather in the contrary sense. This reversion to classical form is all the more remarkable in that the prose-version of *Iphigenie* was begun only five years after the Shakespearean *Götz*: Goethe was not dogmatic in his opposition to French influence.

Despite the change of form, however, the play continues an essentially Goethean preoccupation. The story, as in Euripides, tells of the Iphigenia who is saved from being sacrificed through the intervention of Diana, but who later finds herself, as a priestess of the same goddess, being required by the barbarian King Thoas to sacrifice a victim who is no other than her own brother Orestes. In Euripides' play, the heroine escapes by a ruse: she persuades the gullible king that the statue of Diana has been polluted by the presence of Orestes and his companion Pylades, and must be purified in the sea. Having by this means gained permission for herself and the prisoners to get to the coast, Iphigenia escapes with them in their ship, and would succeed completely but for some interference by Poseidon and Athene which possibly (if Euripides is not being ironical) is meant to show that she needs divine help as well as her own ingenuity in order to succeed. Goethe, however, while taking over essentially the same story, thinks of it in terms of the family of Tantalus (or of Atreus) from which Iphigenia is descended, that is to say, the accursed family whose terrible history is also related in plays by Sophocles and Aeschylus, and is a parallel to the Christian myth of the fall of Man. The issue for Goethe is not simply the local one that it is in Euripides' play, but concerns the whole history of the house, even the whole history of the human race. How can the curse which the gods have laid upon the descendants of Tantalus, and which has caused wife to kill husband, son to kill mother, be lifted? Symbolically, how can the internecine struggles of the human race be brought to an end? Goethe's answer is that if one member of the family can ever achieve pure humanity, all will be redeemed. As he put it in verse many years later:

> Alle menschlichen Gebrechen
> Sühnet reine Menschlichkeit.*

And by this 'pure humanity' Goethe means something very like the trustfulness of Egmont, with the difference that its success is immediate, not deferred. Goethe's Iphigenia, when the crucial moment comes, refuses to deceive King Thoas, to whom she owes gratitude for hospitality and kindness over many years: unlike her namesake in Euripides she casts herself on Thoas's mercy, revealing not only that Orestes is her brother but that she is involved in a plot to effect his escape, and challenging the king, in the name of humanity, to punish her or to withdraw his insistence on the sacrifice of Orestes. Thoas, unlike Egmont's adversary Alba, is mollified by this appeal to his better nature, and allows both Iphigenie and the prisoners to leave.

The final version, mostly in iambic pentameters, conveys an air of great serenity, heard at its best in the recording by the Deutsche Grammophon Gesellschaft,[1] in which Maria Becker plays the part of Iphigenia. The opening speech especially has

---

* All human infirmities are atoned for by pure humanity.

a hushed solemnity which puts it in the first rank of Goethe's
verse:

> Heraus in eure Schatten, rege Wipfel
> Des alten, heil'gen, dichtbelaubten Haines,
> Wie in der Göttin stilles Heiligtum,
> Tret' ich noch jetzt mit schauderndem Gefühl,
> Als wenn ich sie zum erstenmal beträte,
> Und es gewöhnt sich nicht mein Geist hierher.*

There is also verse of entirely different character, racing with
emotion like that in the monologue of Act I, scene iv, or in the
spirit of the 'große Hymnen' which Goethe was writing at
about the same time, in the famous 'Parzenlied'.[1] Suspending
all disbelief, it is very nearly possible to let the great harmonies
of Goethe's verse carry one away into accepting as a reality the
dream it stands for, the dream of a human race redeemed by
sheer human virtue. Moreover, the full scope of Goethe's intentions should be realized: while Iphigenia is a redeemer, she
is decidedly a human one, and the intention is that the re-
demption or atonement should come through human rather
than divine actions (or, at its subtlest, that the divine should
act only through human agents if at all). In the spirit of his
times, he attempts a new realization of the way in which the
'curse on humanity' can be lifted.

One essential feature of Goethe's solution is that it has nothing to do with retribution and justice, right and wrong, as
the Greek plays had, but rather with the achievement of happiness. All through the Greek legend runs the idea that retribution must be exacted: Agamemnon sacrifices Iphigenia (or
so it is believed), therefore Clytemnestra kills Agamemnon,
and therefore Orestes kills Clytemnestra, and therefore, as it
seems in the present play, the gods require through Thoas that
Iphigenia should kill Orestes. Goethe's Iphigenia will have none
of this, but not because she is concerned with whether or not

---

* Out into your shadows, you stirring treetops of this ancient, holy, thickly
leaved grove, as though into the goddess's silent sanctum I step even now
with feelings of awe, as though I were entering it for the first time, and my
spirit cannot accustom itself to the place.

Orestes was right to kill his and her mother. Iphigenia's chief concern is that Orestes shall be saved from the torment of guilt which afflicts him: it is this 'positive' attitude that is typically Goethean, and the first three acts of the play are mostly occupied with it. In Act I Arkas, Thoas's right-hand man, reproaches Iphigenia with her unhappy appearance, exiled though she is; then in Act II Pylades reproaches Orestes in much the same way, each of these scenes stressing the need for an affirmative welcome to life. While these two Acts do relate a good deal of the history of the house of Atreus, they also serve to reiterate the point which Iphigenia herself makes,[1] that the immortals love mankind, and gladly grant men life so that for a while they may enjoy

> Ihres eigenen, ewigen Himmels
> Mitgenießendes fröhliches Anschaun.*

In other words, the gods look on happily at all that happens on earth and in heaven, and enjoy it with those of mankind who are able to enjoy it (*mitgenießend*). Iphigenia is attempting to achieve both for herself and for Orestes a similar joyful acceptance of life throughout the first three Acts, and she is curiously brief in her responses to the dreadful news of Agamemnon's and Clytemnestra's death. In II, ii, she expresses no grief at her father's murder, merely asking for more precise details (she may grieve, inwardly, but Goethe gives us no sign of what her grief is like); in III, i, she feels for Orestes, but not for Clytemnestra, as we may see from these lines:

> Unsterbliche, die ihr den reinen Tag
> Auf immer neuenWolken selig lebet,
> Habt ihr nur darum mich so manches Jahr
> Von Menschen abgesondert, mich so nah
> Bei euch gehalten, mir die kindliche
> Beschäftigung, des heilgen Feuers Glut
> Zu nähren, aufgetragen, meine Seele
> Der Flamme gleich in ewger frommer Klarheit
> Zu euern Wohnungen hinaufgezogen,

---

* The joyful gaze with which in their own, eternal heaven, they join in the enjoyment [of the world].

Daß ich nur meines Hauses Greuel später
Und tiefer fühlen sollte? Sage mir
Vom Unglückselgen! Sprich mir von Orest!*[1]

This response from Iphigenia to the news that her mother has
been stabbed to death by own brother reveals her egocentricity
(apart from the incongruous detail about the 'ever new' clouds,
as though newness of resting-place had something to do with
the gods' perfection) in that it shows her more concerned at the
deceptive way the gods have treated her than at the calamity
which is driving Orestes mad. These murders are for her
shocking because they seem to contradict the recent intention
of the gods to draw her up to themselves 'in eternal devout
clarity', rather than because she is afflicted.

When Orestes is finally cured of his guilt, it is not because
he has seen that it is unjustified, but rather because of two
things. He has sunk into a death-like swoon[2] from which he
recovers, still believing himself to be near the shores of Death,
to drink in imagination from Lethe, the stream of forgetfulness.
That is, like Faust at the beginning of *Part II*,[3] Orestes forgets
the past and is thus enabled to go on living. Secondly, in his
waking vision he sees his ancestors, all of whom hated one
another in life, walking in reconciliation among the shades of
Hades. It is not forgiveness, however, which has caused this
harmony; it is simply a fact that they have all passed through
death and so feel enmity no longer. Orestes, believing himself
dead, can therefore join them:

Verlosch die Rache wie das Licht der Sonne?
So bin auch ich willkommen, und ich darf
In euern feierlichen Zug mich mischen.†[4]

---

* Immortal ones, who live blissfully through the pure day on clouds for ever
new, have you then separated me so many years from men, kept me so
close to you, entrusted me with the childlike task of nourishing the sacred
glow of the fire, drawing my soul like a flame upward towards you in
eternal, devout clarity, only that later I might feel the horrors of my house
more deeply? Tell me of the unhappy man! Tell me about Orestes!
† Did vengeance go out as did the light of the sun? Then I too am welcome,
and may join in your solemn procession.

When the thoughts of guilt are blotted out in this way, Orestes can return to normal life, with the help of the prayer which Iphigenia pronounces over him, and the life to which he returns, again in typically Goethean fashion, is one of activity and joy:

> Die Erde dampft erquickenden Geruch
> Und ladet mich auf ihren Flächen ein,
> Nach Lebensfreud' und großer Tat zu jagen.*[1]

By the end of Act III, then, the first essential step has been taken. Through the intervention of Iphigenia, Orestes has been released from care, anxiety, guilt, all the hampering feelings which Goethean heroes commonly reject or strive to reject, and is restored to healthy *action*. (The significance of the word 'Tat' in the lines just quoted becomes clearer in connection with *Faust*.)[2]

True, there has been no question of atonement here, or of human infirmities being redeemed, as Goethe implied in the couplet of his old age. Rather, Orestes has been freed of his inhibitions and is able to act once more, just as Faust surmounts the encounter with Care and goes on to carry out his final plans: neither of them seems morally any the better, they simply become uninhibited. But the real gist of the play has not yet been reached, for Iphigenia has still to persuade Thoas to give up his demand that she should sacrifice his prisoner.

It is a commonplace of criticism, though a challengeable one, that Goethe weakens his play by making his Thoas too much of an eighteenth-century gentleman, and thus too prone to give way to Iphigenia in the end. (We have seen how Alba treats Egmont in comparable circumstances, and it does not need saying that the brutality of some men is certain to be untouched by any amount of trustfulness.) But the eighteenth-century 'gentleman' is not really the kind of character that Thoas proves to be. True, he is spoken of throughout the play as noble and generous, and Iphigenia herself, who admits these qualities in him, is several times admonished to treat him in a

---

* The earth exhales refreshing odours and bids me enter on her plains to go in pursuit of joy in living, and great deeds.

way more appropriate to the magnanimity he has shown towards her. But, as so often happens in Goethe's plays, we hear a great deal about this magnanimity having been shown before the play begins, and see next to none when it does begin. Since Iphigenia arrived in Tauris, she has dissuaded Thoas from requiring that all strangers be sacrificed, and he has allowed her a measure of liberty. In Act I, however, Thoas finds himself in a new situation. His son has just been killed in war, and he has now no heir to follow him on the throne; he believes that his people are restive, and that only the restoration of human sacrifice will, in their view, persuade the gods to be favourable; he also fears threats of a revolution which will place on the throne a king whose line is assured.[1] Thoas therefore proposes marriage to Iphigenia in the belief that she may bear him a son and re-establish his position. He does, despite this, have the magnanimity to promise solemnly that, if she can hope to return home some day, he will not press his suit. But when Iphigenia reveals for the first time that she is the daughter of Agamemnon and thus can expect to be welcomed back to Greece (so far as they know, for the news of the fate of her parents still has not reached them), he changes his mind, saying with extraordinary frankness, 'Aufs Ungehoffte war ich nicht bereitet.'* He breaks his word as soon as it is given, and never intended to keep it. Stranger still, he now adds that he has been foolish to ignore the murmuring of his subjects so long, and requires Iphigenia to sacrifice instantly the two strangers— Orestes and Pylades, as they prove to be—who have just been captured. Since a moment before he seemed prepared to let Iphigenia go scot-free, this demand can only appear as a kind of blackmail, aimed at compelling her to consent to marriage. Thoas, then, is neither shown as a barbarian to whom sacrifices seem natural—in which case one might feel some greater sympathy—nor as a fundamentally good-natured, if rash-tempered, gentleman, but as a calculating, exacting man, unreliable in his pledged word, and brutally regardless of Iphigenia's dedicated virginity.

* I was not prepared for anything that crossed my hopes.

During the three central Acts of the play we see no more of Thoas, whom Iphigenia and Arkas nevertheless continue to call 'a second father', noble, loyal, serious and reasonable. In the meanwhile, the action turns for a time to the curing of Orestes, then to the final issue of the play, whether or not Iphigenia should tell the truth to Thoas, out of gratitude to him for past benefits. Orestes and Pylades have already left the temple where they were held prisoner, to reconnoitre the path to the shore where their ship is waiting (it is a weakness of the play that they are able to escape without the least hindrance: no guard is placed over them, and Thoas does not know they have escaped till they come back, so that his determination to have them sacrificed looks a little foolish). Iphigenia is left behind to deceive the king while they are away (again, the purpose of the escape plan is left unclear: if the men can walk out, Iphigenia can presumably go with them at once; it appears from IV, iv, in fact, that Pylades, having returned, expects to shoulder the statue of Diana alone, and walk down to the ship with it and with Iphigenia, which makes the reasons for Iphigenia's staying behind till this moment even less easy to comprehend. With prisoners guarded in any normal way, Iphigenia's dilemma would seem more real.) And in this situation Iphigenia's doubts begin to emerge, whether or not she should connive at this deception.

From the beginning of Act IV, the plot begins to waver, indeed the opening lines of the Act are oddly inconclusive. The meaning of Iphigenia's opening thirteen lines[1] is, literally, that if the gods intend to lead a man into many confusions, and shatter him with vicissitudes of joy and sorrow, then they always provide, either near to a city or on some distant shore (the particularity of the last two features is especially puzzling), a friend to help him in his need. This seems to imply that the gods always operate in a dualistic way, providing both trouble and the means of combating it, rather as Faust declares in the 'Forest and Cavern' scene that he has been granted by the Earth-Spirit both peace of mind and at the same time the devil Mephistopheles to shatter every moment's enjoyment—Faust's

77

head, seems spiritless, an inappropriate ending to a poem which began with such vigorous insistence on the *fear* that men should feel for the gods. This Tantalus appears not to fear but merely to have become wearily resigned.

The function of the 'Parzenlied', however, is to reveal how near Iphigenia comes to reversing her earlier belief about the gods—it is an incipient despair which could deprive her of her faith. In the fifth Act, that faith is vindicated to the full, or at least that is the impression Goethe intended to give at the time, and the one which it is all too easy to gain from a superficial reading. Iphigenia stakes everything on telling the truth, and Thoas relents, allowing her to return home with Orestes and Pylades, and even bringing himself, under pressure from Iphigenia, to say farewell with a good grace. Closer examination shows that the issues of the play have altered since the beginning. In Act I, the difference between Iphigenia and Thoas was mainly concerned with the question of human sacrifice. In Act v, this is practically forgotten. At no time in this Act does Thoas refer to his need to marry Iphigenia for political reasons, or to his fear that the people will dethrone him if he remains without an heir, or to the pressure being exerted on him by the people to reinstitute the custom of sacrifice. From the moment that Iphigenia reveals the plan of escape to him, Thoas is only concerned to make sure whether Orestes truly is her brother. The whole ground of the argument has changed. There is no debate, no weighing up of the consequences if Thoas allows his priestess and her prisoners to leave. He is convinced because Iphigenia is able to show him a scar between Orestes' eyebrows, caused by a fall in childhood—surely a trivial point in comparison with his earlier objections—and won over when Orestes re-interprets the oracle which, as he thought, required him to remove from Tauris the statue of Diana.

All this has nothing to do with the atonement for human infirmities which Goethe spoke of in his old age. Iphigenia has shown daring (if it is not foolhardiness, for she confesses after having revealed the plan of escape to Thoas that she has only just realized the hideous danger into which she has plunged the two prisoners: she has not weighed up the consequences of her deed). She has been truthful when it was not easy to be so, and perhaps when it was inadvisable, in view of what we have seen of Thoas's duplicity and hypocrisy. She has also persuaded Thoas not to make her kill her brother, and so a first lifting of the curse on her house may be said to take place. But what she has really achieved is permission to return home and to take the two Greeks with her. It is a personal satisfaction she has achieved, not a reconciliation with Thoas or his conversion from barbarism. If we remember the first Act, which Goethe does not encourage us to do, we cannot help seeing that Thoas is left to face the music, possibly to lose his throne and his life, and Iphigenia's insistence that he should say 'fare well' ungrudgingly is a mark of her obliviousness to everything except the achievement of her own happiness—which has, after all, been the theme of earlier parts of the play. Right or wrong, as we saw, are not major issues: the maintenance of an unruffled serenity is. As Iphigenia says, when Pylades has almost persuaded her that she is being over-scrupulous in her regard for the ruthless Thoas, 'Ganz unbefleckt genießt sich nur das Herz'.*[1] It is only when her heart is kept completely immaculate that it can enjoy itself, and it is this 'self-enjoyment' that Iphigenia is seeking all the while. Thoas's situation affects her only in so far as it may make her feel that she has shown him less than due gratitude; once she is satisfied on that score, she is able to forget the perilous situation in which he finds himself (whether or not she could possibly help him out of it), and to part from him with such a good conscience that she can even insist on his showing some sign of happiness. The appeal she makes to him in one of her last speeches is an indication of her real values and presuppositions: 'Look at us, you will not often have the chance to do so noble a deed.' It is the opportunity to add a meritorious action to his store that Iphigenia offers Thoas, not an appeal to charity or humanity.

This play will always have some effectiveness, although

---

* The heart enjoys itself only when quite immaculate.

we know that the solution it puts forward is no solution. It can also act as a stimulus to plain, truthful speaking, and can only do harm in that respect if it encourages the idea that such speaking is always appropriate. (It is worth remembering that Jesus, with whom Iphigenia is sometimes compared by critics, was prone to give non-committal answers to people who, he thought, were likely to destroy him.) Even its lack of regard for practicalities need not count severely against it; it can have the power of a dream or vision in which such things are of comparatively small account. In the odd way in which such things do happen, it has probably had morally good effects on spectators regardless of the exact formulations which Goethe found. All the same, to ignore the ultimately egoistic basis of Iphigenia's conduct, or the deviousness with which the argument of the play is conducted, is not the way to get at the real sense of what Goethe wrote. There is a good deal to be said for the view that *Iphigenie auf Tauris* is the expression of a sublime intention in which the conception of what 'pure humanity' might mean was never sufficiently clarified. There is too much self-seeking in the play, and too little regard for the weaknesses and rights of characters other than the heroine, to make it appear the morally uplifting work which Goethe, at least at the time of writing, hoped it would be. (Later on, in a bitter mood, he called it 'ganz verteufelt human'—quite devilishly humane.)

In a certain sense both *Iphigenie* and *Egmont* are plays in which the hero or heroine attempts to live in harmony with his society, while being conscious that it makes impossible demands of him. A similar attempt is made in *Torquato Tasso*, in which Goethe set out the problem of reconciling the vocation of a poet, satisfied only by ideal perfection, with the practical demands which society may justly make on him. This was of course partly his own problem at the court of Weimar; the solution he finds may be in accordance with his doctrine of polarity, that is, it may be that the final embrace of the poet Tasso with the man of affairs Antonio is meant to symbolize a fusion of the two. No one can be quite sure, and Goethe himself helped to make the sense unclear by the confusing final speech he gave to the poet. But at least everything tends to show that a reconciliation between Tasso and the society surrounding him is desirable. He is, as Goethe said, a 'gesteigerter Werther', that is, not only a more intense representative of the thwarted love and antagonism to society which Werther shows, but perhaps also a Werther who, in the special sense of 'Steigerung', which implies ultimate identity of 'polar' opposites,[1] is made one with the world he lives in.

Any doubts on this score are caused by the fact that the society surrounding Tasso is made, whether deliberately or not, to look scarcely worth the effort at reconciliation. Of the four other characters, Leonore is made to look the least attractive: she is an unabashed flatterer, as the opening scene establishes, and Tasso has ample evidence for his accusation that she is designing in all she does. She is a complete egoist, as her specious arguments in her own interest show, both in III, iii and III, iv.

But Leonore plays a minor role. More important is that played by Antonio, Tasso's counterpart, of whom it is said that he is only Tasso's enemy because Nature neglected to make a single man out of them both[2]—in other words, he is Tasso's complementary opposite, and needs Tasso for the complete integration of his personality just as Tasso needs him. Antonio is the practical man of affairs, just returned from Rome with the makings of a highly successful agreement with the Holy See involving the handing over of territory to his own state of Ferrara: he is the diplomat and courtier, at home in the world of politics in a way that Tasso, with his scruples and self-doubtings, can never be. However, almost the first words that Antonio utters give one cause to doubt his sagacity. The Pope, he says, is the wise ruler of a State where every man is proud to obey, and in obeying sees that he is serving his own interests, since nothing is ordained but what is right. There is nepotism, Antonio agrees, but neither more nor less than what is just—a Pope who did not look after his own kith and kin would earn the censure of the people themselves.

Further, Gregory honours science 'so far as it helps to rule the state' and art so far as it makes Rome glorious.[1] One need not know that the Pope in question is the one who ordered a jubilee to celebrate the massacre of St Bartholomew's Eve to feel that this picture is roseate as well as threateningly authoritarian, yet there is nothing to suggest that Antonio is speaking with his tongue in his cheek. On the contrary, this speech seems to accord with the idea that Tasso's criticisms of the world in general are undesirable, and that a 'positive' attitude like Antonio's is essential to proper living. As the Duke Alphons, an authoritative figure, says, 'Only one who does not know men can fear them'—the underlying assumption is that there is good will everywhere if only the habit of criticism could be brought to an end. The difficulty about this point of view is that, when applied to the portraying of Antonio, it makes him look politically a simpleton, who too readily takes everything at face-value.

On the other hand, Antonio shows malice towards Tasso from the moment of their first meeting, and scarcely changes, though he does desire Tasso's conversion to a more 'positive' viewpoint, throughout the play. In the famous scene[2] in which Tasso draws his sword on him, Antonio contributes at least as much as the younger man to the exacerbation of emotions, flicking him on the raw time after time until he almost obliges Tasso to challenge him to a duel: his sneers and taunts say little for the maturity of character he is said by some critics to possess. The smugness with which, on the intervention of the Duke, Antonio thrusts all the blame for the quarrel on Tasso,[3] while affecting to be, and to have been throughout, an impartial observer of the poet's uncontrollable rage, is particularly hard to respect. Later, it is true, Antonio comes to apologize for his conduct on this occasion,[4] but the apology itself is annulled by the statement that Tasso has not suffered any insult which a nobleman could resent. Since Antonio has accused Tasso of being a ladies' man, capable of winning victories only at kissing and lute-playing, and one who offers to fight a duel only in the secure knowledge that his challenge

83

may not be taken up in the court, we can only suppose that
Antonio's self-righteousness is playing tricks with his memory.

Antonio is petty in almost every respect. His speech on the
poetry of Ariosto[1] makes a trite impression, not least in the
passage describing an Arcadian landscape:

> Die Schalkheit lauscht im Grünen halb versteckt,
> Die Weisheit läßt von einer goldnen Wolke
> Von Zeit zu Zeit erhabne Sprüche tönen,
> Indes auf wohlgestimmter Laute wild
> Der Wahnsinn hin und her zu wühlen scheint
> Und doch im schönsten Takt sich mäßig hält.*

and again one might suppose that he had his tongue in his
cheek, if he did not apologize at once for this piece of prosiness
as though he had been carried away in rapture. Yet more remarkable is the way in which he is deceived by Leonore's
transparent flattery—in the scene, namely,[2] where she tells him
that Tasso's superior attractiveness to women, in comparison
with Antonio's own, resides in the fact that Tasso frequently
loses his clothes and so needs more looking after than Antonio
does. (Happy the youth, laments Antonio, whose very faults
are reckoned to him as virtues; Leonore must excuse him if it
makes him a little bitter.) But none of this is so cheap as the
scene near the end of the play where Antonio on the one hand
accuses Tasso of falsely imagining enemies all round him,
while at the same time he himself complains to the Duke in a
trivial yet genuinely hostile tone that Tasso eats too much
spicy food and too many sweets, that he fails to mix water
with his wine, refuses to drink unpleasant-tasting medicine or
water either, and blames the doctors for not curing the melancholia which results.[3] This catalogue of peccadilloes close to the
climax of the play, together with the very fact that Antonio
is tattler enough to be troubled by it, makes one sceptical

---

* Roguishness eavesdrops, half hidden in the grass, and Wisdom sends lofty
sayings down from a golden cloud from time to time, whilst on a well-tuned
lute Madness seems wildly to pluck at random, and yet keeps moderately
to the most beautiful measure.

of any benefit to be gained from Tasso's reconciliation with him.

We must look, then, rather to the Duke Alphons and to the Princess for the values which Tasso respects, or which Goethe respects sufficiently to write a play on this theme of reconciliation, and it is true that the Duke is a far more generous man than Antonio. Perhaps his most prominent qualities are frankness and toleration: he does not conceal from himself or anyone else that he keeps Tasso at his court in order to enhance the prestige of his state, Ferrara, but, this much granted, he is always willing to lend an ear to both sides, and several times thinks of a compromise to save the situation; again, he is charitable, as he says, because one ought to practise all the virtues, and Tasso is a deserving case for the practice of this particular virtue.[1] He is coy in his little joke[2] about not being disturbed by Leonore if he is dallying with a pretty girl in the garden, and he is prone to sententiousness, as they all are. Tasso is not inaccurate when he complains that the Duke has treated him like a naughty schoolboy, sending him to his room after finding him with his sword drawn, and putting him on his honour not to come out. But in several ways Alphons is more shrewd than the rest. He does not expect the Pope to be an easy man to deal with; he knows Leonore well enough to see that she is a born intriguer, and when Leonore complains at his teasing of her on this point he has a genial answer, to the effect that he has a good many debts to repay her on that score. Moreover, it is he who tries to bring Tasso into harmony with the rest by gaining his confidence and treating him with continual indulgence. The Duke's weakness is that he never really sees through Antonio. Despite his doubts about the possibility of gaining any advantage from dealings with the Vatican, he accepts Antonio's absurd optimism at face value, and although he is inclined to see that there must be faults on both sides, both Antonio's and Tasso's, he is inclined to allow the former to pull the wool over his eyes. When it comes to the point, moreover, that Tasso asks for the return of the manuscript of his epic poem so that he may revise it, the Duke is sufficiently concerned with his own interest and the glory of Ferrara to withold it from him,[1] and thus supplies the final evidence to Tasso's already masochistically suspicious mind, that the whole world is conspiring against the realization of his poetic hopes. The Duke's frankness and toleration are of a kind which acknowledges the world to be what it is, but is inclined to do nothing about it. Despite his more amiable nature Alphons does not show such highly admirable qualities as would persuade one that the poet should strive to respect them more.

There remains the Princess, sister to the Duke, the ardent student and admirer of the poet, and the occasion of his final downfall in that his attempt at embracing her sets the seal of condemnation on him. Of her, as of the Duke, there is more good to be said. She is more generous and more just than her companion Leonore, whose flattery she perceives even though, like the Duke, she does not let it influence her relationship with her friend. Like all the other characters, she adjures Tasso to forgo his suspicions and negative attitude and to put more trust in others. But she has no distinctive personality, no attachment, no concern in anything that happens, and at every vital moment is either equivocal or helplessly inadequate. Her speech to Tasso[2] on the Golden Age reveals something of the tenor of her thoughts, which waver uncertainly from moment to moment: that Age, the time of ideal perfection, she says, is past, or rather it existed in former times just as little as it does today, or if it ever did exist, it can always return again here and now. Yet the fact of this vacillation is never brought out by the structure of the play.

There is a more serious equivocation in the Princess's attitude (not unlike Faust's)[3] when she first hears of Tasso's disgrace—that is, after he has been sent to his room for his offence against court rules in drawing his sword. She is at first convinced[4] that the fault cannot have been all his, but like the Duke she quickly acts as though Antonio had been in the right. In the course of the scene, far from making any defence of Tasso, she allows herself to be persuaded by Leonore that the poet should be sent away for a time. (Leonore, incidentally, urges this in the belief that she will thus have a chance to attract Tasso's affection away from the Princess to herself.) This in itself is not reprehensible, or would not be, if the Princess made up her mind to it, but she does not. The really disagreeable quality she shows in this scene is a half-hearted yielding which never comes to a decision at all. Her successive answers to Leonore's blandishments run like this—'I will not give assent that this should happen' (namely that Tasso be banished); 'you torture me, and know not if it will avail us aught'; 'If then it must be so, ask me no more'; and 'I still am undecided, yet let it be so'. And being in this wavering determination to let things happen, she does not visit Tasso in his confinement or even send him word of her continuing trust and affection, a silence which he notices and which thus also contributes to his desperation. As a lover or even as an admirer, the Princess shows no constancy or devotion. And, finally, when she and Tasso meet in the garden and he, deceived by her apparent friendliness, impetuously embraces her, she has no more spirit or tact or care for his over-wrought mind than to thrust him off, cry 'Begone!' and run out of sight, never to be seen again in the play.

The court of Ferrara (had it any relation to the court of Weimar?) as Goethe draws it is so egoistically small-minded that one might reject any suggestion that he could ever have wanted his poet to be reconciled with it. But when Tasso himself is seen, the idea at least becomes more credible. He actually admires Antonio's trite praise of Ariosto,[1] which either speaks little for his discernment or for his honesty, and his first private speech to the Princess, to quote only one instance, is so full of redundant repetition and cliché as to throw doubt on his ability to use language at all impressively. The italics in the following passage are mine:

> *Unsicher* folgen *meine Schritte* dir,
> O Fürstin, und *Gedanken ohne Maß*
> *Und Ordnung* regen sich in meiner Seele.
> Mir scheint die Einsamkeit zu winken, mich
> Gefällig anzulispeln: komm, ich löse

Die neu erregten Zweifel deiner Brust.
Doch werf ich einen Blick auf dich, *vernimmt*
Mein *horchend Ohr* ein *Wort* von deiner *Lippe,*
So wird *ein neuer Tag* um mich herum,
Und *alle Bande fallen* von mir los.*

The wordiness of 'uncertainly' followed by 'thoughts without order', of 'my listening ear', and of the 'new day' (not in itself a striking image) which is associated with the falling off of 'all bonds' (certainly not a more original choice) could even rouse doubts about Tasso's sincerity—can a poet not express himself with more power than this? Again, the picture he draws of Ferrara in the same scene is as rosily optimistic as that of Rome drawn by Antonio, and he seems to have a genuine belief that the statesman has all the virtues he himself lacks. However, he is strangely insincere even in his most impetuous moments, and despite the great sincerity he seems to show in his first speech of all. The fervour with which he greets Antonio[1], offering lifelong friendship to him, which does so much to offend the cooler instincts of the older man, seems to be typical of the poet's warm-hearted effusiveness. In reality, Tasso confesses, it was not genuine: having met with no initial success, he declares almost at once, as though excusing himself, that he has done his duty by honouring the Princess's wish that they should be friends—in short, the effusiveness was put on for the occasion. And thus one doubts Tasso's self-knowledge when he laments to himself towards the end[2] that he is now for the first time obliged to practise deceit. He does not remember, apparently, having told both the Duke and the Princess, separately, that each of them has been the sole inspiration of his poetry, or how he has told the Duke to his face that he has learned all he knows of the conduct of affairs from the Duke's rich fund of experience, while behind his back he

---

* Uncertainly my footsteps follow you, o Princess, and thoughts without moderation or order stir within my soul. Loneliness seems to beckon me, to whisper kindly 'Come, I will resolve the newly arisen doubts within your breast.' Yet if I cast a glance at thee, if my hearkening ear hears a word from thy lip, a new day is created about me, and all bonds fall from me.

declares that the Duke has never exchanged a word with him on such matters. No doubt Goethe did not want Tasso to appear in a very favourable light; indeed he makes him appear almost mad with distrust towards the end. Yet there are times when he lets Tasso sink into bathos, grovelling ludicrously as when he offers to do anything at all if only the Princess will not deny him all hope: he will open the windows to air the paintings, dust the stucco on the walls with a feather-duster, polish the floor and weed every blade of grass from between the paving-stones, if she will give him her protection.[1] (These are serious offers; there is not a breath of humour anywhere in this scene.) It is difficult to see what cause Goethe can have had, unless it was unawareness of more civilized manners, to set against an unlikeable court a no more likeable poet, or for that matter a poet who does so little to persuade us that he has poetic gifts.

If there is any solution to be found, it must surely be in the final scene in which Antonio, presumably sincerely, tries to persuade Tasso for the last time that he is not surrounded by actively malicious enemies (as no doubt he is not; it is more often general self-ignorance than deliberate malice that causes his tribulations). By making Antonio extremely reasonable here, while Tasso raves with all the signs of persecution mania, Goethe does much to produce the impression of which Professor Peacock speaks, that the play concerns the education of Tasso to the point where he can see the folly of his ways. ('The real theme of *Torquato Tasso* is the rejection of the romantic dream of simple self-fulfilment and happiness as in itself inadequate to the real problem of living in a society.') Antonio is now patient, considerate, compassionate, and concerned above all that Tasso should recover his talent and become reconciled with the rest of his friends. If only Antonio had not been so full of sneers a few scenes earlier we might be convinced of his sincerity. He even seems able to regard Tasso's present condition as Goethe might have regarded it, as a kind of necessary 'death', like that through which Orestes passes in *Iphigenie*, from which he can emerge to a new life:

Und wenn du ganz dich zu verlieren scheinst,
Vergleiche dich! Erkenne was du bist!*

'Compare yourself; recognize what you are'—these are almost
the words spoken by the visionary figure to the poet in
Goethe's autobiographical 'Zueignung'. There is no possible
doubt that this is meant to be regarded straightforwardly as
good advice, whatever Antonio may have been like before.

The effect on Tasso in the last speech of the whole play
remains, however, quite uncertain. He begins oddly enough
by thanking Antonio and literally 'comparing' himself: that is,
he searches his mind to discover whether any man in the whole
of history has suffered so much as he has, and concludes that
there is none. (The self-comparisons with Christ made by
Werther and Wilhelm Meister and by Faust[1] come to mind
here.) This in itself does not look like a step on the path to self-
knowledge. However, when Antonio steps forward and takes
Tasso by the hand in a last sign of friendship, the poet speaks
the final words, the imagery of which leaves an impression of
total confusion, as Ronald Peacock has observed.

O edler Mann! Du stehest fest und still,
Ich scheine nur die sturmbewegte Welle.
Allein bedenk und überhebe nicht
Dich deiner Kraft! Die mächtige Natur,
Die diesen Felsen gründete, hat auch
Der Welle die Beweglichkeit gegeben.
Sie sendet ihren Sturm, die Welle flieht
Und schwankt und schwillt und beugt sich schäumend über.
In dieser Woge spiegelte so schön
Die Sonne sich, es ruhten die Gestirne
An dieser Brust, die zärtlich sich bewegte.
Verschwunden ist der Glanz, entflohn die Ruhe.—
Ich kenne mich in der Gefahr nicht mehr
Und schäme mich nicht mehr, es zu bekennen.
Zerbrochen ist das Steuer, und es kracht

*   And though you seem to lose yourself entirely,
        Compare yourself! Recognise what you are,

'Sich vergleichen' also means 'to come to terms', but Tasso understands
it otherwise.

Das Schiff an allen Seiten. Berstend reißt
Der Boden unter meinen Füßen auf!
Ich fasse dich mit beiden Armen an!
So klammert sich der Schiffer endlich noch
Am Felsen fest, an dem er scheitern sollte.*

The thought of the first two lines is that Antonio is rock-like in his confidence and solidity within society, whereas Tasso is a wave, lashed by the storm, inconstant and without control over his actions, or so he seems. Yet, the next six lines continue, Antonio should not be overweening in his estimate of his own power: though Nature planted the rock where it stands, she has also given mobility to the wave, which moves with a passionate force unknown to the other. Thus far, then, the point Tasso is making is that both Antonio and he are creations of Nature, each with virtues of his own. In the six lines after these, the implications change. The storm-tossed movement is no longer seen as the poet's passionate spirit, in contrast to the practical man's calm, but rather as a troubled, dangerous state of mind, in contrast to the time when the water reflected the sun and stars in its bosom just as the poet, so to speak, embraces the world within himself. Here the poet and the practical man are no longer equal creations, 'recognizing what they are' in accordance with Antonio's injunction; the practical man, symbolized by the rock, is the superior of the two. But now the imagery changes unexpectedly once again: the poet is no longer represented by the water, but by a ship sailing on it, its rudder broken and its hull bursting as it strikes the rock. Whereas the water could come to no harm from the rock, the ship of

---

* O noble man, you stand there firm and silent, I seem to be no more than a storm-tossed wave. But take good heed and do not presume upon your powers. Mighty Nature, which founded this rock, also gave mobility to the wave. She sends a tempest, the wave flees away, and sways and swells and towers up foamingly. In this wave the sun once was reflected so beautifully, the stars rested upon this bosom, which rocked them tenderly. Gone is that gleam, fled is that peace.—In this peril I know no longer what I am and am no longer ashamed to confess it. Broken is the rudder, and the ship cracks open on all sides. The ground bursts open at my feet. I embrace you with both arms. Thus does the sailor cling to the rock on which he was to be wrecked.

course can, and the poet's position becomes yet more desperate and inferior. In the last four lines, however, the image changes once again, or rather Tasso speaks not of the water or of the ship but of himself, falling through the riven timbers and embracing the rock as his only salvation. As he does so, Tasso embraces Antonio, so that as the curtain falls the two seem at least momentarily united. What this embrace means, it is very hard to say. Is it that Tasso was destined to be wrecked ('scheitern *sollte*') by Antonio in any case, so that he can expect no more than to cling to him in one last desperate hope of safety; is it that, although Tasso was destined to the encounter with Antonio, the very threat to his existence has turned out to be his salvation, even though no very secure one (or perhaps the rock is a real, lasting salvation?); is it that Tasso now embraces Antonio with a genuine recognition of his need for him, in the same way that a sailor is glad of any haven in a storm? Whichever interpretation is adopted—and it must be said that Goethe does not make the choice easy—it is clear that all the virtue attaching to the poet in the earlier part of the speech has been abandoned by the transfer of the imagery from the water (itself ambiguous in meaning) to the ship and then to the sailor, and that this change is abrupt, unprepared, merely bringing a sudden finish to an argument which began by leading in a quite different direction. Ending in so inconsequential and vague a way, the play does nothing to clear up the problems which accumulate in the presentation of such a pusillanimous group of characters.

Like all Goethe's serious plays, *Tasso* suffers from the discrepancy between apparent intention and actuality. The motive for writing each of the four studied in this chapter was at least nominally good: Goethe is concerned with freedom, reconciliation, peace, loyalty, truthfulness, and the mere fact of this is enough to justify some indulgence; it would certainly be unwarrantable to attack him for having written them. Yet in all the plays there is too much under-estimating of the evil in history and in human nature, a negligence in the development of ideas, and a so frequent portrayal of vacillating, spiritless or ruthlessly selfish characters as to make one ask why Goethe so seldom conceived more pleasing or subtler ones, after the style of Klärchen and Oranien. Scarcely anywhere is there a portrayal that arouses admiration or affection; the basest motives are spoken of as though they had sterling worth, and superficial solutions to profound problems are offered with the air of complete satisfaction. Is there a point of view from which these apparent defects can be so appreciated that the plays will rank as highly among the works of Goethe's genius as one would want them to do? To find an answer to that question must be one of the chief concerns of Goethe's readers today.

PART III

THE TURNING-POINT AND THE WHOLE

5

AUTOBIOGRAPHIES AND DIARIES

Goethe's life matters more for the understanding of his works than does the life of many authors, since he himself was particularly conscious of the connections between the two. All his works, he said on one occasion, were 'fragments of a great confession'; he would speak of particular works as 'snake-skins' which he had sloughed off, to emerge as though reborn after having lived through in fiction a possible experience in real life. *Faust* and *Wilhelm Meister* are, though very different from one another, a kind of autobiography, and both of these took some fifty years or more of his adult life in the writing. Some of his biographers, especially towards the end of the nineteenth century, have held, clearly mistakenly, that the smallest details in his art need to be related to the incidents in his real life, and partly as a result of this, we know for long periods what Goethe was doing day by day and almost hour by hour.

Goethe himself gave some encouragement to this interest. At the age of sixty, when he may well have felt that not many more years were left to him, he began writing his auto-biography, *Dichtung und Wahrheit*; for the post-Italian period he kept the *Annalen*, in which a brief note of his doings was recorded; in 1813 he began the *Italienische Reise*, and in 1823 he deliberately employed Johann Peter Eckermann (1792–1854) as a friend who would converse with him and record his spoken words for posterity. Goethe's life and art were very closely linked indeed, and in so far as he was a Romantic he scarcely wanted to separate them: both were the growing em-bodiment of the times he lived through, and almost took their justification from that. As he said in the preface to *Dichtung und Wahrheit*: 'the main task of biography seems to be, to present Man in the conditions of his time, and to show how far the cosmos [das Ganze] has opposed him, how far it has helped him, how he has formed his view of the world and of mankind, and how, if he is an artist, a poet, or a writer, he has reflected it all back again'.

The chief documents are, then, *Dichtung und Wahrheit* (1809–1831), which covers Goethe's childhood and youth up to the year 1775, the letters, which are particularly fascinating in the period 1775 to 1787, the partly fictional *Briefe aus der Schweiz*, (begun 1796), referring to the year 1779, the *Italienische Reise* (begun 1813) referring to 1786–8, and the more vivid letters on which it is based, the wartime sketches *Die Kampagne in Frankreich* and *Die Belagerung von Mainz*, written in and referring to the years 1792 and 1793, the correspondence with Schiller from 1794 to 1805, the purely factual *Annalen*, and the *Conversations* with Eckermann, which, though in some cases based on Eckermann's memories of conversations set down many years after they had taken place, are generally regarded as reliable indications of at least the kind of views Goethe expressed from 1823 until his death.

The mass of detail in all these could swamp a small study such as the present one, and is best left to such works as those by Düntzer, Bielschowsky and Günther Müller. Of all the infinite number of influences and acquaintances that shaped him, Goethe himself singled out Shakespeare (he would have thought, no doubt, of *Götz*, *Egmont*, *Faust* and *Wilhelm Meister*), Spinoza (1632–77), who as Goethe read him, rightly or wrongly, was a pantheist, and Linnaeus or Linné (1707–78), the Swedish botanist to whom we owe the principles of classification of plants. To these must certainly be added the mystical writer Hamann (1730–88), to whose work Goethe as a young man was introduced by Herder, a man of equal importance to him, and all together the Pietists, 'Herrnhuter', 'Stillen im Lande', Swedenborgians, alchemists, and other mystically inclined Christians who worked most powerfully on him in his late 'teens. Lavater the Swiss preacher (1741–1801) continued to press such attitudes on Goethe until 1775 at least, and even though his letters to Lavater show an increasing distaste for his friend's 'Schwärmerei', Goethe continued to find some fascination in the occult to his dying day. On the other hand, he was also keenly interested from his early youth in all that was rational and scientific. French influence was strong, since Frankfurt was occupied by French troops in Goethe's childhood, and not only was a French officer billeted on the family (a man to whom many pages of *Dichtung und Wahrheit* are devoted), but also the French plays performed in the Frankfurt theatre, together with his own puppets, aroused his first enthusiasm for the stage. All this worked in an opposite direction to that of the mystics and irrationalists: Goethe imitated Molière (1622–73) and Racine (1639–99), translated Voltaire (1694–1778), and refused to join in the campaign of national hatred for the French after the German defeat at Jena in 1806, declaring that he could not hate a nation to which he owed so much of his own spiritual culture.

Equally important to Goethe was the world of classical antiquity, which had come alive for his generation through the works of the art-historian Winckelmann (1717–68), to whom he paid tribute in 1805 with *Winckelmann und sein Jahrhundert*. Greece above all captured his imagination as a place of serene beauty, almost a pagan garden of Eden, a civilization where Rousseau's 'noble savage' had been realized to perfection. He read in Winckelmann how the Greek sculptors had fashioned out of the natural human form ideal figures of unsurpassable excellence; he read Homer and saw those same figures in Achilles and Hector, Ulysses and Nausikaa; he imitated Pindar and refashioned Euripides. The longing to go to Greece, or at least to Italy, was one of the ruling passions of his twenties and thirties. And only of slightly less importance was Goethe's interest in the Bible; he was 'bibelfest' all his life, and although his work seldom treats directly of Biblical subjects as it does of Greek ones, his language is strongly influenced, and the number of allusions to Biblical texts scattered through his works runs into thousands.

Outward events were of no less consequence. Goethe is careful, in *Dichtung und Wahrheit*, to draw attention to the existence of the Holy Roman Empire in his youth (by the time he wrote, it had been demolished by Napoleon), as well as to the man who was to pave the way to a German unity greater than any the Empire had known, namely to Frederick the Great, King of Prussia (1712–86). For Goethe was also conscious of living at a time when the German nation was beginning to seek unity in a way that it had not done since the Reformation, and although he was little interested in politics, he was conscious of trying to establish a truly German form of literature, and kept this in mind despite innumerable other activities throughout his life.

Dichtung und Wahrheit is not always a reliable guide to the facts: having been written some forty years after the events, it would be surprising if it were, and moreover Goethe set out, as his title implies, not merely to give a factual account, but one which would represent the truth of his life as he felt it to have been, so that he was not averse to an occasional mis-statement so long as it served his general purposes. All the same his letters bear out what he says in the autobiography, that one of the chief characteristics of his youth was the willingness to accept all, or almost all that happened to him with a completely open mind. In his correspondence with Lavater he often says that while he venerates Jesus he cannot venerate Christianity; it treats only one aspect of all man is and does. In his autobiography he writes that the Book of Job, the Song of Solomon, the Orphic songs and Hesiod all contain truth, and that he had a lot of sympathy in his youth with Epictetus and the Stoics. This is paralleled by the remark about the influence on him of Hamann's teaching that 'everything that Man undertakes...must arise from his collective, united forces'; it is also reflected in the remark in his diary for 1780, one of many similar ones: 'everything *must* eventually come to a single point, but bronze patience, stony endurance'; compare with this, 'it is still a mystery, how to find the point in which the vast variety is joined'.[1] Impressed by Herder's vision of Shakespeare, Goethe had come to regard the artist as a kind of Spinozistic deity in whom myriads of differing personalities had their being, and for whom every kind of philosophy and religion had something to say. He was, as he himself said, a chameleon, adapting himself to every outward circumstance; he had a god to worship for every aspect of being, and the more complete his own acceptance became, the more godlike he was. (Rather as in the system of Leibniz (1646–1716), the perfect monad or individual substance is that which reflects completely all others.)

The struggle to achieve this completeness was often intense. *Dichtung und Wahrheit* gives a glimpse of Goethe's vicissitudes, despite its detached mood and its habitual understatements, when it reveals that he was accustomed to sleep with a knife under his pillow and to try its point against his own breast, testing his desire to go on living. 'Misery', he writes in his diary for July 1779, 'is gradually becoming as prosy to me as a hearth-fire. But I shall not leave off my thoughts, and go on wrestling with the unknown angel even though I wrench out my hip. No man knows what I am about, or with how many enemies I have to fight, to produce the little I do.' To Frau von Stein he writes[1] to say that he deserves forgiveness although she witholds it: 'But so it always is with one who suffers alone in silence, not wishing to frighten his friends or weaken himself by lamentations, and if in the anguish of his soul he cries "Eloi Eloi lama sabachthani" the people say you have helped others, help yourself, and even the best of them translate wrongly and think he is calling on Elias.' In the following year[2] he writes to her again: 'all I am doing and suffering for the sake of the Kingdom of God I would rather not tell you.' There are indeed times when he takes Biblical heroes for his models, just as Werther thinks of himself as a Christ, and as Wilhelm Meister tells Mariane of his hope that from their marriage may come 'the phenomenon so desired by all men, that of the superhuman in human form'. (This expectation may have some connection with the story in the sequel, *Wilhelm Meisters Wanderjahre*, entitled 'St Joseph the Second'. In so far as there is any auto-biographical element at all in this, Goethe seems capable of feeling himself both as a Christ and as the father of a Christ.)

Yet although these struggles were real enough, there was also a sense in which Goethe felt himself to be already at his goal, and this long before the Italian Journey, the 'hegirah' to which the achievement of his goal is usually ascribed. Thus he writes to the novelist Wieland (1733–1813), only a short while after his arrival at Weimar, in such terms as these (he is speaking of Charlotte von Stein): 'I cannot explain the significance—the power which this woman exerts over me—in any other way than by the transmigration of souls.—Yes, we were once man and wife!—Now we know of one another—through a veil, in a spiritual mist.—I have no name for us—the past—the future—the All.' The thought becomes so familiar that he can write jokingly about it, addressing Charlotte with 'My darling A and O, how are you',[1] and, in a most affectionate and endearing tone,

Here my d. Lotte is a letter from Knebel with a good morning, see you soon, my

$$\alpha/\omega$$
G.

With Charlotte he is at peace, perhaps because he recognizes in her the complementary opposite which he needs in order to become whole. For a time at least, so long as he is with her, he can be content with what he has achieved so far, calling it a complete world, and being willing to pronounce the words of Faust to the passing moment: 'stay, thou art so fair.'

A wholeness of vision—even though, paradoxically, it was partial still—was also achievable, Goethe felt, in philosophical terms. It was no doubt his own struggling self that he had partly in mind when he came to write his poem on the Wandering Jew, who, he tells us in *Dichtung und Wahrheit*, was to have been first condemned for having opposed Christ's purpose of driving men into the wilderness—of awakening their sense of sin, as we may interpret. The Jew, had the fragment we still possess ever been completed, would have been doomed to walk the earth until he saw Christ again transfigured, as he saw him on the day of his crucifixion. But this revelation would have come, or else have been supplanted, by the Jew's meeting with Spinoza, from whom, we may surmise, he would have learned to see the transfigured existence of God in all things. In a certain sense, and at certain times, Goethe could feel this 'liebliche, volle Gewißheit',* and even witness it with his own eyes, and this was another source of comfort: 'My confidence in Spinoza rested on the peaceful effect he produced in me, and only increased when my dear mystics were accused of Spinozism.'[1]

Before the Italian Journey, then, Goethe knew the heights and the depths, and a yet further aspect of his inward life is illustrated by the belief in polarity to which he bears witness at the end of Book 8 of *Dichtung und Wahrheit*—in the passage, that is, where he speaks of the cosmology he developed as a young man, in which the origin of the world and its continuance were explained by a series of contradictory movements, expanding and contracting, flowing and stopping. Man, Goethe affirms, must therefore be at one and the same time 'the most perfect and the most imperfect, the happiest and the unhappiest of creatures', and indeed that is precisely what he had always felt himself to be. Moreover, as he continues, 'the whole of creation is nothing else but a fall', while at the same time salvation 'must renew itself over and over again throughout all the time that living beings continue to develop'.[2] Goethe's doctrine in his youth—and there is no reason to suppose that he changed it in later years when he came to write about it—is thus akin to the paradox expressed in his own curious, many-faceted language by James Joyce in *Finnegans Wake*, 'Fall if you but will rise you must'. Every moment is a combination of the two movements, every man is a combination of Prometheus and Ganymede, and the divinity is distinguished only in that it subsumes both sides in an instantaneous fusion, whereas man is compelled to realise first one side of his nature, then the other: 'to fulfil the intentions of the Godhead, being obliged from one side to assert ourselves [uns zu verselbsten], while not neglecting, in a rhythmical pulsation, to empty ourselves of selfhood [uns zu entselbstigen]'.

It was in such terms that Goethe could write to Lavater,[3] 'You say truly that Man is God and Satan, Heaven and Earth,

* lovable, complete certainty.

all in one, for what else are these concepts but conceptions which Man has of his own nature', or again,[1] 'There is an unending purification going on in me, and yet I confess gladly that God and Satan, Hell and Heaven, which you so well define, are one in me'. Moreover, in such speeches Goethe allows us to suspect what he brings out a little more clearly elsewhere,[2] that in his view God is, as Thomas Mann speaks of him in his 'Joseph' novels, good and evil at one and the same time: as the microcosm Man is, so is the macrocosm God. In so far as Goethe could reconcile himself to this thought, as he does in the poem 'Harzreise im Winter', he can be content; in so far as it torments him, he continues to struggle; life is an alternation of these moods and there is nothing else but this. Something of the kind seems to be implied by the passage just quoted, in the 'and yet'. Goethe believes that he is being purified *and yet* gladly confesses that God and Satan are one in him or are in his single person ('gesteh ich gerne Gott und Satan...in mir Einem'): this surely means that, whatever the degree of purification that has already taken place, the ultimate can only be an enhanced awareness of his own duality-in-unity. Yet alongside this thought of God as good and evil runs also the idea of a God who is all-loving. Goethe is never consistent in his beliefs, and there is always some contradictory passage that can be quoted against any passage that is taken to be his true meaning.

This contradictoriness is nowhere better illustrated than in the way he speaks in his autobiography, letters and diaries, of already possessing the knowledge he sets out to acquire. It is as though he were conscious all along that the stage he was about to reach was one he already knew potentially, rather as the Philosophers' Stone of the alchemists, in some ways the object of their search, was also said to be fully present at every stage of the quest. With Charlotte von Stein, Goethe could feel himself to be Alpha and Omega. In much the same way, he could feel the presence of the external world to have been already within him, as though he were a microcosm, unfolding more and more signs of its identity with the macrocosm. Expressions of this feeling are particularly numerous as he starts on the Italian Journey: a simple example is his remark that he has just found a man who is 'the living image of a Söller'[1] (Söller being a character in a play written almost twenty years earlier). 'Thus I gradually discover my people [Menschen]', Goethe adds, as though meaning to imply that the character he had created entirely out of his imagination, as he thought, now proves to exist in the outside world. In the same month, writing of an entirely different matter, architecture, he says 'what pleases me is that none of my old basic ideas is shifted or altered, but rather everything becomes more closely defined and detailed, it all develops and grows to meet me'. He seems to have in mind, in this last phrase, what he had called rather strangely, in September 1780, the 'pyramid' of his existence. The sense is, apparently, that the whole of his existence is pyramidal or triangular, but that his self at any given moment is climbing up one side towards the apex, while, all unseen, the external world is 'growing to meet him' on the other side. On the way to Italy and in Italy itself, he sees himself close to or actually at the apex, and the image occurs to him again and again. Thus he writes[2] of finding 'beautiful confirmations' of his botanical ideas.

But [he adds] it is strange, and sometimes it makes me afraid, that there is so much as it were forcing itself in upon me, so that I cannot defend myself, and my being grows like a snowball, and sometimes it is as though my head simply could not grasp it or bear it, and yet it all develops outwards from inside, and I can't live without that.

The strange sense that what is forcing itself in upon him from outside is also forcing itself outwards from inside is another expression of the feeling intended by the pyramid image, another way of saying that Goethe is no longer swaying between the opposites but about to subsume them both in himself in a quasi-divine or superhuman unity. Indeed Goethe almost uses these very terms in a letter copied into his diary on 30 September 1786, 'My darling, how I rejoice that I have devoted my life to the True, as it now becomes so easy for me to move over to that greatness which is but the highest, purest point of the True.' This was the apex he had hoped to reach; his pyramid, the 'summit of existence' of which he spoke in *Egmont*,[1] was almost complete and attained.

The revolution which I foresaw [he went on] and which is now going on within me, is the one which has arisen in every artist who has long and zealously been loyal to Nature, and then seen the remnants of the great, ancient Spirit; his soul has welled up and he has felt a kind of inward transfiguration of himself, a feeling of freer life, higher existence, lightness and grace.

The moment which Goethe's Wandering Jew was to have found was realized in the transfiguration of all existent beings which Goethe now experienced. And still the sense continued, of this all having been known to him before. 'How Roman history climbs upward to meet me!' he cries,[2] evidently with the same image of the pyramid in mind; and, seeing Roman antiquities, 'it is really as though I were not merely seeing these things, but seeing them again'.[3] In a letter to Charlotte he writes again: 'You know my old manner of treating Nature, I am treating Rome in the same way and already it is climbing to meet me.'[4] Everything, he had written in 1780, must come to a single point: here in Italy it was beginning to do so. Evidence was crowding in on all sides that his intuitions had been right, that he in some way contained all this knowledge before it ever manifested itself to him in the real world, just as he could only explain the fascination Charlotte von Stein held for him by saying that she and he had known one another in some earlier existence. 'I am here and at peace', he wrote to his friends in Weimar from Rome 'and at peace for my whole life, it seems. For one may well say that a new life begins when one sees with one's eyes that Whole which one partly knows already, within and without oneself.'[5]

The rebirth in Italy was like a convergence on him from all sides of all he had hitherto believed in. It was symbolized externally in the idea he formed of Sicily, which he visited in

1787, for Sicily itself, with its rich historical past, seemed to him a focal point. 'Sicily points me towards Asia and Africa, and to set foot oneself on that strange point, on which so many radii of world history converge, is no small matter.'[1] It was no small matter because it would encourage a similar 'centripetal' movement in himself, and Goethe had already begun to experience what that meant. Not only botanical ideas and architecture and Roman history were 'climbing to meet' him, but everything he had ever admired became more real, even transfigured, and he rejoiced in it, above all in his experience of the Greeks. As Humphry Trevelyan has shown, he came to a realization of the Greek gods, with whose images he now surrounded himself, not as the kindly beings he had portrayed in *Iphigenie* but in the spirit of Karl Philipp Moritz's *Götterlehre*: Zeus, Hera, Mars, Apollo the 'destroyer' were anything but humane, as Iphigenie's gods were. Conflict and violent destruction were part of the order of Nature, and the Greeks in their wisdom knew that even the dreadful, hateful, highest powers, who ruled the very gods, were beautiful. 'Everything', said Moritz, whose ideas influenced Goethe profoundly at this time, 'is light and easy for the unlimited highest Power. Nothing laborious or difficult exists on this plane; all opposition ceases at this culminating point'; there, there was only unimpeded power. The sight of the Apollo Belvedere, the Zeus of Otricoli, and the Ludovisi Juno, 'had carried Goethe past the barrier that we know as the problem of good and evil ... The tendency that was fundamental in him, to admire what was great, beautiful and powerful, though it might be in no way beneficent on the human plane, now found itself supported and justified by the wisdom of the Greeks'.[2] In other words, Goethe felt himself not only at the culminating point so far as ideas were concerned, but also at the place where good and evil met and were transcended; from the almost divine position he now felt himself occupying, distinctions no longer existed; subject and object, self and the world, good and evil were one, and in the zestful enjoyment of them he was as though born into new life.

In the despondency which followed on the Italian Journey ('a kind of gloom and hesitancy which I am unable to master', were the words used by Goethe in a letter of 27 August 1794), like a return to the cycle of depression and elation he had already experienced before going to Italy, Goethe almost lost sight of what the experience had meant to him. Was it ever, one wonders, more than a high peak of elation? It required the encouragement of Schiller, who for ten years was to be his closest companion, to restore his confidence. For Schiller, by an uncanny instinct, told Goethe the very things he most wanted to hear. Goethe, Schiller told him, was the very reverse of himself and yet in a sense complementary to him. Goethe had not only married the Nordic spirit with that of the Greeks, he had proceeded in a purely intuitive way to grasp the whole essence of whatever he had undertaken to study. Where Schiller was speculative and analytic, rational in his approach to all things, and far less creative and many-sided than Goethe, the superior genius of the latter was natural, spontaneous, and free—and yet each supported and confirmed the other.

At first sight it may well appear that there could be no greater opposites than the speculative mind which proceeds from a unity, and the intuitive, which proceeds from a variety [of phenomena]. But if the first chastely and loyally pursues experience, and the other seeks the law with an independent, free power of thought, they cannot fail to meet half way.[1]

Had Schiller deliberately set out to flatter Goethe he could not have said anything more to his liking. It amounted to saying that, while others might laboriously pile up fact after fact, idea after idea, poetic invention after poetic invention, Goethe could achieve the same result with sovereign ease. Though Schiller could not know it, Goethe had indeed written something very similar in his diary on 26 February 1780:

I see that I labour in vain to learn my way from the detail into the whole, I have always been able to develop only from the whole into the detail, aggregation means nothing to me, but when I have dragged together wood and straw for some time, trying in vain to warm myself, for all that there are coals beneath and smoke everywhere, the flame does at last sweep over the whole in one mighty gust.

Goethe was evidently the type of poet whom Schiller in a famous essay described as 'naïve'—not in the usual sense of the word but in the sense, specially defined by Schiller, of the poet who '*is* Nature', whereas the 'sentimentalic' or reflective poet, like Schiller himself, rather 'seeks' Nature. If it emerged that the naïve poet could achieve almost effortlessly what the sentimentalic poet could achieve only by laborious effort, so much the greater might the naïve poet seem.

Your mind [Schiller wrote][1] works intuitively to an extraordinary degree, and all your powers of thought seem as it were to have subordinated their differences, to support the imagination as their common representative. Fundamentally this is the highest that a man can make of himself, when he succeeds in generalizing his point of view and making his feeling legislate for all. That is what you have striven for, and to what high degree have you already achieved it! My own reason works rather more in a symbolizing way, and thus I hover indeterminately between concepts and actual observations, between a general rule and a particular feeling, between technical ability and genius.

All this was equivalent to saying that Goethe had reached, or very nearly reached, the apex he had aimed at. Where Schiller merely symbolised, Goethe revealed the 'open secret'—as he was accustomed to call it—of the presence of the real in the ideal and the ideal in the real. Where Schiller could merely portray characters, Goethe grasped at the very idea of mankind, the 'Ur-mensch', and the feelings of such a man were not mere chance emotions but the archetypes of love, friendship, hatred, loyalty: Goethe's characters were individuals with the characteristics of their whole type or species.[2] The intuitive genius could rejoice that, all unawares, and by sheer honesty in his openness to truth, he had reached a position identical with that which speculative reason had reached from the contrary method of working.

Yet Goethe was not always in need of outside help to gain confidence. Schiller helped him somewhat as Charlotte von Stein had done, by his complementary nature, but at times Goethe could feel himself containing both opposites within himself, and abandon himself to them with complete trust. He was driven by a daemon which to some seemed nothing else than the assertion of his ego, to others an almost divine will. As his friend Fritz Jacobi (1743–1819) said,[1] he was 'a man possessed...who is almost never permitted to act of his own will. I do not mean to suggest by that,' Jacobi added, 'that no change for the better and lovelier is possible in him, but it is possible only in the way that a flower unfolds, a crop ripens, or a tree grows aloft and bears its own crown.' Goethe himself could speak in similar terms, 'may my existence develop enough, may the stem lengthen and the flowers break forth more richly and beautifully'.[2] He could also speak almost as a Christian might have done, and this at a time when he was far from professing Christianity. 'So much I can assure you of', he wrote to Charlotte,[3] 'that in the midst of all my happiness I live in a perpetual renunciation, and with all my toil and labour I see daily that it is not my will, but the will of a higher power which is being exerted, whose thoughts are not my thoughts.' In all this, he seems entirely at the mercy of every gust, incapable of choosing his direction. Yet at the same period he can also write in his diary in such terms as these:

New secrets are revealed to me. I am in for a rough time...By God there is not a chancelry clerk who cannot talk more sense in a quarter of an hour than I in a quarter of a year, God knows—ten years. But then I also know what none of them know, and do what none of them know, or do know for all I care [sic]. I feel gradually a general confidence, and God grant I deserve it, not in that it's easy, but as *I want it*. What I have to endure in myself and others nobody sees. The best part is the deep stillness in which I live and grow against the world, and am gaining what they can never take from me by fire or by sword.[4]

The iron will which Goethe seems to reveal here is strangely in contrast to the subservience to the divine which he speaks of elsewhere, and one can never be sure how much he distinguishes between the two.

Had he been asked, Goethe would probably have spoken to this point as he did in his sixties, looking back over his youth at the conclusion of so much of his autobiography as had been written: he had always sought the ineffable until at length he realized that it was better to turn away from it, not to probe too deeply into its mysteries. For he had discovered, he thought,

in both animate and inanimate Nature, something which manifested itself only in contradictions and therefore could not be summarised in any concept, still less in a word. It was not divine, for it seemed irrational [unvernünftig], not human, for it had no sense [Verstand], not diabolical, for it was beneficent, not angelic, for it often gloated over misfortune. It resembled chance, for it displayed no logical sequence, it resembled Providence, for it suggested coherence. All that confines and limits us seemed no obstacle to it; it seemed to play arbitrarily with the necessary elements of our existence, it contracted time and expanded space. It seemed to enjoy only the impossible, and the possible it spurned with contempt.[1]

This was the 'Daemon', 'das Dämonische' of which Goethe also spoke to Eckermann on a number of occasions. (He speaks of it too in the poem 'Urworte. Orphisch'.) Of all the countless topics on which Goethe touched in these conversations, from Byron to Victor Hugo, from Herder, Lessing and Manzoni to Molière, Mozart and Napoleon, from Rossini, Schiller and Scott to Shakespeare, Sophocles and Sterne, perhaps this one may be singled out. There was in great men, Goethe believed, something peculiarly open to the daemonic; it was most operative in his relationship with Schiller, and had seemingly brought about their meeting at just the right time.[2] Thus it would appear to have been providential, not Chance, as he had called it in the autobiography. Similarly, he spoke of certain hindrances to the completion of a certain work as having proved ultimately beneficial: 'such things have often happened in the course of my life, and one comes in such cases to believe in a higher influence, something daemonic, which one worships without presuming to explain it any further'.[1] At times he seemed to identify the daemonic with God,[2] despite the disclaimer in *Dichtung und Wahrheit*; moreover, he denied that it could exist in the Mephistopheles of *Faust*, the devil being much too negative: 'the daemonic expresses itself in a thoroughly positive energy [Tatkraft]'.[3] This, again appearing to contradict the account in *Dichtung und Wahrheit* which speaks of the daemonic as gloating over misfortune—an action in which it is impossible to conceive of any positive motivation—serves to render Goethe's meaning the more confusing. (The notion of gloating also seems to require a person, rather than an impersonal force.) As he says, the daemonic does move in contradictions. All the same, his stress lies on the whole on the idea of energy, effectiveness, the mysterious and attractive personality in such men as Peter the Great, the Duke of Weimar, and Byron.[4] The phrase he used in one of his poems comes to mind: 'ewiges lebendiges Tun'.* If he urges that men should also oppose the daemonic, not yielding to its power,[5] he may mean no more than that by doing so the energy they display will derive from the daemonic also, for he makes it quite clear elsewhere that men must yield themselves unconsciously to it, believing all the while that they are acting of their own free will.[6]

The essential point remains the contradictoriness of the Daemon. Unlike the 'daemon' of Socrates, which was a kind of instinctive prompting which told him when he was about to commit some wrong in thought or deed, and unlike the Holy Ghost of Christian theology, to which it also bore some resemblance, the force or person which Goethe worshipped and to which he submitted was incalculable and incomprehensible in nearly every way. Almost nothing can be affirmed of it that cannot also be denied. The one thing which remains constant throughout, and which can never be contradicted, is

* eternal, living doing.

the energy of the daemon: it seems to be at times a kind of amoral life-force with no other purpose than that of exerting itself. And if Goethe sometimes calls this force by another name, that of love, we can never be sure that he does not mean something quite different from what is usually meant by the word, something more akin to what he wrote of to Katharina Fabricius on 27 June 1770: 'When I say love, I understand by that the rocking emotion in which our hearts float, moving backwards and forwards for ever on the same spot, whenever some stimulus shifts it out of its usual path of indifference.' This definition of love in terms of movement, as though it were the pendulum of some great mechanism, has much in common with what Goethe spoke of in old age as the daemon. As in *Faust*, the overruling factor is always the deed, the action, the movement, in contrast to passivity, calm, stillness, and this is simply life in abundance, nothing else. ('The aim of life is life itself' as he wrote to J. H. Meyer.)[1] Strangely, for one who at times paid so much regard to formal qualities, Goethe never thought of it as requiring discipline or rule, moral law or truth. His garden remained as it were unweeded, full of powerful shoots but always running the risk that, as Hamlet says, 'things rank and gross in nature' would possess it exclusively. That they did not, but only showed their heads from time to time, was a tribute to the sympathy, humour and good sense he was always capable of showing and which make of him so ambiguous and tantalizing a figure. That they appeared at all was later to help produce some calamitous results.

6

SCIENCE

Goethe's scientific writings take up fourteen volumes of the Weimar edition, which allots sixty-four volumes to his literary work. They bulked at least as large in his estimation of their worth, and, like *Faust*, they were a principal preoccupation throughout his life.

Strictly speaking, Goethe's first interest was in alchemy, which, because of the religious symbolism attached to it, he began studying in the winter of 1768-9, in company with the Pietist Fräulein von Klettenberg, and which he continued to study until at least 1770. The confusion in the alchemical writings displeased him, however, and he resolved to develop their teachings more consistently, first by studying the theosophist Swedenborg (1688-1772), who resembled the alchemists in that he used scientific facts and theories in order to symbolize inward states of mind, then by helping his friend the Swiss parson Lavater in his compilation of a work on physiognomy, published in 1775, which again sought to relate the external with the internal world.

These early stages had an evident occult tinge. It was not until Goethe moved to Weimar that he began to direct his attention more conscientiously to objective facts. Here he assumed control of the ducal estates; the care of the parks, greenhouses, mines and museums demanded a grounding in forestry, botany, geology and many other branches of knowledge. Goethe studied Linnaeus, the great Swedish botanist; he collected geological and anatomical specimens, and in 1784 made a remarkable discovery, that the 'intermaxillary' bone, which most anatomists believed not to exist in man, was present in the human jaw. (Goethe made this discovery independently, though he was not the first to do so; its importance lay in the fact that it demonstrated a further link in man's affinity with the brute creation.) This was in the modern sense of the word a scientific discovery; in Goethe's eyes, however, it had a special significance, it was the 'keystone to Man'; it showed how every creature was 'only a tone, a shade in one great harmony'. Man was no longer as he had been thought to be, a special creation from the hand of God, but one facet of a great whole which might manifest itself in countless forms. This was an idea peculiarly close to Goethe's heart, and much of his later scientific work was to reflect it.

Meanwhile his botanical studies were also taking a more serious turn, especially from 1785 onwards, when he acquired a microscope and began a herbarium. These studies also quickly bore fruit, although it was some years before Goethe made known his ideas. But already in July 1786 he was writing to Frau von Stein in terms as enthusiastic and confident as these:

What pleases me most at present is plant-life. Everything is forcing itself upon me, I no longer have to think about it, everything comes to meet me, and the whole gigantic kingdom becomes so simple that I can see at once the answer to the most difficult problems. If only I could communicate the insight and the joy to someone, but it is not possible. And it is no dream or fancy; I am beginning to grow aware of the essential form with which, as it were, Nature is always playing, and from which she produces her great variety. Had I the time in this brief span of life I am confident I could extend it to all the realms of Nature—the whole realm.[1]

The staggering claim Goethe makes is a reminder of the real nature of his scientific inquiries. Like Faust, he was not interested in mere practical information or partial knowledge. From his study of alchemy onwards, he too had wanted to know

> ...was die Welt
> Im Innersten zusammenhält,*

and this knowledge was precisely what he felt his botanical studies had brought him. The 'essential form' of Nature, which, so far as plants were concerned, he called the 'Ur-pflanze', was still only an idea, it is true. Goethe had not yet had time to

---

* What holds the world together at its heart.

show how it applied even to one of Nature's realms. All the same, it was so vivid in his mind, that on travelling to Sicily in 1787 he was confident of finding a real confirmation of his intuition. 'Faced with so many new and renewed forms', he wrote, thinking of the great wealth of flora on the island, 'my old whim occurred to me, that perhaps in all this host I might find the 'Urpflanze'. For there must be one. Otherwise, how should I know that this or that form is a plant, if they were not all fashioned after one pattern?'[1]

Goethe was thinking here of the Platonic notion that there is an 'ideal' form of all natural phenomena, implanted in human minds, by means of which we recognize them as belonging to one species or another. (Other philosophers, however, have held that we group objects according to certain common features, but that the groupings are sometimes only verbal—the 'idea of a house' which would include Blenheim Palace, an igloo, and the 'house of Stuart' would, for instance, be either vague or useless.) The special feature of Goethe's belief was that this 'Idea' might actually be found in concrete form. To Schiller, for whom the very notion of an Idea implied abstraction, the finding of a real specimen was an absurdity. Still, for Goethe the combining of the real and the ideal, and the ability to see the one in the other, had a strong fascination, and all his investigations were directed towards it.

The first published work on botany was the *Versuch, die Metamorphose der Pflanzen zu erklären*, of 1790, to be followed by many more treatises as well as by the poem 'Die Metamorphose der Pflanzen'. In the next two years he published the first and second of his *Beiträge zur Optik*, a comparatively minor work, which was to be followed in 1810 by the more important and lengthy *Zur Farbenlehre*, and again by a variety of lesser writings. Here too, his interest dates back to about 1770, although optics and chromatics rather gave way to botany for the remainder of Goethe's youth. And once again, his purpose was not purely scientific, but aimed at combining a stringent scientific and objective discipline with a symbolical and subjective interest. Just as, in his botanical work, Goethe speaks of sepals, cotyledons, and reproductive organs in a manner far removed from the vague references to Nature in Boehme (1575–1624) and Swedenborg, so in his chromatic studies he refers to prisms, mirrors and beams of light. Yet all this has, as he himself declares, 'a spiritual meaning', and light and darkness are words denoting not merely physical but allegorical opposites. 'We are dealing', Goethe wrote, 'with phenomena which must be present both to the bodily eyes and to the eyes of the spirit.'[1] Indeed colours were just as much an expression of the 'ideal in the real' as plants were.

Goethe's other scientific studies, which included meteorology, geology and anatomy, developed less systematically than those in chromatics and botany, although they give some evidence of the same intentions, especially in so far as they attempt to range the phenomena they deal with into groups of contrasted opposites. For this was the clue to Nature which Goethe looked for and believed in 1787 that he had found: the presence of 'polar' forces everywhere in the universe, opposed yet complementary powers which were in conflict and which could nevertheless be brought to a synthesis, to a unity in which their opposition was subsumed. This is an idea prominent in neo-Platonist writers, whom Goethe read while quite young, and in alchemy, where the twin opposites are often designated 'Mercury' and 'Sulphur' (these being symbols rather than chemical substances), and where their union is called the Philosophers' Stone. It is also found in Jacob Boehme, who strongly influenced the Pietistic circles in which Goethe's mentor Susanna von Klettenberg moved, and in Swedenborg, who borrowed heavily from Boehme. Goethe's literary work shows traces of it, in the dual view of Nature shared by Werther and Faust, for both of whom she is, in the words of Faust's Earth-Spirit, 'Geburt und Grab, ein ewiges Meer',* in the division of *Werthers Leiden* into two contrasting parts, in the contrasted opposites of Goethe's two poems 'Prometheus' and 'Ganymed', written within the same year yet expressing completely incompatible religious attitudes, and above all in

---

* Birth and the grave, an eternal sea.

Torquato Tasso, which not only opposes the poet to the man of action but also hints at the possibility of their combining, and thus suggests something of the concomitant of 'polarity' which Goethe called 'Steigerung', meaning 'intensification' or 'heightening'. There are also signs of a transference of these theories in his novel *Die Wahlverwandtschaften*. Goethe was as a rule, however, less schematic in his literary works than he was in his scientific ones, so that the latter are often useful as pointers to overtones of meaning in his plays, novels and poems, even if also temptations to overschematize them.

Bearing this in mind, and also bearing in mind that Goethe's scientific writings themselves do not lay emphasis on the schemes of symbols they contain, allowing these rather to emerge incidentally during a long exposition, a summary outline can be useful.

Goethe's fundamental pattern in his Colour-Theory is based on the idea that all colours belong either to a group deriving from the primary yellow or to one deriving from blue: these in turn stand for light and darkness, and are representative of the duality in all Nature: repulsion and attraction, above and below, action and reaction, activity and passivity, male and female. This duality, however, is a constant source of strife (one thinks here of Faust's famous speech 'Two souls there dwell, alas, within my breast' and of his tragic division between earthly and heavenly striving); the tendency of Nature, it is true, is to restore a balance, but the conflict nevertheless takes place so long as there is one-sidedness and individuality. We see this natural process at work in the tendency of the eye to see complementary 'after-colours': presented with a powerful purple image we see afterwards the complementary colour green, which stands at the opposite rim of the so-called 'colour-cycle', and thus, Goethe suggests, the too obtrusive colour is balanced out. The eye 'strives for a whole', attempting to embrace both opposites together. (Again one thinks of Faust's desire to taste experience in all forms, 'painful enjoyment', 'enamoured hate', 'refreshing annoyance'.)[1]

This natural tendency to achieve a unity is also visible,

Goethe argues, within the realm of colour itself. For both yellow and blue, he says, have a barely perceptible tinge of red, which can be increased by various methods so as to produce pure red. All these methods involve what may be called an 'intensification': thus, a sheet of parchment held in front of the pin-hole of a *camera obscura* will cause the light from outside to appear yellow; if further sheets are added, increasing the degree of opacity, the yellow will take on a reddish tinge, and this at length 'passes into red'. Conversely, if darkness is seen through a semi-opaque medium it will appear blue, but as the opacity increases the blue will become mauve or violet, introducing an element of red. Similarly a yellow or blue liquid in a vessel, seen from above, will take on a reddish tinge as more of the same liquid is poured in: there is a greater concentration of the liquid, and the red colour appears as a result.

Red, however, is not meant purely as a physical colour. It gains overtones of meaning from remarks dropped by Goethe such as that it is the 'culmination'[1] of a process, that it is the colour which will spread over the sky on the Day of Judgement, and that it contains either in actual fact or potentially all other colours, besides being a source of bliss. From such phrases, some of them very surprising if one thinks only of the physical colour, the reader gains an impression that red is for Goethe a kind of symbol of the divine, conceived in neo-Platonist or similar terms. Nor is this entirely unparalleled, for the colour red in alchemy stood for the Philosophers' Stone, which some alchemists called Christ or God, and which trans-muted metals into gold, as some maintained, in the sense that God could transform men into his own likeness. On these terms it is easier to understand Goethe's meaning when he says of red that 'in the union of the intensified [or enhanced: gesteigert] polar opposites it is imaginable that an actual quietening [of the sensations] takes place, a feeling which we should like to call an ideal satisfaction'.[2] He has in mind that, whereas in the world of phenomena there is division and polarity, in the deity there is a duality-in-unity or a unity-in-duality which contains the polarity and yet transcends it. And this pattern in the macrocosm is repeated in identical terms in the microcosm of the world of colour (rather as the solar system is repeated in the structure of an atom, with its 'planets' in orbit around the nucleus).

Goethe's botanical ideas also reflect his belief in polarity, although here the opposites are not light and darkness but expansion and contraction, which he sees as a pulsation operating in a sevenfold rhythm from the 'contracted' seed to the 'expansion' of the stem, thence to the 'contraction' of the calyx, and then alternately from the corolla to the reproductive organs, the fruit and the seed, which completes the cycle by returning to the origin: Alpha and Omega are one and the same. The pattern of the 'Urpflanze' must have been essentially one comprising this dialectical movement, although Goethe never gave any explicit definition of the term. It must surely have been, like the colours, an exemplification within the plant-world of the same all-embracing divine nature. At the same time, the sequence of expansion and contraction symbolized the temporal extension of the deity, for in another formulation Goethe declared that 'Alles ist Blatt'. All is leaf: by this he meant, as he said, that throughout its length, 'backwards and forwards, the plant is nothing but leaf, so inseparably united with the seed to be, that the one cannot be thought of without the other' (just as man, Goethe may have wanted to suggest, cannot be thought of without his origin and end in God). The leaf was 'the true Proteus, which could conceal and reveal itself in all forms'. And indeed petals, for example, can truly be described as coloured leaves; Goethe was able to find some specimens in which a series of leaves could be seen passing through barely perceptible stages until they had, so to speak, become petals. An example which particularly attracted his attention was that of a tulip, in which one of the stem-leaves had grown into the corolla, where its upper half had become united with one of the petals. This, he remarked, was 'a curious case of a leaf being at one and the same time a stem-leaf and a petal'. But, although these instances bore witness to Goethe's concern for detailed demonstration, they were also servants of his larger purpose, which was to show that, as Plato had said in words which Goethe had copied down in his early twenties, 'the parts must resemble each other and the whole'. Just as the presence of the intermaxillary bone had shown that Man was not a special creation from the hand of God, but a tone, a shade in one great harmony, so, within the limited unity of the plant, forms as apparently distinct as petals and seed-coverings were modifications of one single fundamental organ. In this way the leaf was at one and the same time its own individual self and the basic form of the whole plant. Or, as Goethe expressed it in one of his most moving poems:

> In tausend Formen magst du dich verstecken,
> Doch, Allerliebste, gleich erkenn' ich dich;
> Du magst mit Zauberschleiern dich bedecken,
> Allgegenwärt'ge, gleich erkenn' ich dich.*

He was thinking not merely of plants and leaves but rather of something akin to the experience which made him let Wilhelm Meister see the form of his love Natalie first in one woman then in another, without ever finding abiding satisfaction in any of them. The leaf was the unity pervading all manifestations of life, corresponding to the colour red which, as Goethe so strangely declared, contained all other colours in itself. The leaf might take this form or that, expand or contract as the moment demanded, but ultimately there was only its one ineffable self which no definition could ever exhaust.

Within this quasi-divine unity of the leaf (corresponding in some ways to the opening and closing scenes in Heaven which encase the action of *Faust*) much could happen. Goethe advances the theory that the sap is purified and refined as it advances higher up the stem, perhaps with a human parallel in his mind. When the reproductive organs are reached, something quite exceptional takes place. 'Why', Goethe asks,

---

* Though thou hide thyself in a thousand forms, yet, most-beloved, at once I recognize thee; though thou cover thyself in a thousand magic veils, yet, ever-present, at once I recognize thee.

in language which has unmistakably symbolical overtones, 'should not this pollenization also be a liberation from the burden of matter, so that at the last the plenitude of the profoundest, innermost depths may come forth with all its living and fundamental power, and partake in an infinite generation?'[1] He is clearly thinking here of some apotheosis of man, whereby he becomes—almost in a sexual sense—a Creator, rather than of the plant in any strictly scientific sense. One thinks here of such phrases as 'auf zur höheren Begattung' (up to a higher sexual union) in the poem 'Selige Sehnsucht',[2] or the words from 'Wiederfinden':

> Allah braucht nicht mehr zu schaffen,
> Wir erschaffen seine Welt.*

Within the pattern of life which is in any case a pattern of the divine life itself, there is the possibility of progressing towards complete realization of our identity with the divine. This was what Goethe saw in the life of the plant, and, although he illustrated his vision with a wealth of concrete detail, it was still essentially the vision of the mystics, the neo-Platonists, the alchemists and Jacob Boehme. Goethe was more concerned to demonstrate his vision than to give a scrupulously scientific account of the outside world—which in any case he regarded as a fruitless undertaking.

Goethe's whole notion of scientific inquiry was against the purely objective collection of data, the strict testing by repeatable experiments, the exact tabulation of results, all of which was for him equivalent to placing Nature on the rack and forcing her to reveal her secrets (an image which Francis Bacon himself, one of the founders of modern science, had used). He preferred to see Nature almost as a mistress coming to meet him, confirming what he already intuitively perceived, revealing her identity with his own inward nature rather as, in his novel *Die Wahlverwandtschaften*, the lovers Eduard and Ottilie grew more and more like one another. 'How the plant-world climbs up towards me', he wrote in a

* Allah needs no longer to create; we procreate his world.

In comparison with Boehme and Swedenborg, Goethe does present much more detailed evidence for his belief, and his symbols are much more intricate and more subtly worked out, even though they often remain arbitrary in their associations. The fact that they are non-scientific is not the only important thing about them, so long as the things they have to say by analogy about the inward life of human beings are illuminating, and this they sometimes are. Goethe's greater respect for scientific data, however, did bear fruit in unexpected ways, especially in the biological field. While one historian of biology writes of his science that 'it is romantic philosophy from beginning to end [and] bears no resemblance whatever to modern natural research', another holds that 'the subject of developmental morphology received its greatest impetus from ...the Poet-Philosopher Goethe', and another adds: 'if Goethe succeeded it is because he was a man of genius, and was more interested in Nature than in his own method'. Distinguished botanists of recent times like W. Troll and Agnes Arber have certainly found inspiration in Goethe's science, and there has been a revival of interest in it through such writers as Lancelot Law Whyte, Erich Heller, and Rudolf Steiner (the founder of the anthroposophical movement, who claimed a spiritual descent from Goethe), principally on the grounds that Goethe provides at least a glimpse of an exit from the increasing departmentalization of modern science, and its disregard of subjectivity and symbolism. The work of Teilhard de Chardin and of the philosophical historians Arnold Toynbee and Oswald Spengler is akin to Goethe's in its attempt at combining theological or 'weltanschaulich' views with the facts of history and science. The musical theories of Anton Webern are directly indebted, as the composer shows in his book *The Path to the New Music*, to the symbolical aspects of Goethe's science. Yet one is left finally with the impression of what Goethe would have liked to prove true and believed to be true, rather than with any sense of his having even remotely proved it. As Sir William Dampier writes in his *History of Science*, the basis of Goethe's Colour-Theory was one that 'could not stand the simplest physical analysis, and was supported by nothing but Goethe's abuse of Newton and the compromising help of the Hegelians. It is not surprising that the men of science learnt to ignore the writings of the philosophers'.

What Goethe believed perhaps more fervently than any-thing else was defined in his words to Eckermann, quoted by Sir Charles Sherrington in his brief essay *Goethe on Nature and on Science*:

Let people serve Him who gives to the beast his fodder, and to man meat and drink as much as he can enjoy. But I worship Him who has infused into the world such a power of production, that, when only the millionth part of it comes out into life, the world swarms with creatures to such a degree that war, pestilence, fire and water cannot prevail against them. That is *my* God!

It was the god whom he celebrated in the love-feast in the Aegean Sea in the Second Part of *Faust*, in the Earth-Spirit of Part One, and indeed in the whole of his own tremendous creativity. Did it matter, that this creativity was often foiled or spoiled? That is the issue in all genuine study of Goethe's work, and with more of his literary work reviewed, we are closer to being able to answer the question. Despite what can be said in its favour, Goethe's science is so arbitrary in its associative techniques that we still have to look elsewhere for signs of really important achievements in him. There can be no more proper place to look for them than in *Faust*, and his lyric poetry.

7

'FAUST PART I'

When Goethe wrote the first monologue in the original version of *Faust*, he had in mind the style of Hans Sachs (1494–1576), the poet and dramatist of the Reformation:

> Hab nun, ach, die Philosophei,
> Medizin und Juristerei,
> Und leider auch die Theologie
> Durchaus studiert mit heißer Müh.*

This is nearly the same rough wood-cut language as that of the 'cobbler of Nuremberg', from whose play *Der farend Schuler im Paradeis* Goethe must have borrowed the theme of the scene in which the devil Mephistopheles meets the house-wife Marthe. The four-stressed line with its irregular beat and archaic spelling of 'Philosophie' evokes a picture of a Faust with crude, vigorous features such as one sees on old broad-sheets. It was not the language of Goethe's day, and he did not keep it up, in the *Urfaust* version, for more than thirty lines. In the final version the roughness is smoothed down:

> Habe nun, ach! Philosophie,
> Juristerei und Medizin,
> Und leider auch Theologie
> Durchaus studiert, mit heißem Bemühn.

This more mellifluous rhythm, though still reminiscent of Sachs's 'Knittelvers', allows Faust to develop more credibly into the speculative genius with whom Goethe was really concerned. The sixteenth-century language would not only have sounded like pastiche; had it been sustained throughout it would have made it difficult to introduce the new interpreta-

---

* I have now, ah me, studied philosophy, medicine and law, and, alas, theology, too, from end to end, with zealous toil.

tion of the Faust legend which Goethe eventually gave, an interpretation which had more to do with developments of thought in his own time than with those of Luther's day. What we hear in the remainder of the final version of the monologue are echoes of the sixteenth century, not a renewal of its speech, iambic tetrameters usually being substituted for the syllabic count of the original 'Knittelvers'.

In going back to the sixteenth century at all, Goethe was deliberately looking to the period when German culture had last shown itself in all its vigour, without the French influence—especially in its rationalistic form—which the generation of Goethe's youth deplored. The humanists of the Reformation, Reuchlin, Wimpfeling and others, influenced by the Renaissance in Italy, had themselves tried to give new meaning to the name 'Germania'. In the second half of the eighteenth century, Germany's second experience of the Renaissance, Lessing had called for 'a German play'[1] and pointed to the Faust legend as providing admirable and popular material; Herder had inspired Goethe to look for subject-matter among the folk-songs of the ordinary people of Germany; and Frederick the Great, paradoxically for such a Francophile, had sparked off the political trail which was to lead within a century of his death to the first unification of Germany. For Goethe, then, the Faust legend was an ideal theme. The first references to Faust, who may have been a real personage, had been made in Germany, between 1507 and 1540. The *Historia von D. Johann Fausten, dem weitbeschreyten Zauberer und Schwartzkünstler* had been published by Johann Spies in 1587, to be followed by the moralizing collection by Widman in 1599, and its revision by Pfizer in 1674. Through the *Faustbuch des christlich Meynenden*, of which the first extant dated copy was published in 1725, and which was very widely sold at fairs, the legend became extremely well known. In addition, Marlowe's dramatic version, *Doctor Faustus*, written shortly before his death in 1593, soon became known in Germany through touring English players, and gave rise to many vulgarizations and to puppet-plays, so that once again the subject was widely known to the common people. It is true that, unlike Shakespeare, Goethe had no popular audience in the theatre to write for. The people who knew the Faust legend best were the least likely to have contact with the literary circles in which Goethe moved. All the same, the German-ness of his subject was indisputable, and the scenes he wrote, requiring a high-vaulted Gothic chamber, a beer-cellar, a timbered house, a witches' sabbath on the Brocken mountain, a fir-forest, a Gothic cathedral, were the first ever to achieve such local colour.

As events proved, the choice of Faust was epoch-making: the next century and a half in the literary history of Germany was fascinated by the legend, partly symbolized by it, and Faust came to be thought of by some as the embodiment of the German people, so that it had political importance too. Already in Goethe's lifetime, Schelling called the play 'the poem peculiar to Germans', while in 1855 Jakob Burckhardt wrote 'it is a definite, inescapable destiny of educated German youth at a certain age to delve into *Faust* and ponder deeply about it'. There were versions in dramatic, epic, or novelistic form by Weidman (1775), Maler Müller (1777), Klinger (1791), Chamisso (1804), Grabbe (1829), Lenau (1836), Heine (1847) and Thomas Mann (1949)—the last of these construing Faust's pact with the devil as the equivalent of Germany's adherence to Hitler—and there were musical settings on the theme by Mendelssohn, Schumann, Spohr, Liszt, Wagner, Mahler; outside Germany the theme attracted Coleridge (who never achieved his ambition of writing a 'Faust' in *Michael Scott*), Byron, in *Manfred* (1817), and Shelley (who was enthusiastic and translated several passages of Goethe's work), Philip James Bailey (*Festus*, 1839), Gérard de Nerval, who translated Part One into French, Paul Valéry (*Mon Faust*), the Hungarian Imre Madach (in *The Tragedy of Man*, which borrows from Goethe, though Faust himself does not appear), the Russians Lunacharsky, who wrote a Faust of his own, and Pasternak, who made a modern translation, and in music Gounod, Mussorgsky, Boito, Busoni and Berlioz. Ibsen's *Peer Gynt* is a Norwegian treatment of the same theme, and indeed the figure became so 'universal' a type that almost any work of metaphysical aspiration came to be known in Germany as the author's Faust.

Yet the scenes which Goethe wrote in his early youth, known from the *Urfaust* manuscript discovered in 1887, scarcely treat the old Faust-theme at all. It is true, they include the first 248 lines of the first scene: Faust's monologue, his encounter with the Earth-Spirit, and the interruption of his thoughts by his famulus Wagner. But all that follows in the final version, including the pact with the devil, up to the beginning of the scene in which Mephistopheles catechizes and confounds the student, is not yet written at the *Urfaust* stage, which has only two more scenes, one in Auerbach's Cellar, the other entitled 'Landstraße' (of four lines, omitted from the final version) before the 'Gretchen-tragedy' begins. This was Goethe's first concern, the telling of the tale of Gretchen's betrayal by Faust, reflecting partly his own betrayal of Friederike Brion. Except for the insertion of the scenes 'Forest and Cavern' and those of the 'Walpurgis Night', and the turning of some prose passages into verse, this section of the *Urfaust* is essentially the same as the latter half of *Faust Part I*, although this was not published until 1808. Yet this part of Faust's story has nothing essentially Faustian about it; it is at most barely suggested in the later Faust-books, and could just as well have been told of any pair of lovers, apart from the fact that it is the devil who both leads Faust to Gretchen and compels him to abandon her. Only later, in *Part I*, did it become possible to interpret the Gretchen-scenes as belonging to the whole story of Faust as Goethe conceived it.

For the time being, Goethe had concentrated on telling a simple tale with ballad-like simplicity. There is no plot to speak of in the Gretchen-tragedy. Faust sees Margarete, falls in love with her, obtains her trust through Mephistopheles' persuasions, gets her with child, and attempts in vain to rescue her from prison where she awaits execution; at the last, Mephisto hales him off to what seems to be his eternal perdition. So far as narrative goes, that is all there is to it: there is no intrigue, no great array of characters, no deep inquiry into motivation. There is, however, a distinctness of outline such as is to be found as a rule not in plays but in ballads. Each scene of the Gretchen-tragedy is like a verse in a poem: as a ballad moves on from one statement to another, sometimes with only a tenuous connection which has to be guessed at, so the play proceeds by isolated portrayals. Faust sees Margarete pass by and desires her. He goes to her bedroom and feels his passion calmed at the sight of its cleanliness and purity. He learns that the present he left for her has been confiscated by a priest. Mephistopheles engineers a meeting. Faust and Margarete play at hide and seek in the garden; she confesses her love for Faust and her fear of Mephistopheles. All this might have been the enacting of one of those 'Moritaten' or 'Bänkelsänge' which used to be sung at market-places while the singer pointed to pictures illustrating his theme. It is not until the seduction of Margarete that the story acquires really dramatic impact: in the scenes 'At the Well', 'The City Wall' (*Zwinger*) and 'Cathedral' Margarete is suddenly struck down by three hammer-blows, as the recognition of her guilt overpowers her and unhinges her mind. From here to the end, with its fine portrayal of Margarete in her madness, the play leaves the ground and maintains itself, for all its still fragmentary character. It seems meant, in the *Urfaust* form, for the simplest of stages, and is ideally suited to a troupe of strolling players.

This is as much as to say that there is no tragedy here in the grand manner, nothing to compare with the Antigone of Sophocles or the Phèdre of Racine. Goethe is not concerned with that kind of effect; there is no choice confronting his heroine; she has no notion of any evil consequences until they have already begun to batter her down. One of her most moving passages is that in which, lamenting her sin, she adds: 'Doch alles, was dazu mich trieb / Gott, war so gut! ach, war so lieb!'* Margarete is without subtlety, an innocent, hard-working girl overcome with embarrassment at receiving so wealthy a lover as Faust appears to be. There is a childlike

* But all that led me to it was, oh God, so good, ah, so loving kind.

simplicity in the way she plucks the petals from a flower to see whether his love is genuine, and although she may be of an age with Juliet, she has none of Juliet's wit or fire, or any of Juliet's desire that 'strange love, grown bold' should 'make true love acted simple modesty'. True love in this sense, in the physical sense which Shakespeare emphasizes through Mercutio's speeches, would take Margarete completely by surprise —she has no notion, until the play is almost over, of what it means, and although she is called 'schnippisch' ('pert') by Faust, she never shows any such quality after her brief first appearance. She is sympathetic, shy, devoted, humble and trustful, but has only brief occasions to show how much she is also spirited, self-reliant, perceptive. Turgenev was obtuse to find her stupid, and Ruskin unkind to speak of 'mere maidenhood', for as a critic has said, she yields to Faust 'with a naïve readiness that would either be stupid or dissolute, if it were not the most innocent acceptance of the burden of love'. Her real distinctiveness is in the strength of her passion. Goethe borrows for her from Desdemona (in her singing a song while undressing) and from Ophelia (in the 'mad' scene) and gives her the innocence of both without their maturity (she has not the experience needed to speak Ophelia's lines 'O what a noble mind is here o'erthrown'). But she is too unconscious of all that is going on about her for her fate to be more than pathetic. When Goethe added the final word of the First Part, capping Mephisto's exultant cry in *Urfaust*, 'She is condemned', with a 'Voice from above' declaring 'She is saved', he expressed the feeling most people have about her, that she has not deserved the hideous punishment we have seen her suffer, and deserves comfort now. But she has been a quite helpless victim.

On the other hand, Gretchen has musically the best passages in *Urfaust*, not only the songs 'Es war ein König in Thule' and 'Meine Ruh ist hin', but also the speech 'Ach neige, du Schmerzensreiche'. And in these she is given a power of speech which seems to come to her in her misery of desolation:

> Mein Schoß, Gott! drängt
> Sich nach ihm hin.

> Ach dürft ich fassen
> Und halten ihn
> Und küssen ihn
> So wie ich wollt,
> An seinen Küssen
> Vergehen sollt!*

and

> Wer fühlet,
> Wie wühlet
> Der Schmerz mir im Gebein?
> Was mein armes Herz hier banget,
> Was es zittert, was verlanget,
> Weißt nur du, nur du allein.†

There is a vigour in these rhythms which one would scarcely expect from some other parts of the play, and it is when Gretchen's suppressed passion breaks out that she is at her most alive:

MARGARETE. Sieh das Kind! Muß ich's doch tränken; da hatt ich's eben. Da! Ich habs getränkt! Sie nahmen mirs und sagen, ich habs umgebracht, und singen Liedcher auf mich! — Es ist nicht wahr — es ist ein Märchen, das sich so endigt, es ist nicht auf mich, daß sie's singen.

FAUST (*der sich zu ihr hinwirft*). Gretchen!

MARGARETE (*die sich aufreißt*). Wo ist er? Ich hab ihn rufen hören, er rief: Gretchen! Er rief mir! Wo ist er? Ach, durch all das Heulen und Zähnklappen erkenn ich ihn, er ruft mir: Gretchen! (*Sich vor ihm niederwerfend.*) Mann! Mann! Gib mir ihn, schaff mir ihn! Wo ist er?

FAUST (*er faßt sie wütend um den Hals*). Meine Liebe! Meine Liebe! (*Margarete, sinkt, ihr Haupt in seinen Schoß verbergend.*)‡

---

* My womb, God!, urges to receive him; o that I might grasp him and hold him and kiss him as I want to do; I would die of his kissing.

† Who can feel how the pain rages in my bones? What my poor heart fears, how it trembles, what it desires, you, only you can know.

‡ MARGARET. Look, the child! I must give it a drink; I had it just now. There! I *have* given it a drink. They took it away from me and said I killed it, and now they sing songs about me.—It isn't true—it's an old tale that ends like that, it's not me that they're singing about.
 FAUST (*casting himself at her feet*). Gretchen!
 MARGARET (*struggling to her feet*). Where is he? I heard him call, he called

It is in her madness that Margarete uses phrases which make her sound like a girl of the people, phrases like 'Wie? Was? Bist mein Heinrich und hast's Küssen verlernt?'* and (in answer to Faust's urging her to escape) 'Da hinaus? Nicht um die Welt',† and, as the day of her execution dawns, 'Tag! Es wird Tag! Der letzte Tag! Der Hochzeittag! Sag's niemand, daß du die Nacht vorher bei Gretchen warst.'‡ In all this there is a spirited woman, laughing at Faust, even feeling horror at him, but loving him at the same time. This was latent in the pure maiden whom we saw earlier; that it emerges only in her insanity makes the ending the more powerful.

The Gretchen-tragedy of *Urfaust* culminates in this prison-scene: it is complete in itself, except that we do not yet know how Faust comes to be associated with Mephistopheles, and to all intents and purposes the devil might be no more than an evil but human friend.

Within the whole of *Part I*, however, this sequence of scenes is no more than an episode. In recasting the play, Goethe returned seriously to the Faust legend proper, to give it the new interpretation which in his eyes it demanded. After a moving Dedication, and a Prologue in the Theatre, both of which are usually omitted from stage-performances, Goethe presents a Prologue in Heaven in which, as in the Book of Job, the temptation of the principal character by the devil is agreed upon. Structurally this scene and the last in *Part II*, showing Faust's ascent to Heaven, encase the remainder of the action, indicating that all that takes place is within the divine compass —not so much providentially guided as permitted within the

---

'Gretchen'! He called me! Where is he? Ah, through all this howling and gnashing of teeth I know his voice, he's calling me, 'Gretchen'! (*falling down before him*) Man! man! Give him to me, get him for me, where is he?

FAUST (*savagely grasping her by the neck*). My love, my love! (*Margaret sinks down, hiding her head in his lap.*)

* Eh? What? You my Heinrich, and forgotten how to kiss?
† Out there? Not likely!
‡ Daylight! It's daylight! The last day! My wedding day! Don't tell them you were with Gretchen the night before.

divine framework. There is no divine intervention in Faust's life, indeed the divinity is above all conflicts, as the archangels at the beginning of the Prologue declare. Whereas earth spins round from day to day, exchanging 'paradisal light' for 'deep, awe-inspiring night', and storms rage from land to sea and sea to land, in other words, whereas the earth and Faust himself are subject to the 'polarity' of opposites and the laws of change, the angelic hosts revere 'Das sanfte Wandeln deines Tags'.* The Lord, like the Spirit in Hegel's philosophy or the noumenal world in Kant's, is beyond all dichotomies, proceeding smoothly and undisturbedly as the sun in the heavens:

> Der Anblick gibt den Engeln Stärke,
> Da keiner dich ergründen mag,
> Und alle deine hohen Werke
> Sind herrlich wie am ersten Tag.†

It is this magnificence and splendour which is to be contrasted with the human condition throughout the play: an unassailable felicity and 'schaffende Freude',‡[1] of which Faust has an occasional glimpse, once through the Earth-Spirit,[2] once in the sight of the sun itself,[3] and for which he longs in the speech[4] where he sees himself sweeping over land and sea in the wake of the setting sun, never again subject to darkness and longing. There are times in the Prologue when the Lord does indeed seem to be the Sun, or so identified with it as to leave very little distinction. And it is against the background of this ever-living light that the 'first wager' is made between the Lord and the devil (the second being that between the devil and Faust). In effect, the Lord affirms, Faust can never go wrong, never so wrong as to deserve damnation. 'Es irrt der Mensch, solang' er strebt',§ for so long as he strives he remains within the dichotomies, he is trying to escape, and does not yet enjoy the divine clarity and unity-in-duality. Mephistopheles may seek

---

* The gentle turning of thy Day.
† The sight of Thee gives strength to the angels, though none can fathom Thee, and all Thy mighty works are glorious as on the first day.
‡ creative joy.
§ Man errs so long as he strives.

to divert Faust from his 'Urquell',¹ the primal source of his
being which we may regard as his knowledge of this unity and
light, but he will ultimately fail, since

> Ein guter Mensch in seinem dunklen Drange
> Ist sich des rechten Weges wohl bewußt.*²

A good man may have urges and longings, which inevitably
belong to the world of darkness (since in the light all longings
vanish), but he knows the right path nevertheless. The Lord
does not seem concerned whether the man follows this path,
it is true. The implication appears to be that the divine light
will be there in any case, and this is sufficient to guarantee
salvation no matter what actions the man performs. (There is
a parallel in Luther's qualified insistence on faith rather than
works.) And dramatically speaking, there is some disadvantage
in this, for the fate of Faust can strictly never be at stake, and
consequently there can be no tension, no dramatic conflict,
so long as the wager is borne in mind. True, we are not reminded of it in any later part of the play until at the end the
angels descend to catch up Faust's soul to heaven, when they
declare (in words which Goethe emphasized in conversation
with Eckermann),³ 'Wer immer strebend sich bemüht / Den
können wir erlösen.'⁴ He who strives unceasingly they can (not,
perhaps, must) redeem: there would seem to be a paradox here
too, if not a contradiction, for in the Prologue erring was said
to be inseparable from striving, whereas now striving seems to
be a condition of salvation. Possibly sheer contradiction can
be avoided if we conclude that however much Faust strives
he will still err, and yet if he abandoned his striving he would
forgo any chance of salvation. It remains true, however, that
the 'first wager' removes some potential dramatic tension.
Indeed the whole purpose of the diabolic temptation, as the
Lord defines it, is not to afford Mephistopheles any chance of
winning Faust's soul, but of urging Faust onwards, refusing him
the opportunity of relaxing, in short of forcing him to continue
that striving which without the devil's help he might give up.

---

* A good man, in his obscure impulsion, is well aware of the right path.

Man needs this help; the angels, by contrast, exist to rejoice in 'die lebendig reiche Schöne'*[1] and 'Das Werdende, das ewig wirkt und lebt'†[2]—this beautiful unfolding of living action, 'werdend', that is to say continually developing and growing in time, is the invincible panoply that ensures the devil's defeat.

The chief addition Goethe made to the *Urfaust*, apart from the Prologue, was the pact scene, filling the 'great gap' between Faust's first monologue and 'Auerbach's Cellar'. Here Goethe's new intentions really become apparent. In all the earlier versions of the legend, Faust's aim had been to enjoy supreme knowledge and power, in exchange for which he had been willing to sign away his soul after death. 'A sound magician is a mighty god', Marlowe's Faustus had said: 'Here, Faustus, tire thy brains to gain a deity.' There had been something of the serpent's temptation in the garden of Eden about the temptation offered: 'Ye shall be as gods', or as Goethe's Mephistopheles puts it, misquoting the Vulgate: 'Eritis sicut deus', 'You shall be as God.' In Goethe's version, this is partly changed. Faust no longer seeks knowledge, he is weary of that when the play begins; instead, he seeks the widest possible experience of all that human life means. Just as the 'monads' of Leibniz, the simple units which were akin to men's souls, were at their most perfect when they reflected all the rest of the cosmos—indeed they were godlike when they did—so Faust will expand his individual self to cover all other selves,[3] becoming what Mephistopheles mockingly calls a 'Herr Mikrokosmus'[4] or 'cosmos in miniature'. It is this experience which Faust demands of Mephistopheles, rather than knowledge in the sense of learning. And because it is every experience that he asks for, he does not expect happiness: 'von Freud' ist nicht die Rede'‡[5]. Rather he expects a sequence of paradoxes, painful enjoyment, loving hatred, refreshing annoyance; all the polar opposites of which earthly existence consists. He will dash

* the living, rich beauty.
† the growing, changing power that for ever acts and lives.
‡ There is no question of happiness.

136

into 'das Rauschen der Zeit', 'das Rollen der Begebenheit',*¹
letting pain and pleasure follow one another as they may:
activity is all that matters. 'Nur rastlos betätigt sich der
Mann.'†²

In this, Faust comes very close to identifying himself, though
he is not aware of it, with the Goethean divinity whose chief
characteristic is constant movement and who is at the same
time still, whose nature involves both sides of every dual
polarity. He does in a way seek to 'gain a deity', both in the
sense that he seeks the totality of human experience, and in that
he moves forward with 'das Rauschen der Zeit'. In so far as
God may be conceived in such terms, Faust still seeks to be
godlike. In addition to this, however, Faust makes a wager
which runs contrary to the wager in the Prologue. Traditionally,
Faust merely bargained away his soul for earthly power.
Goethe's Faust inserts a proviso: his soul is only to be forfeit
to the devil if he ever remains satisfied with the passing moment,
if he ever becomes so enamoured of such a moment that he
would like it to remain his for ever. (There is a certain incongruity about Faust's words³ in that he speaks at one moment of
reclining on a bed of ease, and at another of achieving so much
that he can say to the passing moment 'Verweile doch, du
bist so schön!'‡—in the one case he would be passive, lethargic,
in the other actively enjoying, and we cannot be sure that
Goethe had this distinction in mind.) Now this rejection of all
expectation of delight seems to run counter to the Lord's
wager that Faust could never be prized away from his 'Urquell',
his primal source. The Lord reproaches Mephistopheles in the
Prologue with finding nothing on earth to his liking, and
confidently challenges him to make Faust of like mind to
himself. Yet here, in the 'second' wager, Faust suspects life so
much that he challenges Mephistopheles to make him contented with any earthly experience whatsoever. He expects
only destruction to await him at the end of his career,⁴ and

* the rushing sweep of Time; the onward rolling of events.
† Only by restlessness can a man be active (i.e. transform his passive being
  into activity).
‡ Tarry a while, thou art so fair.

137

dissatisfaction to attend every moment of it. If any man were disillusioned enough to be thought to have already lost contact with the primal source of divine strength within him, it is surely Faust. As Coleridge said, 'the *incredulus odi*' (turning away in disgust at whatever is presented—the words come from Horace) 'is felt from the very first line'.

To make matters more difficult, Mephistopheles misunderstands Faust's proviso and continues to talk as though the legendary pact were in operation—that is, as though he were sure of Faust's soul and only needed to parade some specious wonders before his victim's eyes during his short mortal span in order to ensure his eternal torment. When Faust says that he neither wants nor expects satisfaction, Mephistopheles replies that nobody could ever digest the sour dough that life is: he does not begin to display the finest illusions at his command in the hope of tricking Faust into a momentary confession that he has found felicity. Mephistopheles does not try to win the pact, and as soon as Faust has left the devil soliloquizes to the effect that he will drag his victim through so much flat triviality that he will long in vain for refreshment.[1] He intends to taunt Faust's insatiability to the full, rather than use the one means he has of winning the wager, which is to satisfy Faust.

In doing this, Mephisto is acting in the role ordained for him by the Lord, of pricking Faust on to further discontent, ensuring that he continues to strive. Yet by this very fact he makes it impossible for the wager to have any real significance. The opposition is simply not meant to try, nor does it try, for Mephisto is true to his word and does drag Faust through flat triviality, first in Auerbach's Cellar, which Faust finds merely boring (although in the *Urfaust* he took an active part, performing magical tricks himself rather than standing by as an onlooker), and then through the Witches' Kitchen, which Faust finds not much better, though he does at the end of it see in a magic mirror the face which will haunt him for the remainder of his life. Even when Faust is on the point of pronouncing the fatal words of the proviso, sealing his own doom, Mephisto fails to take his chance. In the 'Forest and Cavern'

scene, Faust gives thanks to the Earth-Spirit for granting all
he asked (which was, to enjoy all that life had to offer); he is
near to the gods, and coming ever closer to them in his
ability to embrace the multiplicity of human experiences[1]—
yet at this point Mephisto enters to ask how such pleasures can
possibly give Faust lasting enjoyment, and to press him to go
on to something new. In much the same way Mephisto disturbs Faust in his courting of Gretchen, as though preventing
him from gaining delight with her, and he will do the same in
Part II, intervening between Faust and Helen of Troy.[2] One
contradiction follows another. The Lord challenges Mephisto
to make Faust discontented, Faust challenges him to make him
contented; the Lord employs Mephisto to make Faust discontented so that he may continue to strive, although to
strive is to err; Faust declares he will always strive, and Mephisto
ensures that he will have to. Ultimately striving is to be the
basis on which Faust's salvation becomes possible.

It does not seem possible to resolve these contradictions.
They seem rather to be inherent in the paradoxical world-view
which Goethe had come to adopt. From Goethe's standpoint, the contradictions may indeed have appeared unimportant. He may well have thought of Faust as essentially right
in his very striving for totality, and thus have come to disregard any incidental logical fault. He wrote at a time when the
idea of contradictoriness as an inherent part of life was particularly strong. Kant, in *The Critique of Pure Reason* of 1781,
had sought to show that reason was bound to arrive at diametrically opposite conclusions (such as that the world both
has and has not a beginning in time, or that the principle of
cause-and-effect is and also is not the only way in which
phenomena can be explained); this, Kant argued, was because
philosophers erroneously regarded the world as a thing-
in-itself, which was not the case. Hegel spoke in the early
nineteenth century of all history as a self-contradicting mani-
festation of the World-Spirit, which yet stood outside its own
manifestations, and Schelling found in electricity, because it
had both a positive and a negative pole, an image of the

World-Soul. All these, and several later philosophers, show some similarity to Goethe's *Faust*, where the Lord remains outside the 'polarity' of his creation, and yet seems also to participate in it. If the pact and the wagers are mutually contradictory and self-contradictory, it may be because Goethe was untroubled by a phenomenon which in his day was so often regarded as a necessary result of mortal limitations. He himself had already come across something of the kind in the occult, alchemical and neo-Platonist works he read in his early twenties.

The fact remains that consistency in the action of the play is not to be expected. When the terms of the wagers are so opposed, and the characters themselves fail to understand them, the particular episodes can have no relevance to the winning or losing of Faust's soul and must be seen as existing in their own right—as the Gretchen-tragedy especially does, having presumably been written before the ultimate formulation of the pact between Faust and the devil occurred to Goethe.

This discreteness of the individual scenes, the lack of development from one to another, is a feature of the structure of both *Part I* and *Part II*. The Gretchen-tragedy does present a series of connected events, especially in the *Urfaust* version, and must be regarded as different in structure from the rest of the play. Yet even here the additions made later by Goethe tend towards what we may call the 'discrete' structure. A signal example is the Walpurgis Night's Dream which follows abruptly on the Walpurgis Night scene, and which consists entirely of epigrams, some of them of ephemeral significance and none with any relevance to the Faust-theme. This is a kind of appendix, akin to the sets of epigrams which Goethe arbitrarily inserted in *Die Wahlverwandtschaften* and *Wilhelm Meisters Wanderjahre*. The Walpurgis Night itself is also inserted with unexplained abruptness, though it may be that its vivid evocation of evil is meant to portray the depths of Faust's or Gretchen's mind after his murder of Gretchen's brother. Valentine having been run through by Faust's sword, and Gretchen exposed to fierce popular disapproval, it is strange to find that Faust has abandoned and apparently forgotten about her while he goes in search of truth at Satan's court.

The placing of the 'Forest and Cavern' scene is still harder to explain. In the *Fragment* which Goethe published in 1790, it appeared after the scene 'At the Well' in which Gretchen realizes that she is pregnant and open to the reproaches of such girls as Lieschen. It was inappropriate in that position, since it contained the very fine speech[1] in which Faust thanks the Earth-Spirit for having given him all he ever asked for—a speech written by Goethe in Italy and expressing his own thanksgiving for the new access of life gained there, but tinged with an unwanted irony in the context of the *Fragment*, where it could not properly be placed after the catastrophe of Gretchen's fall. Perhaps because of this, Goethe moved the scene forward when he published *Part I*, avoiding the awkwardness of making Faust give thanks just at the moment when disaster was striking at Gretchen, and altering the circumstances so that his speech followed the first courting of her. It was still slightly surprising that Faust should leave Gretchen so suddenly after having gained her love, to sit alone in a cavern, but the incongruity was lessened. Unfortunately, the second half of the scene contains a speech, originally part of the *Urfaust*, where it was meant, very appropriately, to follow on the death of Valentine; in this Faust denounces himself for his inhuman destruction of Gretchen's happiness and calls on Mephisto to take them both quickly out of this life to their damnation. This is quite unsuitable at a moment when Faust has barely met Gretchen at all, and should either have been omitted or placed at some later moment in the play. As we have it, the halves of the scene conflict with one another, referring to different moments in the story.

These inconsequentialities result in part from the time Goethe took over writing *Part I*: it was nearly forty years after its inception that it was published, and Goethe's mind had changed profoundly in that time. Other 'discrete' aspects of the structure are in the scene 'Outside the Gate', also added at a stage later than the *Urfaust*, in which individuals or groups of citizens come forward to speak a few lines typical of their condition and then pass by: they remain almost entirely without contact with one another, and the earlier part of the scene resembles the masque in Act I of *Part II*, where a similar sequence of types appears, rather than the Gretchen-tragedy. Here perhaps a deliberate intention can be sensed: Goethe appears to have wanted this discreteness for a special purpose. The same is true of the scenes following the pact; 'Auerbach's Cellar' and the 'Witches' Kitchen' have no connection with one another, but are merely episodes in the life through which Mephisto conducts Faust.

Indeed within the scheme of the whole work, *Part I* and *Part II* alike, the Gretchen-tragedy becomes one more such episode, one of several more to follow, and it becomes clear, viewing the play as a whole, that this episodic structure is quite congruous with the nature of Faust's mode of living. He himself expects no pattern or logical sequence in his life: 'Des Denkens Faden ist zerrissen'[1]—the thread of thought is broken, and he expects only an aimless succession of pleasure and pain which will change and change about as best they may,[2] and end ultimately in disaster.[3] His very proviso in the pact is based on the idea that life can never have any vital moment for him that is to be prized above all others, and thus he can never have in mind the attainment of a goal, for this would imply satisfaction, and this in its turn implies damnation. (Or better, to do justice to Goethe's ambiguities, it would imply both salvation —as it seems to do in Act III of *Part II*—and damnation at one and the same time.) True, Mephistopheles seems to mock at this flitting restlessness as an alternative to enjoyment:

> Beliebt's Euch, überall zu naschen,
> Im Fliehen etwas zu erhaschen,
> Bekomm' Euch wohl, was Euch ergetzt.*[4]

But Faust is deaf to this mockery and we can only suppose that Goethe thought it enough merely to state the Mephistophelean

---

* If you fancy nibbling here, there and everywhere, grabbing what you can as you flee past, I hope what you fancy does you good.

objection. Certainly *Part I* is built as though in harmony with Faust's intention, dipping into experience here and there without any coherent form.

This is reflected, moreover, in the belief in 'activity' ('Tätigkeit') which plays so important a part in Faust's ideas. 'Nur rastlos betätigt sich der Mann'[1]—it is only by restless activity that a man displays his worth. In a similar vein is the passage[2] in which Faust, like a new Luther, attempts a translation of the opening of St John's Gospel, where the creation of the world is set forth. Faust cannot accept the straightforward translation 'In the beginning was the Word', although the Greek 'logos' does mean 'word'; a mere word, he argues, cannot have such great significance. Turning to a rough equivalent of the overtones usually associated with the Greek, he rejects also the idea that in the beginning there was 'der Sinn'—the sense, or meaning, or the intention. And his reason for this rejection is significant: it is that it cannot be mere meaning 'that effects and creates everything'. The word is too close to the rationalism which the 'Sturm und Drang' had rejected as cold and uncreative, for Faust to believe in it as the origin of all things. He looks for something more dynamic and spontaneous, is tempted to write 'power', but decides finally on the momentous words 'Im Anfang war die *Tat*!' In the beginning was the deed—what Faust tries to convey here is his complete break with all moral conceptions of the world, which he conceives as springing by an instantaneous fiat from the being of God. There was no premeditation, no intention that the world should be this or that, no purpose which it was to fulfil, nothing but the unprepared, utterly meaningless flash by which the world came into existence and by repetitions of which, presumably, it continues to exist. Thus there could also be, one supposes, no coherent sequence in the world, no reason why one deed should follow another, and no pattern or purpose beyond that of 'Lebensfreud',[3] or of giving expression to what Faust calls 'die ewig rege...heilsam schaffende Gewalt'.*[4] Creativity is the criterion: 'schaffend, Götterleben zu genie-

---

* The eternally stirring, healing, creative might.

ßen',*[1] regardless of what was created (whether, that is, it was good or evil, high or low). And this was often Goethe's own belief, revealed in such phrases as 'was fruchtbar ist, allein ist wahr'† and 'das wahre Leben ist des Handelns ew'ge Unschuld'.‡ Not that Goethe ever held any belief to the exclusion of another—to have done so would after all have been to run counter to the whole idea of 'Tätigkeit' and 'sich betätigen' as we have just seen him express it. All the same, he held to this idea sufficiently closely for us to see that it informs the structure of *Faust*, which is in reality a succession of creative inspirations conceived at different periods of Goethe's life and without any binding plan. Whether this was ultimately to the advantage of the play, whether it led to confusion or neglectful obscurity rather than to a creative masterpiece, is a matter on which judgement must be postponed for the time being.

This stress on creativity is enough to account for, though not necessarily to justify, the often-noted absence of any really evil nature in Mephistopheles. He is, it is true, bent on tormenting Faust, and this is in itself an evil thing. He is also destructive in purpose, wishing an end to all existence.[2] Yet for a great part of the time he appears rather as a humorous, cynical, witty and sharp-sighted man, whose unsuccessful function is to bring Faust to face facts, to destroy his sentimentality and make him accept responsibility for his actions, rather than to deceive him, or inveigle him into doing what he does not want to do. It is he who points out the absurdity of Faust's desire for all human qualities (how, as he says, is Faust to be both magnanimous and sly, both a naïve lover and a cunning flirt?);[3] it is also he who gives the Biblical-sounding advice that Faust cannot add by his own efforts one cubit to his stature. His attack on learning, and the bewildering of Faust's pupil, are without apparent malice, and one of his remarks, the famous

> Grau, teurer Freund, ist alle Theorie,
> Und grün des Lebens goldner Baum,§[4]

* In creating, to enjoy the life of the gods.
† What is fruitful, that alone is true.
‡ True life is the eternal innocence of action.
§ Grey, my dear friend, is all that theory is, and green the golden tree of Life.

is often quoted by people who have no intention of invoking the devil's opinions. He has all Faust's scorn for mere book-learning, with the difference that he is more entertaining in expressing it, and his whole attitude to Faust is rather that of a supercilious *bon viveur*, impatient with his victim's prudery and dispirited qualms. He takes much the same tone with the carousers in Auerbach's Cellar, disdaining both them and their wines, but showing almost a delight at their discomfiture when his own wine shows its diabolical origin. His scenes are often the most striking and subtle in the entire work, as here, at the moment when the revellers have each tasted the wine magically supplied from holes bored in the table-top:

FAUST. Ich hätte Lust, nun abzufahren.
MEPH. Gib nur erst acht, die Bestialität
    Wird sich gar herrlich offenbaren.
SIEBEL (*trinkt unvorsichtig, der Wein fließt auf die Erde und wird zur Flamme*). Helft! Feuer! helft! Die Hölle brennt!
MEPH (*die Flamme besprechend*). Sei ruhig, freundlich Element!
    Zu dem Gesellen.
    Für diesmal war es nur ein Tropfen Fegefeuer.*[1]

Mephistopheles admires the bestiality with the knowledge of a connoisseur; his compassionate address to the fire, as an element peculiarly close to his heart, is nicely taken, and his words to the drinker have a sharp double edge—they sound like a consolation, yet conceal a hideous threat. But even so, he does not treat his victims badly—he stops short when his practical joke could cause them in error to cut off each other's noses, and the scene leaves no bad taste in the mouth. Similarly, in the scene in the Witches' Kitchen, the devil deprecates the ugliness of the surroundings and offers, ironically no doubt, the alternative means of rejuvenation through living a blame-

---

* FAUST. I should like to depart now.
    MEPH. Just watch a bit, they'll make marvellous beasts of themselves.
    SIEBEL (*drinks incautiously, the wine spills to the ground and turns to flame*).
     Help! Fire! Help! All hell's alight!
    MEPH. (*to the flames*). Be quiet, my friendly element. (*To Siebel*) For this once it was only purgatorial fire.

less life in bovine simplicity. 'Schelm' and 'Schalk'—'rogue'
and 'rascal'—are the worst names that he is given or deserves
for the greater part of the play, and Faust's stronger language
'Du Spottgeburt von Dreck und Feuer'*[1] is in reality a pro-
jection of Faust's disgust at his own wrongdoing.

There is even a portion of good will in Mephistopheles. He
is impressed, in an amused way, at the cleanliness of Gretchen's
room, and even a little awestruck at her quite unsuspecting
manner when he first meets her, saying of her in an aside (which
cannot, therefore, be meant as flattery), 'Du gut's, unschuldig's
Kind!',†[2] and telling her—sincerely, to all appearances—that
she need feel no shame before any monarch on earth.[3] His
self-mockery is perhaps the most undiabolical thing about him:

> Bei aller verschmähten Liebe! Beim höllischen Elemente!
> Ich wollt', ich wüßte was Ärgers, daß ich's fluchen könnte!

and

> Ich möcht' mich gleich dem Teufel übergeben,
> Wenn ich nur selbst kein Teufel wär!‡[4]

These are observations that can only make Mephisto more sympathetic: they witness to a humorously self-deprecatory frame of
mind which it is surprising, not to say incongruous, to find in
one of his nature. The Mephistophilis of Marlowe carries his
hell about with him and never ceases to be tormented; Goethe's
is gay and almost blithe by comparison. And at no point does
he perform (except for some obscenities on the Brocken) any
evil deed. He provides the casket which tempts Gretchen, and
arranges the assignation, but it is Faust who woos her; he para-
lyses Valentine's arm but it is Faust who kills him; he supplies
the entry to Gretchen's prison-cell but it is Faust who gives up
trying to save her. Mephistopheles is rather a means towards
doing evil, an encouragement to evil propensities, than himself

---

* You misbegotten son of filth and fire.
† You good, innocent child!
‡ By all despised love! By hell itself! I wish I knew something worse to
  swear by.
  I would give myself up to the devil, if I weren't a devil myself.

evil. He is also like a good conscience, reminding Faust of his responsibilities, barring off his attempts at self-delusion. It is he who brings home to Faust his own share in causing Gretchen's downfall, just as it is he who persuades Faust to go back to her after his sudden departure for the woods.

All this makes the untroubled course of the Lord in the Prologue the more easily understood. The Lord has no adversary to speak of; indeed, Mephisto does in many ways seem to fulfil the purpose laid down for him, of pricking Faust on to further striving. Whether Mephisto's word can be trusted when he calls himself 'Ein Teil von jener Kraft / Die stets das Böse will und stets das Gute schafft'*[1] is another question. Apart from whether he really does always want evil—often enough he seems concerned rather to achieve truth—it is hard to see how the result of his actions is in reality good, though the lines are often quoted as though they were accurate. In his relationship with Faust, the opposite is usually the case.

Faust's virtue is that he seeks a higher realm which, it is often held, Mephisto is incapable of understanding. In the famous 'Zwei Seelen' speech[2] Faust himself portrays his divided nature, torn between love of this earthly life and love of the next, or the higher life.

> Zwei Seelen wohnen, ach! in meiner Brust,
> Die eine will sich von der andern trennen;
> Die eine hält in derber Liebeslust
> Sich an die Welt mit klammernden Organen;
> Die andre hebt gewaltsam sich vom Dust
> Zu den Gefilden hoher Ahnen.†

It is not clear what life this may be—Faust gives no more definition to it than 'the fields of lofty forbears', but we may guess that it is in some sense divine. That it is identical with that life which Faust describes in answer to Gretchen's question

---

* A part of that power that always intends evil and always produces good.
† Two souls there dwell, alas, within my breast, and one would cut itself away from the other; one of them clutches with lustful senses at the world it loves, the other rises powerfully from the dust to reach the fields of lofty ancestors.

asking if he believes in God, is possible, although what he speaks of here[1] is rather earthly life transfigured than any heavenly realm beyond. For Faust at this moment there is only, so to speak, the ground of Being; it is not possible either to say that one does or does not believe in God (Faust foreshadows here many of the vaguer developments in twentieth-century German and British theology), but only to rejoice in the sheer facts of earth, sky, love and happiness. If it helps to call this God, he is content; for his own part the experience itself is enough, the name is of no consequence. But it is difficult to know how seriously this speech is to be taken. It does of course go clean against the proviso in the pact, for it surely implies that to be wholly blissful while alive is to know God, whereas the proviso implies that to do so is to be in the devil's power (we surely must not be legalistic and regard the proviso as valid only if Faust avoids pronouncing the fatal words *verbatim*). The speech to Gretchen also suggests that Faust is no longer divided as he is in the 'Zwei Seelen' speech, for that implied a contrast between clutching desperately at this world, and violently struggling to rise above it. In short, Faust does at this point seem both to have ceased to strive and to have ceased to think striving necessary for his salvation. Thus the speech does something to undermine the idea that a *loftier* calling distinguishes Faust from other men. In a sense he does—at any rate for a moment—regard earthly life not as a delusory snare, but as a revelation of 'heavenly fire'.

In portraying Faust thus, however, Goethe may have meant to show how his beliefs led him to a certain blindness which helped to further his decline into Mephistopheles' power. For in seeing heaven all about him Faust ignores the evil which at other times he desperately welcomes as a necessary part of life, and in saying 'Feeling is all'[2] he places a reliance on emotions which is soon shown to be misplaced. Immediately after Faust's speech, Gretchen voices her doubts about Mephistopheles, whose identity she does not know, only to be told by Faust not to worry her head about such trifles. Faust's duplicity at this moment, when sincerity seems his whole creed, is a poor sign of his love. Gretchen is not to fear Mephistopheles, he tells her; there have to be such odd fish, and she has merely taken an irrational dislike to him. To cap this, Faust reproves Mephistopheles for not seeing into Gretchen's frame of mind with more sympathy. All this seems (but perhaps only seems) meant to cast a doubt on Faust's creed of emotional sincerity.

As the play progresses the possibility of admiring Faust becomes increasingly remote. In the earlier scenes of *Part I* he is for the most part concerned with abstract or philosophical matters, and so scarcely appears as a character, although he does show some aloofness towards his famulus Wagner and the crowd outside the city-gate. Only in the Gretchen-tragedy does he have any real relationship with a human being, and here he displays a certain pusillanimity. His first desire for Gretchen is purely lustful; not until he has seen the cleanliness of her bedroom does his love become more adoring, and for a moment he determines, presumably out of repentance, not to see her again. Even here, he is curiously detached, looking at his emotion as though it were degrading to a resolute man of action. Yet when Mephistopheles arrives with the casket intended as a gift, Faust hesitates—'Ich weiß nicht, soll ich?'*[1]—and when Mephisto shows annoyance he simply gives in without another word. Thus he neither decides nor refuses to go on with his wooing, but falls into it half-heartedly. It is doubtful sometimes whether he realises he has made a pact at all: when Mephistopheles later suggests that they should gain access to Gretchen by telling lies to her friend Marthe, Faust is as indignant as though his earlier violent rejection of the traditional virtues[2] had never happened; but again he gives in just the same.[3] Even the rhythmically very fine nuanced speech 'Erhabner Geist'[4] is in the end curiously vapid. For all its imagery and musicality, the impact of the speech declines after the first dozen lines. In these, Faust gives thanks to the Earth-Spirit for the insight into Nature it has granted him, and there is here a subtle manipulation of stresses and currents of emotion which has great effect, as have the enjambements and onomato-

* I don't know; should I?

poeia in the succeeding section, where Faust contemplates the destructive power which he also knows to be in Nature:

> Erhabner Geist, du gabst mir, gabst mir alles,
> Warum ich bat. Du hast mir nicht umsonst
> Dein Angesicht im Feuer zugewendet.
> Gabst mir die herrliche Natur zum Königreich,
> Kraft, sie zu fühlen, zu genießen. Nicht
> Kalt staunenden Besuch erlaubst du nur,
> Vergönnest mir, in ihre tiefe Brust,
> Wie in den Busen eines Freunds zu schauen.
> Du führst die Reihe der Lebendigen
> Vor mir vorbei und lehrst mich meine Brüder
> Im stillen Busch, in Luft und Wasser kennen.
> Und wenn der Sturm im Walde braust und knarrt,
> Die Riesenfichte stürzend Nachbaräste
> Und Nachbarstämme quetschend niederstreift
> Und ihrem Fall dumpf hohl der Hügel donnert,
> Dann führst du mich zur sichern Höhle, zeigst
> Mich dann mir selbst, und meiner eignen Brust
> Geheime tiefe Wunder öffnen sich.
> Und steigt vor meinem Blick der reine Mond
> Besänftigend herüber, schweben mir
> Von Felsenwänden, aus dem feuchten Busch
> Der Vorwelt silberne Gestalten auf
> Und lindern der Betrachtung strenge Lust.*

Yet the meaning of the later part of the speech is merely that, while Faust rejoices in the kindlier gifts of Nature, when faced

---

* Exalted Spirit, you gave me, gave me all my heart's desire. Nor did you turn in vain your countenance upon me in the flames, but gave me resplendent Nature for my kingdom, strength to embrace, enjoy her body. No cold, dumb amazement is my portion, for you afford me insight into her bosom, as in a friend's deep heart, with loving gaze. You lead the orders of all living things before my eyes, teach me to see my brothers in air and water, in the silent bush. And when the storm strikes crackling on the forest, the giant fir-trees toppling crush their neighbours, trunk, branch and bole are ripped and ground to ashes while all the hills resound with hollow thunder, then do you lead me to the silent cavern, then you show me my own self, and my own breast yields up its deep and secret mysteries. And if before my sight the limpid moon moves upward, calming me, then from the rocky cliffs, from dripping coverts silver shapes of ancient times rise up, and relieve the dour delight of contemplation.

by her harsher moods he can retire into himself and, apparently, ignore them. The speech is one of the best in the play, musically speaking, yet it also shows that veering away from a confrontation with an unwelcome experience which we have already observed as typical of Faust as a man.

How far Goethe meant to make Faust so evasive and sometimes small-minded is not certain. People have often looked on Faust as a hero despite these unheroic qualities, and references to his Titanism and his assaults on heaven abound, although there is little to show for them. On the other hand, in the scenes added later to the *Urfaust*, or the revisions, it appears several times that Goethe deliberately emphasized the least praiseworthy aspects of his central character, just as he did in *Clavigo*, whose plot is a close parallel. It must have been his intention, even in the *Urfaust*, that Faust should kill Gretchen's brother Valentine, for the preliminaries to the deed were already written in that version, and Gretchen reproached Faust with it in the prison-scene, but we do not know just how the murder was to have been done. As we see it in the final version, it is as despicable an action as might be conceived: Mephistopheles having first paralysed Valentine's arm, Faust pierces the helpless man with his sword and runs away. (In Delacroix's magnificent illustration, Faust appears here with a smooth, mask-like face almost exactly like that of Mephistopheles, seeming to act as in a trance.) No thought of Gretchen or of anything but his own safety seems to cross Faust's mind, and to see him almost immediately after this assassination climbing the Brocken, enjoying the landscape, wishing he might more quickly reach the summit where Satan sits, dancing with a young witch, is to ask whether any sanity, love, or human regard remain in him. Even when the wraith of Gretchen with a tell-tale red line round her throat appears before him he is no more than amazed, says merely that he cannot stop gazing at it, and allows himself to be diverted by the absurdly inappropriate 'Walpurgis Night's Dream', with its no less inappropriate allusiveness to Shakespeare's play. Goethe did intend at one time to bring Faust to the summit of the Brocken, and a fragment of this scene is extant, showing Satan in all his obscenity, but the scene was never completed, and as though recognizing his own unwillingness to portray real opposition to the divine serenity announced in the Prologue, Goethe smudges off the scene with the 'Dream'. It may be, then, that Faust's comparative insouciance at the sight of Gretchen, the inadequacy of his reaction 'How strange...' was not so much a consciously placed observation of his character, as part of a development whose originally intended end we do not see.

The scene 'Trüber Tag. Feld', however, almost identical in its *Part I* version with the version in *Urfaust*, leads to equal doubts about Faust's human concern and sense of his own responsibility. In this scene Faust upbraids Mephistopheles for having provided him with entertainment while, all unknown to him, Gretchen was being tormented in prison; he contrasts his own mental sharing of her suffering with the devil's inhuman coldness. His anger is almost beyond expression; yet, as Mephistopheles reminds him, he has Valentine's blood on his hands, and from the spectators' point of view it is almost incredible that Faust should have allowed himself to be entertained at all in these circumstances. His protestations, couched in the wildest 'Sturm und Drang' language, sound hypocritical, and Mephistopheles' reminder of Faust's own principal part in the seduction of Gretchen is wholly appropriate. True, Faust does have enough determination to return to the town where Gretchen is imprisoned and attempt to rescue her. But even this attempt is half-hearted. Faust's first words on entering Gretchen's cell are an indication of his frame of mind: he thinks not of her, but of his own grief, which he magnifies out of all proportion: 'The misery of all mankind grasps hold of me'.[1] After this, his speeches are no more than interjections between Gretchen's much more moving lines: urgent pleas that she should escape at once with him, coupled with exclamations of grief which once again sound oddly self-centred: 'Werd' ich den Jammer überstehen!',[*2] 'O wär' ich nie geboren!',[†3] and, strangest of all, 'Laß das Vergangene vergangen

---

* Shall I survive this grief!   † O that I had never been born!

which this implies, some of the characteristics just touched upon may be due to the length of time Goethe spent on the play and a certain negligence in relating scenes written at one period with those written at another. Some of them, however, seem part of a conscious intention (one can never be quite sure), and thus make it the more difficult to understand those who have written about Faust as though his attitude and conduct were admirable. The philosophers Fichte and Schelling and the youthful Hegel regarded *Part I* as 'the absolute philosophical tragedy', and there is no doubt they did so because they regarded Faust himself as a representative of humanity: they saw in his philosophical questioning a profound portrayal of matters essential to human existence. But few men are philosophers, and Faust's almost total disregard of moral claims makes him an inadequate protagonist. However poorly one thinks of men, at any rate they pay a nominal respect to their moral responsibilities, whereas Faust pays none of any consequence, except at the moment of his return to Gretchen's cell. A violently expressed criticism of the play was indeed heard in the mid-nineteenth century, when the Liberal Wolfgang Menzel declared 'If Faust deserves to go to heaven for having seduced and abandoned Gretchen, every pig that wallows in a flower-bed deserves to be made head-gardener'. Similarly the theologian Kierkegaard compared Faust with a medieval magician who required the blood from the heart of an innocent child to nourish his sick soul, and in 1892 Wilhelm Gwinner declared that the whole German nation was being led astray by its reverence for Faust. This was, however, at the other extreme from the view of the influential Herman Grimm, who at the time when Bismarck's 'Reich' was beginning to establish itself declared that both Faust and Mephisto, were they to appear before the 'Reichstag', 'would immediately size up the situation, choose the right moment, and with a few penetrating ideas create for themselves an attentive audience!' And again, though without drawing any political consequences, the standard biographer of Goethe, Albert Bielschowsky, speaks of the poet as one who 'grasps the world in the warm embrace of a Faust and again spurns it with the annihilating contempt of a Mephistopheles'. Somewhere in the play Bielschowsky found evidence of a Faust who could even be identified with Goethe, if only partially, and it is clear from the context that this is no intended slight on the author. Indeed, Marshall Montgomery could write of Faust: 'he is not a mere average man, but greater by far than most'; '...he remains "der gute Mensch", however much he fails to "keep his soul unspotted from the world"'.

The moral issue cannot, however, be taken in isolation. It would not be worth mentioning at length, were it not that critics of high standing have denied the obvious fact, that Faust's conduct in *Part I* is often pusillanimous or despicable, and that he performs only one deed which is morally worth admiration. But for the dispute which these denials arouse, it would be possible to come straight to the literary issue: what kind of a work is the whole play (*Part I*, that is) in which this almost completely unattractive character appears? A variety of answers have been offered to this question, by commentators as various as Baumgart, Burdach, Minor, Erich Schmidt, Traumann, Gundolf, Trendelenburg, Petsch, Rickert, Viëtor, Beutler, Staiger and Emrich, to mention some more outstanding names of the last seventy years in a roughly chronological order. (Among non-German authors the best known have been Brandes, Croce and Santayana.) To give even so much as a summary of these views would be beyond the present scope—in fact as early as 1906 a proposal for a kind of 'variorum' *Faust* would have meant, it was discovered, a work comprising seven volumes of dictionary size: publishers refused to handle it.

The issue from a literary point of view has been whether *Faust* nevertheless has a unity, whatever the human shortcomings of the hero may be; whether its admittedly multifarious content 'grew' as one critic puts it '...from a relatively small beginning to a vast symbolical scheme, keeping, in the circumstances, a remarkable degree of coherence', or whether it is rather 'an agglomeration of great and small fragments, additions, and dove-tailings, showing all too plainly new phases of thought and style, and achieving a unity so partial and strained that many inconsistencies remain'. In short, is Goethe's work a mosaic which, viewed from close by, seems an assortment of stones, but which from further away assumes a shape and form, or is it a mere heap?

The seeing of a shape is so often, though not always, a matter of an individual's capacity and desires, that a final answer is seldom possible. The various features already mentioned—the contradictoriness of the wagers, the misunderstanding by the devil of what the wager with Faust is about, the comparative absence of evil in Mephistopheles, and the extreme weakness of Faust as a character—all seem to militate against either comprehensibility or dramatic tension or tragic quality. It was all very well for Goethe to say to Eckermann, possibly in ironic mood, that the more 'incommensurable' a poetic work was, and the more incomprehensible to reason, the better.[1] He cannot have meant to say that a completely incomprehensible work would be perfection. Thus the attempts at showing a comprehensibility and a unity in *Faust* are very necessary, and, although most of them refer to both Parts, it is a good thing to introduce them here so that their validity can be borne in mind also while studying the Second Part.

It has been claimed to be a matter of fact established by research that the guiding conception of *Faust*, its *Leitgedanke*, has been discovered by Konrad Burdach, and that it is the thought expressed by Leibniz in the following words from his *Principles of Nature and of Grace*:

It is true that supreme felicity (by whatever *beatific vision*, or knowledge of God, it may be accompanied) can never be complete, because God, being infinite, cannot be entirely known. Thus our happiness will never consist (and it is right that it should not consist) in complete enjoyment, which would leave nothing more to be desired and would make our mind [*esprit*] stupid; but it must consist in a perpetual progress to new pleasures and new perfections.

There is in this, it is clear, a general similarity to the proviso added by Faust to the pact. But it is not a precise similarity, for

Leibniz is talking about the knowledge of God, and of the impossibility that the bliss in having this knowledge could ever be complete. The counter-argument must run that Faust, by contrast, is not expecting bliss at all—'von Freud' ist nicht die Rede';[1] he is denying that earthly pleasures could ever give him satisfaction, not proceeding from one stage momentarily supposed to be perfect to another yet more perfect. All the same, those who accept Burdach's argument will naturally find in Faust an ever-renewed desire and ceaselessly striving toil which prepares him at his death for his ascent to God. Within *Part I* the evidence of Faust's higher yearnings will be found especially in the lines 'Daß ich erkenne, was die Welt / Im Innersten zusammenhält',*[2] and 'Wo fass' ich dich, unendliche Natur',†[3] in the dramatic appeal to the Earth-Spirit,[4] in the attempt 'Götterleben zu genießen',‡[5] in the 'Zwei Seelen' speech,[6] in the reason Faust gives for his dejection, namely that the God within him has no power in the outward world,[7] in his further dejection at the thought that all his accumulation of experience will bring him no nearer to the infinite,[8] in the enthusiasm with which he sees, in the witches' magic mirror, the body of Helen as 'den Inbegriff von allen Himmeln',§[9] and in the very fact that after such a vision he can find happiness in the simplicity of such a woman as Gretchen. Faust does desire an infinity of experience, he *can* find perfection, or think to find it, despite the pessimistic speeches of the pact-scene, and there is a sense, as we shall see, in which the perfection he experiences in loving Gretchen is intensified in his love for Helen (in *Part II*), only to prove imperfect in its turn, so that he does progress in this regard from one stage of bliss to another.

Even within *Part I*, there is clearly a continual desire for infinity in Faust, and this is what some critics mean when they say that the unity of the play is to be found in the unity of his character. This, however is specious, for the unity of a play

* That I may know what holds the world together at the heart.
† Where may I grasp thee, infinite Nature?
‡ To enjoy the life of the gods.
§ the quintessence of all heavens.

as Aristotle observed[1] does not consist in the unity of the hero. The same consideration applies to the argument that unity is provided by the theme of Faust's striving. There is of course a sense in which this striving can seem repugnant: if we consider Faust to be striving not only past the dissatisfaction of his encounter with the Earth-Spirit, with the carousers, and with the witches, but also past his love of Gretchen, we may see him as altogether too calculating a man, with one eye always on advantage in the metaphysical world beyond, rather than on the human being in front of him. However, to take a single instance, we can see that his resolution to overcome his rejection by the Earth-Spirit is rewarded later in the play (in 'Forest and Cavern') by the vision granted to him by that same Spirit; we can also see that this in its turn proves unsatisfactory to Faust in that, though exalting in itself (with the reservations made on p. 150 above), it involves him in isolation and precludes that enjoyment of Gretchen's body which Faust also urgently desires.

This 'one-sidedness' of all human satisfactions—the way in which having one enjoyment makes another impossible—is also one of the features of the play which tend to hold it together. The doctrine of polarity, which Goethe developed more and more explicitly in later life, is concerned with this very fact of complementariness, and we have already seen how in the Prologue in Heaven earthly life is regarded as a mere alternation of paradisal brightness and horrifying darkness, while the Lord lives in unchanging light. Mephistopheles makes much the same point when he says of the Lord:

> Er findet sich in einem ew'gen Glanze,
> Uns hat er in die Finsternis gebracht,
> Und euch taugt einzig Tag und Nacht.*[2]

Faust may vacillate, in that at times he seems to want no more than 'day and night', that is the alternation of opposites inherent in mortal life, whereas at others he may want the

---

* He dwells in eternal light; us [the devils] he has consigned to darkness, and you [human beings] have only day and night.

'eternal light' which, as Mephistopheles tells him, is only intended for a god. Certainly, when Faust speaks of wanting
'verliebter Haß' and 'erquickender Verdruß'*1 he wants light
and dark in one, although when he speaks of his kinship with
all creation and the love he has learned for it through the
Earth-Spirit, he seems devoted to the light alone. Yet this idea
of the polar opposites is a valuable one and may even help to
explain how Goethe could to all appearances deliberately make
Faust an unrepentant murderer, an ultimately faithless lover,
and a man so dedicated to evil that he can ascend Satan's
mountain in search of truth.[2] For the doctrine of polarity was
coupled with the doctrine of 'Steigerung', according to which
an intensification or heightening of both sides of a pair of
opposites could lead to their fusion.[3] The important point here
is that, in Faust's case, he does proceed on two different planes,
rising higher in that his disdain for other men, his desperation
and his lust give way to his love for Gretchen, descending in
that he not only makes a pact with the devil but yields to his
temptations, gets Gretchen with a child for which he takes no
care, kills her brother, leaves her in misery for the pleasures of
the Brocken, and finally abandons her. Whether or not Goethe
ever visualized the play in this schematized way, it could well
be that, almost instinctively, he allowed the two developments
to take place from some ulterior feeling that they could end in
the fusion which Faust was seeking. If we take this view, which
at least tallies with certain known patterns of Goethe's thought
outside the play, we are able at least to see in what way *Part I*
could have appeared a unity to him, rather than the mere
conglomeration which he surely cannot have wanted to write.
A decision on this vital issue is best deferred, however, until the
First and Second Parts have been seen together, as the whole
which Goethe intended them to be.

* enamoured hate; refreshing annoyance.

8

'FAUST, PART II'

At what stage Goethe realized that there would have to be a second Part to *Faust* is not known: it has been argued that he envisaged the play in its entirety from its first inception, but even that would not necessarily have involved the present division. Once the First Part was near completion, however, it must have become apparent that a new start must be made. You could not simply turn over the page after Gretchen's despairing cry and start on the next adventure. But it was not the scene which now opens *Part II* that Goethe wrote first. In 1800, eight years before *Part I* was published, he had already begun to write what was to become Act III, with its traditional encounter between Faust and Helen of Troy, and although he did not take up the Second Part again till 1825 (his seventy-sixth year) he had drawn up an overall plan around the turn of the century. Goethe's whole method of writing was different, in the six years he finally spent on *Part II*. It was much more schematic and disciplined, much more a matter of regular stints, thought out of an evening and written down the following morning. Goethe was also more conscious that this was his testament to posterity; when he finally sealed up the manuscript in August 1831 after some sixty years, he regarded the remainder of his life, as he said, as a 'sheer gift'. *Part II* was published after his death, in 1832.

Despite Goethe's schematic method of working, there have been critics like Benedetto Croce who have seen in *Part II* a kind of loosely assembled bouquet of reminiscences, an anthology of fine lyrical passages strung together on the theme of Faust, rather than a coherent whole. This is not surprising, since the work is even more a series of disconnected epigrams or fragmentary scenes than *Part I* is, and the total structure is not easy to discern, so that Goethe's own indication of his intentions is particularly valuable. The essential feature of the plan he wrote round about 1800 is the definition of the relation between the two parts:

Lebens-Genuß der Person — von außen gesehen — 1. Teil. — In der Dumpfheit Leidenschaft.
Taten-Genuß — nach außen — 2. Teil. — Und Genuß mit Bewußtsein. Schönheit.
Schöpfungs-Genuß — von innen — Epilog im Chaos — auf dem Weg zur Hölle.*

and what he clearly has in mind is a threefold progression in Faust, in which the whole of the First Part is contrasted with the first two-thirds or more of the Second Part (ending perhaps at the marriage with Helen in Act III, as seems to be indicated by the word 'Beauty'); finally both these sections are contrasted with a third which must begin at that moment in Act V when Faust, blinded by the allegorical figure of Care, grows suddenly aware of an inward light and returns zestfully to the creative work which he might have been on the point of abandoning. (The epilogue on the way to Hell probably refers to Mephistopheles, not to Faust, and may have been meant for the scene which now appears shortly before the end, showing the devil cursing his bad luck in losing Faust's soul.)

It is perhaps not fanciful to see in this scheme a more conscious employment of the doctrine of polarity and enhancement than Goethe had used earlier. Certainly the first two sections are contrasted almost word by word, subjective experience being contrasted with 'Taten-Genuß', in other words receptivity with activity, the mode of vision being now 'von außen', now 'nach außen', and the 'Dumpfheit' of the First Part—that is to say, Faust's unawareness of the meaning of what is happening to him—being contrasted with his conscious, purposeful behaviour in the Second Part. By the time the scheme was

---

* Enjoyment of life in the person—seen from outside—1. Part.—passion in obscure desire.
Enjoyment of deeds—towards the outside—2. Part.—And enjoyment with awareness. Beauty.
Enjoyment of creation—from within—Epilogue in Chaos—on the way to Hell.

written, Goethe had been to Italy, he had felt the key to all the realms of Nature in his grasp, and had rewritten *Wilhelm Meister* to show how a man might be led by unseen powers to knowledge of the Truth. Something of the same awareness that Goethe had enters into Faust in the earlier Acts of the Second Part.

But if it is true that there is a kind of polar opposition in the scheme, it may also be true that the third stage represents that synthesis or godlike fusion which Goethe speaks of in his Colour-Theory and elsewhere. The three words which Goethe wrote above the part of the scheme just quoted might also point in this direction. 'Lebens — Taten — Wesen':* the first two seem to correspond to the 'Lebens-Genuß' and the 'Taten-Genuß', while the third, 'Wesen', or 'essential being', might correspond to the 'Schöpfungs-Genuß'. Even in *Part I* we have seen[1] how creativity is the mark of the divine life, and indeed, from Goethe's 'Sturm und Drang' days onwards, to create was to be at least like a demigod. Was it perhaps his intention to show Faust, in the final scenes shortly before his death and ascent to heaven, enjoying the god-like life of a creator here on earth? Faust does, after all, with almost his dying breath pronounce the words which would hand him over to Mephistopheles, were he not to make his acceptance of the moment still conditional, still postponed. Is the fact that he can now even foresee the day when he *could* pronounce the words not a mark of his almost divine condition (for as the Prologue in Heaven shows, the splendour of the divine creation demands acceptance, and the Lord proceeds always on an untroubled course)? That Faust would also lose his soul by pronouncing the words is not necessarily a counter-argument. The moment of salvation and of damnation oscillates with lightning speed between one and the other just as it must seem to do in all syntheses which combine twin opposites in one. You can only say that it is a synthesis at all by pointing to the opposites which form it, and yet ultimately it is (if it exists at all) a unity which subsumes them both, a true 'Doppelreich',† as Faust calls it.[2] Per-

---

* Life's—Deeds—Essence.   † Double realm.

haps some such broad pattern as this was in Goethe's mind. Faust was ultimately to find not the mere alternation of opposites or even the sweet-sour combination of them, which he spoke of in the pact-scene,[1] but as near as might be a godlike realization of what Goethe had called, in one of the earliest passages to be written, 'Alle Würkungskraft und Samen.'*

Within this broad pattern, minor patterns can be seen, though dimly, through the mass of detail and digression. The first three Acts, roughly speaking, are concerned with Faust in his relation to Helen, the last two with his acquisition of land and his decision to reclaim land from the sea, with all the allegorical significance which that acquires. Again, a certain structure emerges from both Parts if we see them in terms of Goethe's own life. In these terms, *Part I* corresponds to Goethe's youthful metaphysical and religious struggles, and his love for Friederike Brion, while Act I of *Part II*, taking place at the Emperor's Court, corresponds to Goethe's move to Weimar. The quest for Helen which occupies most of Act II is partly a reflection of Goethe's love for Charlotte von Stein, partly of his yearning for Italy, which is then as it were fulfilled in Act III, when Faust and Helen are united. Act IV is a difficult, not to say tedious Act, by any standards, yet it is not inappropriate that, just as Goethe returned from Italy to Weimar, so Faust here returns to the service of the Emperor. Act V reflects through Faust's leadership of the people in their struggle against the sea Goethe's own sense in later life of a social mission to be fulfilled, and of his dominant position in European letters and thought. While none of these comparisons requires that every detail should be relatable to Goethe's life, a certain autobiographical interest is undeniable.

Equally evident is the parallelism between the two Parts, not only in that the last scene of Faust's ascent to Heaven is like a reply to the Prologue, but in smaller details. In both Parts, Faust is dissatisfied, in one case with knowledge, in the other with the superficialities of the Emperor's court; in *Part I* he

---

* All efficacy and seed.

seeks metaphysical satisfaction in calling on the Earth-Spirit, whose presence is so fearsome that he is on the point of committing suicide, in *Part II* he makes the descent to the mysterious realm of the 'Mothers', from whom he takes the shade of Helen, only to be flung senseless to the ground, as though by an electric discharge, when he tries to take her to himself. Each of these encounters with a power greater than Faust himself, which totally dominates him, is followed by a scene in which Wagner appears, and a meeting between Mephisto and a student (the order is reversed in *Part II*). The Classical Walpurgis Night appears earlier in *Part II* than its counterpart does in *Part I*, but in its whole conception it is clearly meant as a parallel, with the difference that it ends in a festival of Love where the other was to have ended in a festival of Evil. Faust's love for Helen is also explicitly related[1] to his love for Gretchen (Mephistopheles also interrupts each time),[2] and this too ends, though less catastrophically, in the death of their child and Faust's relinquishment of Helen. Thus all that section of *Part II* which must represent 'Taten-Genuß' and appears to be in polar opposition to *Part I* bears a close formal relationship to *Part I*. It is as though Goethe were pointing to a basic similarity between the two spheres of 'Lebens-Genuß' and 'Taten-Genuß' (a similarity which all polar opposites are said to have) and contrasting this with the completely new final section of 'Schöpfungs-Genuß', in which the parallelism ceases.

As well as this much greater formal awareness, there is a detachment seldom to be found in *Part I*. Goethe makes us very conscious from time to time that it is a play we are watching (not that he is likely to have envisaged some of the scenes being performed in the theatre—the festival in the Aegean Sea, for instance, or Faust's long ascent heavenwards, and many other effects impossible to stage convincingly, even though the attempt is still being made in 1966). Thus Mephistopheles is required by a stage direction to speak 'ad spectatores'[3]—to the audience, that is, in the theatre; at the end of Act III he is seen 'within the proscenium arch', while in Act V the Jaws of Hell are actually brought on stage[1] by a group of subordinate devils, while Mephisto encourages them to give the sinners in the audience a thorough fright. All this is of a piece with the humorous, sometimes jaunty or even boisterous tone in which a good deal of the work is written—with the screechingly bad rhyme, for instance, which Mephistopheles makes between 'Neusten' and 'erdreusten' (for 'erdreisten').[2] As Goethe said on more than one occasion, *Part II* is a series of 'very serious jokes', 'seriously intended jokes'. It is integral to his whole conception, this oxymoron that runs through it, for just as there is a fusion of opposites in the final scene, so we are meant to take it both seriously and not seriously at one and the same time. We are to concern ourselves with the profoundest issues of heaven and damnation, and yet be aware that we are watching nothing but a stage-performance, perhaps with the suggestion that life itself (being, as the final chorus has it, only a simile or parable)[3] is an illusion.

Part II remains, for all that, a difficult work to enjoy. Indeed it is only comparatively recently that it has begun to be acclaimed as equal to, or even better than *Part I*, which is of course much more stageable and so at once more popular. In the nineteenth century poets such as Mörike, Hebbel, Keller, and Meyer could find little value in *Part II*, and thought Goethe had become incapable of handling such material poetically in his old age; in the twentieth century, by contrast, T. S. Eliot has declared a preference for the Second Part, and André Gide has spoken in similar terms, while opinion among German scholars has leaned towards seeing in *Part II* the poet's crowning glory.

The difficulty remains, that for long passages of the play, for hundreds of lines together, the action is lost completely from view, and the masques or the series of persons declaiming occasional verse, who occupy the stage, have very little of dramatic interest to offer. The Furies appear at the Emperor's Court to announce that they will tell tales to lovers about the duplicity of their sweethearts and that they will make trouble between married couples; all this in the mildest of accents.[4] If these fall short of their expected awesomeness, Avarice, who offends the ladies of the court by rolling his gold into a phallus, is observed by the Herald with the unemphatic words 'I am afraid he enjoys himself when he offends morality'.[1] The Fates also appear, one to announce that there is much to be thought about in spinning the thread of life (she does not say what), and that those who dance too boisterously should beware of snapping the thread, another to say that she has often made mistakes as a young woman, in cutting off people's lives too soon, and that to keep herself under control she has placed her shears in a sheath, while the third says she is afraid of what might happen to the world if she were to forget her proper function.[2] There is a great deal, especially in the First Act, in this bathetically comfortable tone, so flat as to cause surprise in a work of these pretensions.

Nor is the absence of a continuing thread confined to Act I, dominated as that is by the masque, for the next three acts are almost as full of the same kind of material, relieved only here and there by more stirring passages. Most remarkable of all, in the first four thousand lines or so, Faust has less than three hundred to speak, and, in the seven and a half thousand in *Part II* altogether, he has less than nine hundred. (He has more, if one supposes that he plays the part of Plutus in the masque, but this is a surmise without a hint from Goethe, and at all events the role of Plutus tells us nothing of Faust himself. It is also suggested sometimes that Homunculus and Lynkeus are aspects of Faust.) Despite the 'Taten-Genuß' of Goethe's scheme, Faust in *Part II* does little. He presumably has some part in organizing the masque; he courageously descends to the realm of the Mothers in quest of Helen, and is struck down when he touches her; he is taken to Greece and at once goes in search of Helen again; he admires the Sphinxes and dreams of Zeus wooing Leda; he inquires Helen's whereabouts from Chiron and rides the centaur in search of her, but in all this we catch only the briefest glimpses of him, and at length he meets Helen not as the result of his search, but because she is brought to him by Mephisto. Goethe leaves us in no doubt about the urgency of Faust's desire, but he affords little time for it to manifest itself. Not until the middle of Act III does Faust occupy the stage continuously for a coherent action over a long period.

The scene 'Innerer Burghof', in which Faust and Helen are united, is the climactic centre of the Second Part. Here, momentarily at least, Faust enjoys what he has been striving for, the knowledge of perfect beauty, and we are to see symbolically in this union a synthesis of North and South, German and Greek, a temporary resolution of polar oppositions. Although the action is more consecutive, the structure does not differ much from that of the masque scenes or the Classical Walpurgis Night. There are two snatches of dialogue, forming less than 50 lines in the whole scene, which is some 450 lines long. Most of the remainder takes the form of a series of poems, differing in metre and verse-form from one another and often treating some theme adjacent to the main theme without really developing it. Lynkeus the watchman tells how Faust's treasure was amassed, Faust tells how the Germanic tribes overran Greece, and paints vividly the landscape of Arcadia; the chorus reflects on the need for strength in arms for the defence of womanhood. Even this climax, then, is not so much dramatic as lyrical in form; there is little development from one moment to another.

This absence of development is still more striking in relation to the play as a whole. Although in Act II Faust was last seen urgently in quest of Helen, that is now over, and he is in his castle, presumably waiting for her. When she comes, it is not because of any action by Faust, but through the magical intervention of Mephistopheles (disguised as Phorkyas); the reason for this intervention is not given, and perhaps we are not expected to ask why Mephisto brings Helen now, when he could not do so before, in Act I. Thus Faust's quest is to all intents and purposes dismissed, as though it had never been— and indeed we did not see very much of it. Moreover, he is now a different man, living in a different age. We last saw him at the medieval Emperor's court, which he left, as though in a dream, for the land of classical Greece. Now suddenly he is the

ruler of a castle near Sparta, at the time of the Crusades so far
as one can tell, though he also appears to be the leader of the
ancient tribes of Goths, Germans, Franks, Saxons and Normans
who once overran most of Europe. The change is unheralded:
Goethe presents this new situation without warning and we
assimilate the new facts from the implications of what is spoken.
Clearly, then, Faust can no longer be regarded as a character in
the normal sense. His military virtues and capacities must be
thought of as magically acquired, and the scene is to be
appreciated above all in its symbolical portrayal of Classicism
and Romanticism in one. . ..

Despite Faust's former yearning, however, his greeting to
Helen is muted. Nothing like Marlowe's 'Is this the face that
launched a thousand ships' crosses his mind. Though, presumably, he knows who Helen is (there is no actual indication
in the text that he either expects her or recognizes her), his
first speech to her is a long, pedantic apology for the fact that
his watchman failed to see her coming and give due warning
so that she could be properly welcomed.[1] It is all rather prim
and formal, and Faust does not, apparently, realise that Helen
has been spirited to the place by Mephisto-Phorkyas, so that
his formality is all the more remarkable. You might expect him
to be overwhelmed by the sudden appearance of a Helen in his
courtyard. When Lynkeus has proffered his excuse, and Helen
has begged forgiveness for him, Faust still remains strangely
calm.

> Erstaunt, o Königin, seh' ich zugleich
> Die sicher Treffende, hier den Getroffnen;
> Ich seh' den Bogen, der den Pfeil entsandt,
> Verwundet jenen. Pfeile folgen Pfeilen,
> Mich treffend. Allwärts ahn' ich überquer
> Gefiedert schwirrend sie in Burg und Raum.[*2]

There is no life in these rhythms, no spirit in the imagery.
Faust announces that he too is smitten by Helen's beauty in

* Astonished, O Queen, I see at once her who aims surely, and him she has
smitten; I see the bow which dispatched the arrow, and see him wounded.
Arrows follow arrows, striking me. On all sides I sense them crossing, in
feathered flight whirring across the castle and its space.

the abruptest of tones, with 'Mich treffend'. The whole passage sounds more like a polite compliment than a protestation of adoring love, and Faust's later offer to present Helen with great riches looks, in these circumstances, a rather materialistic gesture. So does his next offer, made in the belief that she is unsatisfied,[1] to give her all that his castle contains. It is munificent, but it is not what you might expect him to be saying to such a woman or even to such a symbol.

The next section,[2] with its pretty sequence in which Faust the Northerner teaches Helen the Greek how to rhyme, and uses rhyme as a sign of love, is of entirely different quality. So is the passage[3] in which the increase of passion is represented by an intensification of rhymes which pour out in such profusion between Helen and Faust that their complementary fulfilment is vividly realized.

HELENA. Ich fühle mich so fern und doch so nah,
  Und sage nur zu gern: Da bin ich! da!
FAUST. Ich atme kaum, mir zittert, stockt das Wort;
  Es ist ein Traum, verschwunden Tag und Ort.
HELENA. Ich scheine mir verlebt und doch so neu,
  In dich verwebt, dem Unbekannten treu.
FAUST. Durchgrüble nicht das einzigste Geschick!
  Dasein ist Pflicht, und wär's ein Augenblick.*

Yet between these two passages comes one spoken by the chorus which casts a strange light on this love-making. They say, in effect (but they have been hostile to Helen throughout the Act), that their mistress has never been particular about the men she yielded to, whether golden-haired shepherds or bristling black-haired fauns: all enjoyed her just as chance offered, just as Faust enjoys her at this moment. She is, after all, they reflect, a prisoner, and no one could blame her for sur-

---

* HELENA. I feel so distant, yet so near, and say so willingly, here am I, here!
  FAUST. I scarcely breathe, I tremble, stumble for words, this is a dream, all time and place are gone.
  HELENA. I seem worn out, to death, and yet so new, woven in you, and faithful to the unknown.
  FAUST. Ponder not on this strangest of destinies. Existence is a duty, though it be but for an instant.

rendering now. Whether this is meant to indicate why Helen yields is not clear: no other motive for her yielding than this submissive prostitution is given. Similarly Faust is not presented as specially noble; he has, according to Mephisto,[1] been letting his men ransack the country as they pleased for the last twenty years, and has himself exacted, not a tribute, but 'free-will offerings' from the inhabitants. He too is presented in no other guise than this of the successful freebooter: the two together, Helen and Faust, seem oddly inadequate symbols of what they are supposed to stand for. Nor is the case altered when Mephistopheles breaks up the love-scene (against all his interest in winning the wager) with the news that Helen's husband Menelaus is on the war-path. Once more the chorus intervene, to comment[2] that Faust has won Helen by flattery but he had better defend her with weapons or someone will filch her from him. They conclude that both Helen and Faust are likely to gain great glory, since Faust's soldiers are most loyal, being so aware of their own advantage (presumably because the soldiers will continue to exact free-will offerings), that they will always defend him. These speeches are again materialistic and cynical in their implications, and since neither Helen nor Faust shows any qualities to contradict these interpretations of their conduct, we are left with an incongruous idea of their nature. The Germanic qualities are presented almost entirely as those of ruthless plunderers, while the Greeks, in so far as Helen represents them, are shown as not much more than gold-diggers.

At this point, moreover, the dramatic sequence is quite forgotten. The leaders of Faust's army assemble to hear his orders for the fight against Menelaus. Faust, however, does not give them; he begins instead a long lyrical portrayal of the pastoral beauties of Greece and at length, letting Menelaus slip completely from consciousness, he invites Helen to join him in an Arcadia which is still quite close to Sparta. (A kind of fusion of opposites may be meant here too.) With this the scene changes to Arcadia, and all talk of war and defence disappears from the play. Anyone looking for a connected sequence of

the world; he also regards the dam which he has built as 'the masterpiece of the human mind'[1] (although it has been constructed mainly by magical and diabolical means), and speaks of reclaiming sufficient land for 'many millions' of people.[2] Although only a strip of land was awarded to Faust in Act IV, it thus seems that by Act V he is on the way to seeing himself as a kind of world-ruler: he has a palace, thousands of workmen, and, as he says, his empire extends infinitely before him.[3] Despite all this, however, a petty thought nags at his mind. An old couple, Philemon and Baucis, named after the man and woman who in antiquity were renowned for their hospitality, and who in this play seem also to represent the Christian faith, still occupy a small cottage of their own. The small area in which they live, with its lime-trees and ruinous church, arouses Faust's envy: he wants to shelter in the shade of the trees which 'spoil my possession of the world'[4] and to build a look-out there from which to survey his dominions. The free exercise of his almighty will, he declares in what might be a god-like way, is hindered by this patch outside his control, and he 'rages' with impotence.[5] Growing weary, as he says, of the attempt to be just,[6] he gives instructions to Mephistopheles and three piratical companions who have just returned with the plunder from an expedition, that the old couple are to be removed and provided with some other place to live in.

Faust has never done anything quite like this before. The removal of Philemon and Baucis is made by Goethe to look utterly selfish, inspired by the most trivial of motives. (Even on a symbolical level, it is hard to see why Faust should act so tyrannically merely in order to be able to build a look-out tower, and a good deal of what he says suggests nothing better than spite.) Baucis indeed suggests that Faust has been lusting for the possession of their hut for some time: it is also she who reveals that the dam shutting out the sea has been built through bloody human sacrifices. For the first time in *Part II* Mephistopheles (whose magic is presumably responsible for these sacrifices) is made to appear really diabolical. It is thus all the more surprising that Faust entrusts the commission of his plan to the devil, who is after all unlikely to use the most humane methods.

While Faust is congratulating himself at the thought of the old couple's eventual recognition of his magnanimity towards them,[1] he learns that Mephisto has been impatient. Since neither Philemon nor Baucis replied to his beating at their door, he burst in with his companions and dragged them out: they died of shock and the devil set fire to the cottage to make a kind of funeral pyre for them. Reading this passage today, one cannot avoid the uncanny feeling that Goethe had some foreboding of similar events during the Second World War. Faust, however, though he is angry at the devil's rashness, will accept no responsibility for the deed, it was exchange he wanted, not robbery,[2] and he refuses to regard his own orders as implicating him in the blame. Thus it appears that, just as at the end of *Part I*, so at the end of *Part II* Goethe is concerned to present his hero in an increasingly unfavourable light, for Faust was clearly implicated by sending the devil to effect his plans at all, and his disclaimer has a shabby look.

In the scene immediately following, however, there is considerable ambiguity. Out of the smoke ascending from the burning cottage the allegorical figure of Care ('Sorge') shapes itself and slips through Faust's keyhole, to torment him, as we may at first suppose, with remorse for his deed. But this interpretation is not quite satisfying since another similar figure, Guilt ('Schuld'), can obtain no entry, and Care does not directly accuse Faust of any share in the death of Philemon and Baucis. Instead, she seems rather to be a representation of all that 'taking care for the morrow' which Egmont rejected (he too has a scene in which he almost succumbs to 'Sorge'): she attempts to make Faust unaware of the present moment, to make him concerned only with the future, only with the darkness of boredom at this life. So her connection with the Philemon and Baucis episode is only tenuous, despite first appearances. She has really next to nothing to do with Faust and his guilt. Yet more curious, however, is Faust's reply to her: although she has just been saying that a man who falls into

her clutches can find no enjoyment in anything, Faust stops her
to protest that she will not win him over in that way. Such
temptation, he declares, might make the wisest man infatu-
ated—and despite the profusion of commentators none has explained why Faust should find Care's speech so attractive. (One
can understand that he rejects Care, in this sense, but not that
he should speak as though she had made herself particularly
desirable or powerful.)

All the same, the end of this scene marks the final turning-
point which is implied, in Goethe's scheme for *Part II*, by the
words 'Schöpfungs-Genuß — von innen', for now that Care
can establish no dominion over Faust she revenges herself by
blinding him, saying as she does so:

> Die Menschen sind im ganzen Leben blind,
> Nun, Fauste, werde du's am Ende!*[1]

The suggestion that Faust, unlike the majority of mankind,
has hitherto not been 'blind' is unexplained, and is surely contradicted by most of his conduct up to this point. However, the
point of this blinding is not so much in the deed itself as in its
consequences for Faust, for as a result he now becomes aware
of an inward light[2] which inspires him at once to renewed
activity. Here is the 'enjoyment of creation, from within' of
which Goethe's scheme spoke: from now on Faust enters on a
final period in his life. (One is reminded of Goethe's poem
'Vermächtnis', with its promise of guidance by an inward light
which shall be 'Sonne deinem Sittentag'.)†

But what is this inner light, and has it any bearing on Faust's
most recent misdeed? It scarcely seems to have any, in fact its
function seems rather to renew Faust's ability to act—that is,
to continue to stress deeds rather than reflectiveness—not to
awaken in him any moral sense. Here indeed is a crux of the
play, for we are now about to enter the scene in which Faust
dies and in which he ascends to heaven, and the question whether

---

* Men are blind their whole lives through; now, Faust, be you blind as life
ends.

† Sun to your moral day.

he is a changed man, or whether the whole conduct of his life in itself qualifies him for salvation, has aroused a great deal of discussion. Those who argue that he is changed, and that this change makes his salvation more readily acceptable, have in their favour the argument that in the scene with Care Faust not only wishes that he might be free of all magic—and thus, presumably, of the devil also[1]—but furthermore deliberately refuses to use the magic formula which would rid him of Care completely.[2] These points do, it is true, suggest that Faust is changing: he has never sought to be rid of magic up to this moment. On the other hand, he does not explicitly reject Mephistopheles, and it is hard to see what such a rejection might amount to, in view of the pact and wager. Moreover, in the following scene Faust continues to use the devil's help, though once again it is not clear whether he knows it or not. Presumably Faust is aware that his dam has been built with diabolical help and in a diabolical way,[3] yet he does not address Mephistopheles by name in the scene which follows, and, being blind, Faust may just not know who it is who answers when he calls for the 'overseer'. The fact is, Goethe leaves this vital point obscure: Faust's desire to be rid of magic is set in the conditional mood ('Könnt' ich Magie...'); he continues to use Mephisto's help in practice, and he makes no explicit dismissal of the devil.

A similar ambiguity runs through Faust's final speech[4] in which he announces his final scheme, the project with which he can peacefully end his days. Like Wilhelm Meister, who becomes a surgeon in the final pages of the *Wanderjahre*, Faust devotes himself to a socially useful purpose: the soil which has been reclaimed is to serve the needs of a vast new populace which is to live in freedom, to build up 'a paradisal land'. Then the floods outside may rage as they will, the communal spirit of the people will prevent their entry and at the same time drain off any impurity which may remain within the frontiers of the new realm. (One may read this too as symbolism if one chooses.) With this thought in mind, Faust pronounces almost his final words:

Das ist der Weisheit letzter Schluß:
Nur der verdient sich Freiheit wie das Leben,
Der täglich sie erobern muß.*[1]

—which sounds very close to John Philpot Curran's famous words, pronounced in 1790, that 'the condition upon which God hath given liberty to man is eternal vigilance', although the implications are not quite the same. Foreseeing a future realm in which such vigilance will be always present, Faust declares himself able to anticipate the time when he could bring himself to speak the words to the passing moment, 'Tarry awhile, thou art so fair'. The pact of *Part I* is vividly recalled to mind at the instant before Faust dies.

Yet, like so much else in *Part II*, this reminder comes abruptly, and it is not clear why Faust should suddenly find himself close to pronouncing in real earnestness these after all fatal words. Faust has not shown any regard for social freedom hitherto; at the Emperor's court he had some part in distributing paper money, as a new invention, but this was a purely financial measure and had no useful results; at the time of his union with Helen he was a kind of robber baron, who thereafter gave help to the feudal Emperor of Act IV. In Act V, up to this point, he has depended for his power on magic, human sacrifice and piracy, and he has not hesitated to order the removal of Philemon and Baucis for purely personal reasons, however much he may reject the brutal means used by the devil for carrying out his orders. In the speeches immediately preceding his final one he has continued to speak if not as a tyrant, at least as an autocrat who expects complete obedience: the master's word is all that matters;[2] he rejoices at the crowd of workers who, as he believes, are slaving for him ('die mir frönet':[3] the verb is used of enforced labour, vassalage); he gives instructions to Mephistopheles to get help in the building of the dam by any means, payment, enticement or capture ('presse bei'[4] is an instruction to use press-gangs). That Faust should begin to talk

* This is wisdom's final conclusion: only he deserves freedom and life who daily has to conquer them.

of freedom in his last twenty lines, and that the freedom he means should be left so undefined, leaves a final impression of inconsequentiality. One would like to know what is so valuable about social freedom, in contrast with beauty or religious faith or knowledge of the innermost workings of the world, or the love of someone like Gretchen, that Faust should want the endurance of the moment now envisaged rather than any of the others that he has experienced. This is not to say that social freedom is unimportant, but rather to point out that the reference to it is perfunctory, and that the reasons for its supreme importance to Faust are never made apparent. One's hesitation about the final speech is increased by the fact that the last words of all concentrate not on the benefit to society but on the fact that Faust will be remembered for ages to come:[1] this is at least a large element in the 'highest moment' which he now greets, and it reflects the egotism which has been prominent in Faust from the outset.

Critics like Benno von Wiese, who have observed that Faust's dying moments are a 'tragic illusion' (an illusion brought out by Goethe in the scene where Faust imagines his workmen are digging a trench ('Graben') when in fact they are digging his grave ('Grab')) may go on to say that 'in this passionate, amoral determination to act, Faust's creative disquiet lives on, seeking to fight down chaos and opposition'. They see these final moments, in other words, as a further prolongation of Faust's 'will to act', and are able to quote sayings of Goethe himself to the effect that 'the man of action is always conscienceless, nobody has a conscience except the man of meditation'. There may well be some justice in this, in the sense that such an attitude may reflect Goethe's intentions. On the other hand, the 'discreteness', not to say disjointedness, of the scenes may lead one to think that Goethe has left a large number of themes at a superficial level. He does not allow Faust to confront Guilt, he is ambiguous about his relation with Care, and about his renunciation of diabolical help, abrupt in his introduction of the theme of freedom and vague in his treatment of it. When Faust, as we know, is to be saved after all this, we may feel that a less indeterminate, irresolute and erratic man and a clearer treatment would have carried more conviction.

Seen in terms of what he achieves on earth, indeed, Faust accomplishes little even in this last scene. As Mephistopheles points out, Faust is still chasing phantoms, and his enjoyment of 'the last, bad, empty moment' is of no consequence. This view is as valid, perhaps (from Goethe's standpoint), as Faust's own: the final moment is at one and the same time Faust's greatest and his least, just as, in *Part I*, the pusillanimous Faust was possibly, within the system of polarity, meant to appear a glorious Titan as well. What we have been witnessing hitherto has been the earthly life in which, as the Prologue announced, Paradisal brightness alternates with hideous night. What we are now to witness, in the closing scenes of the whole play, is the return to the divine world where the Lord's progression is of unending smoothness, and where all are justified, nothing is condemned. The way for this is prepared by the battle between Mephistopheles' devils and the angels for Faust's soul. The point about the roses scattered by the angels, which burn those who hate but bless those who love, is that they are capable of bringing comfort to 'all natures',[1] as they proceed to show. For the effect of the roses is demonstrated on Mephistopheles himself, who, from feeling an anguish of fire, comes to realise that this is the anguish from which lovers suffer, and, being what he is, begins to feel a homosexual love for the angels themselves. This is not a joke, or if it is, it is a serious one; Mephistopheles begins to be aware of a strange force at work within him,[2] and though he continues to speak humorously, asking the angels whether they are not of the same race as Lucifer (as indeed in a way they are, for Lucifer was of their number before he fell), it becomes clear that he does genuinely admire the angels as well as desire them erotically. This is an intensification of the moment at the end of Act II, when the festival of love was at its height. Gradually, through the power of Love (from which Eros is not excluded), the devil himself is being won round. For the purpose of the roses and their flames,

as the angels sing, is to heal all those who condemn themselves:[1]
it is self-condemnation, denial rather than affirmation, that
excludes men from the eternal splendour of the divine light
which sees no shadows: 'die sich verdammen, heile die
Wahrheit'*—it is not a question of whether self-condemnation is appropriate in a particular instance, but rather a declaration that all such criticism hinders activity, the divine attribute
which has continued since, to use Faust's words in *Part I*, 'in
the beginning was the Deed'. Thus Mephistopheles, though
covered with blisters from the flames, and filled now with
horror at himself, at the revelation of what he is, triumphs at
the same instant, and rejoices that 'the noble diabolical parts'
—he means the sexual organs—are also saved. This passage[2] is
particularly difficult to construe, and deserves special attention.
The basic idea is this, that Mephisto now recognizes himself as
part of the divine plan: he knows how diabolical he is, and
accordingly feels horror; he also knows that sex is of the devil,
and since he is now able to have some sexual enjoyment in
the knowledge that this too is divinely blessed, he rejoices too;
finally, he reverts to his diabolical (and allotted) role to curse the
entire company 'as is right and proper', as he significantly adds.
This is Parolles in *All's Well That Ends Well*, affirming 'simply
the thing I am shall make me live', or Thersites in *Troilus and
Cressida*, denying very truly that he is a man of honour, and
thereby escaping with his life—as we feel he should—by
affirming to Hector 'I am a rascal; a scurvy railing knave; a
very filthy rogue'. Similarly, Mephistopheles now knows himself not merely to be the devil, but to be accepted as the devil
within the divine plan. The words from Goethe's 'Paria',
addressed to Brahma, are relevant here—'du lässest alle gelten'
—all are allowed their validity, including the devil. He feels
love, absurd though it is,[3] and in this there is at least a token
of his being taken up into the radiance of which the angels have
sung:

> Heilige Gluten!
> Wen sie umschweben,

* let those who damn themselves be healed by truth.

Fühlt sich im Leben
Selig mit Guten.*[1]

As Goethe wrote in the poem 'Wiederfinden'—'Sei's Ergreifen, sei es Raffen, wenn es nur sich liebt und hält'[2]—the sus-
taining power everywhere is love, which brings all creatures
together, regardless of whether they feel tenderly or violently
—it is not so much a human feeling as a centripetal force
bringing all into unity:

Um in dem Allverein
Selig zu sein.†[3]

And thus, although Mephistopheles is still left at the end of the
scene outside the heavenly circle, rueing his loss of Faust's
soul, the process of his involvement in the cosmic glory (or of
his becoming aware that he is so involved) has begun.

The last scene of all, 'Bergschluchten' (which passes im-
perceptibly into 'Himmel') realizes the same idea in terms of
Faust himself. In the earlier lines of the scene, the omni-
presence of love is announced, as the hermits in their cliff-face
cells sing of love being the pressure of rocks on their own
foundations or the upward thrust of a tree's trunk (one notices
the contraries here). The raging roar of the waterfall exists so
that the valley below may be watered; the lightning flash
swoops down to improve the atmosphere (here the lines become banal in expression), and both these apparently fearful
manifestations are messengers of love. The Pater Profundus,
deep down in the ravine, in whom we may catch a glimpse of a
part of Goethe himself, longs for the same power to set on fire
his mind which dwells too much with cold, rational speculation.

Into this atmosphere, of a love which attempts to break
through everywhere with the knowledge that all things are
acceptable, enter the angels bearing Faust's immortal soul, and
singing the now famous lines:

Wer immer strebend sich bemüht,
Den können wir erlösen

---

* Holy fires! Him whom they enfold feels himself blessed in life with all that
are good.　　　　　　　　† To be blissful in the cosmic union.

to which they add the equally important, though rhythmically jaunty and nonchalant ones:

> Und hat an ihm die Liebe gar
> Von oben teilgenommen,
> Begegnet ihm die selige Schar
> Mit herzlichem Willkommen.*1

Faust's salvation is thus not solely due to his own striving, but, in accordance with traditional Christian ideas, or so Goethe observed to Eckermann,2 to the fact that divine love has shown him favour. How far indeed the striving was necessary at all is open to question, since love is all-approving: we are perhaps confronted here with a paradox which will not answer to pressure. It is more pertinent in some ways to ask how Faust has striven, for apart from his quest for Helen he has played a rather passive role, leaving vital actions such as the bringing of Helen to Sparta, the winning of the battle against the anti-Emperor, and the building of the dam, to Mephistopheles; again, Faust has several times in the course of the play ceased to strive. All such questions are, however, against the spirit of these final passages, in which the mood is perhaps best expressed by the Doctor Marianus (seen by some commentators as an embodiment of Faust) in the lines, addressed to the Virgin Mary:

> Höchste Herrscherin der Welt!
> Lasse mich im blauen,
> Ausgespannten Himmelszelt
> Dein Geheimnis schauen.†3

That is to say, perhaps, that just as the blue sky spreads over all, so all live under the canopy of love, and all are saved, whether they know it or not. One thinks of Prince Andrew Bolkonski in *War and Peace*, lying wounded, mortally as he thinks, on the field of Austerlitz:

---

* He who strives unceasingly, him we can redeem, and should Love from on high have taken his part, then the blessed host meets him with hearty welcome.

† Supreme queen of all the world, let me see thy secret in the blue, outspread canopy of heaven.

Above him there was now nothing but the sky—the lofty sky, not clear yet still immeasurably lofty, with grey clouds gliding slowly across it. 'How quiet, peaceful and solemn, not at all as I ran', thought Prince Andrew—'not as we ran, shouting and fighting, not at all as the gunner and the Frenchman with frightened and angry faces struggled for the mop: how differently do those clouds glide across that lofty infinite sky! How was it that I did not see that lofty sky before? And how happy I am to have found it at last! Yes! All is vanity, all falsehood, except that infinite sky. There is nothing, nothing, but that. But even it does not exist, there is nothing but quiet and peace. Thank God!...'[1]

Or Goethe's own lines come to mind:

> Und alles Drängen, alles Ringen
> Ist ew'ge Ruh in Gott dem Herrn.*[2]

This is, indeed, the meaning of the last two lines of *Faust Part II*: 'The eternal feminine / Draws us on high.' It has that sense of being taken up into an infinite vault where all earthly distinctions vanish, such as can come from standing beneath a blue sky.

Faust is thus taken up in the final scene into that 'gentle turning of God's day' which the angels adore in the Prologue. He is at the least one of those who, in the words of Doctor Marianus, are in process of transformation:

> Blicket auf zum Retterblick,
> Alle reuig Zarten,
> Euch zu seligem Geschick
> Dankend umzuarten.†[3]

By giving thanks for his existence, be it what it may, he is changed and saved. By objecting, by finding fault, he would merely rank himself with the devil.

Yet it has to be seen that these are the terms with which the play really operates throughout. Though it talks occasionally of good and evil, it really deals in terms of what Nietzsche was

---

* And all thrusting, all wrestling, is eternal quiet in God the Lord.
† Look up at the saving eyes, all tender hearts that rue, transforming gratefully your whole natures into a blessed destiny.

later to call 'Ja-sagen' and 'Nein-sagen', 'affirmation' and 'denial'. And when Faust is saved within the love which approves him, it should not be lost from sight that his whole attitude throughout the play has been one in which he has always declined to consider the faults and crimes he has committed. Like Egmont, he has sought to live within the moment, looking neither forward nor backward, and his relation with Gretchen, for instance, is of a piece with this attitude. In forgetting all his abandonment of her, his murder of her brother, the death of their child and of Gretchen's mother which he partly caused, as well as in declining to accept any responsibility for the deaths of Philemon and Baucis, or for the lives sacrificed to the building of his dam, Faust is himself adopting that frame of mind which, though knowing what has been done, will not condemn it. Despite Goethe's remark to Eckermann, he does not reiterate the Christian tradition in this scene, for Faust at no time shows any repentance or sorrow for any of his misdeeds: he is impatient at being saddled with responsibility for them, and disquieted by them, but never gives any sign that he is deeply affected. He does not deserve to be described as one of the 'reuig Zarte' or 'tender hearts that rue' in the speech of the Doctor Marianus just quoted.

Indeed the unsatisfactory aspects of the play as a whole are part and parcel of the ideas which permeate it. On the one hand there is the mood of adoration, joy and acceptance which is so characteristically German and which has parallels, though distant ones, in such works as the 'Sanctus' in the B Minor Mass, or the final movement of the Choral Symphony or the Hallelujah Chorus, as well as in the concluding paragraphs of Leibniz's *Monadology* and the exuberant architecture of Neumann's Vierzehnheiligen-Kirche. This establishes itself most securely in the mountingly ecstatic speeches of the Magna Peccatrix, the Mulier Samaritana, and Maria Aegyptiaca, in the final scene of *Part II*. On the other hand, there is the action of the play on earth, in which nothing that happens seems to have much significance, all is either undermined with ironical detraction or self-contradictory or perfunctorily treated. This is one perennial feature of what Germans know as 'die deutsche Innerlichkeit', the traditional concentration on an ineffable inward world in which all is well, man is saved, struggle is unneeded, with an accompanying disregard of ephemeral affairs. Not that this disregard necessarily accompanies all manifestations of 'inwardness'. Goethe's *Faust* stands apart from Bach's *Sanctus*, for instance, in that it transfers the heavenly blessedness to the world of here and now, suggesting that the insufficiencies of earthly existence are not merely insufficiencies but divinely appointed ones, with an absolute justification. Thus Mephistopheles finally curses the angels 'as is right and proper', since it is his nature to do so. Similarly, it will be seen how the houris in the paradise of the *West-östliche Divan* ceased to offer men perfect beauty and substituted a beauty more suited to their less cultivated tastes.[1] Heaven adapts itself to human frailty, not merely accepting imperfection out of mercy and love, but not requiring anything better. This is, we may suppose, the meaning of the words pronounced by the Chorus mysticus in the final speech:

> Das Unzulängliche
> Hier wird's Ereignis... *[2]

That which is 'inadequate', these words declare, is not made adequate in heaven (or perfect, we might interpret); rather it becomes 'event', that is to say it really happens, intensely and with all its nature involved. The immediately following lines reiterate part of this thought:

> Das Unbeschreibliche
> Hier ist's getan.†

That which cannot be described, or expressed in words, is not expressed in heaven either; it is done, performed, it is deed and action (we remember how in *Part I* Faust rejected 'word' as a translation of 'Logos' and substituted 'deed'). Goethe reiterates

---

* The inadequate, here it becomes event.
† The indescribable, here it is performed.

here the thought which had occurred to him in Italy: 'how true, how existent!' Morality is dismissed; the world is accepted in all its inglorious glory, as the creation of God's hand.

But the weakness of this attitude is that it supplies no spur to reach perfection. Faust greets Helen as though she were a royal personage inspecting his factory; his achievements are at best questionable, sometimes positively evil; the play is often confused and disjointed, precisely because it is assumed that the inadequate can be apotheosized, and the self-contradictory can be welcomed. In some ways, the negligence about mundane matters actually leads Faust into evil and the play into artistic failure. As George Santayana says, 'the literary merits of Goethe's *Faust* correspond accurately with its philosophical excellences', and the correspondence extends to a mutual influence. The play is almost deliberately inadequate, as though Goethe had said, with Luther, 'Sin boldly', and had added 'but rejoice that the worst of your artistic faults will be swallowed up in the everlasting glory'. It gives the paradoxical impression, for a work in which striving leads to salvation, of having been written by a man who had ceased to think striving important. Such a paradox is of course typical of Goethe; it helps just a little to know this when one is trying to appreciate his work. Perhaps it helps more to remember that Faust was saved not only by striving but also by a love which took no account of shortcomings. That thought is central in all Goethe's work.

9

'WILHELM MEISTER'

Opinions of *Wilhelm Meister* differ extremely. For Friedrich Schlegel it was, together with Fichte's theory of knowledge and the French Revolution, one of the great events of the age; Novalis denounced it as an enemy to poetry. It was the first of a long line of novels, deriving partly from Rousseau's *Emile*, partly from the picaresque novel and its eighteenth-century off-shoots, which took as their theme the development of a man's life—it was the first important 'Bildungsroman', leading on to Keller's *Der grüne Heinrich*, Stifter's *Der Nachsommer*, Thomas Mann's *Der Zauberberg*, and to *David Copperfield*, Disraeli's *Coningsby* and Flaubert's *L'Education Sentimentale*. In parallel with *Faust*, and likewise being written at intervals throughout Goethe's mature life, it is a story of a quest for wisdom and experience; Goethe's deepest preoccupations are reflected in it. Yet the youthful Henry James noted that already in his day it was said to belong to 'the class of the great unreadables'; James felt obliged to take the wisdom on trust, and did not find it one of the world's most gripping tales.

This is strange, since the theme is a fascinating one and its treatment a tantalizing invitation to read on more than one level at once. Some part of an explanation can be found in the fact that the first novel of the two which make up the cycle, *Wilhelm Meisters Lehrjahre* (the *Years of Apprenticeship*, published in 1795–6) was rewritten on the basis of the earlier and more vivid draft called *Wilhelm Meisters Theatralische Sendung* (the *Theatrical Mission*, begun about 1775 and discovered by chance in 1910). But even in the *Sendung*, although it is concerned mainly with Wilhelm's vocation to the stage, and apparently ends with the realization that this is the true path for him to follow, there are signs of the symbolism of the final version. Wilhelm in the *Sendung* meets the same motley crowd of actors and theatre-managers as he does in the *Lehrjahre*; he also meets the strange, hermaphrodite young dancer Mignon who threads a mysterious path through the whole narrative, as well as her guardian and friend, the almost insane yet well-wishing Harper, and has a glimpse of the ideal figure of Natalie, the 'beautiful Amazon' whom he is about to marry in the final pages of the version published by Goethe—indeed it is with a vision of Natalie crowning his endeavours that the *Sendung* ends. All this is an initial exploration of the divided self which Goethe was to make more prominent, and yet treat more distantly, in the *Lehrjahre*.

For although the novel is full of minor incidents and digressions, it is bound together by the developing relationship between Wilhelm and Mignon and the Harper, and by Wilhelm's intermittent quest for the 'Amazon' who appears to him in almost visionary splendour as he lies wounded after an attack by robbers.[1] Just as in *Faust* the plot is partly concerned with the tragic dichotomy in the hero, the 'two souls' in him which are in conflict,[2] so Wilhelm Meister, though himself a placid and comparatively unadventurous character, is aware of similar dichotomies outside him and of the possibility of their fusion into a harmonious unity. Some of this awareness takes the shape of the mysterious, intuitive, yearning Mignon, with her dual sex (in the *Sendung* she is referred to both as 'she' and as 'he', as though Goethe himself were still uncertain about her). Though the full nature and meaning of Mignon is impossible to define, she does represent that still unbroken unity which Goethe sometimes felt to be at the roots of his own being, and which he felt to be lost in the one-sided individuality, the 'Vereinzelung' of human life, in contrast to the all-embracing divine life. The Harper, on the other hand, is not a unity but rather a man tormented with the awareness of extreme opposites in his experience: where Mignon, at least at the outset, hovers fleetingly between either extreme of sex, the Harper has suffered from his experience of the greatest oscillations: in his youth, he relates at one point—and there is evidence that Goethe could have spoken of himself in identical terms—he abandoned himself entirely to an alternation of mystical bliss and dreadful desolation. 'I am entitled to speak', he says, 'for

I have suffered as few men have, from the supreme, sweetest exaltation to the most terrible deserts of helplessness, vacuity, annihilation and despair, from the loftiest intimations of super-terrestrial beings down to the most radical disbelief, to disbelief in myself.' In many ways the Harper represents that side of Goethe which could write *Faust*. But he has sought release from his psychological malaise not as Goethe did, but by means of incest with his sister, in which he saw a symbol of the rejoining of complementary opposites such as Goethe himself could not have accepted.[1] 'Consider the lilies', the Harper says in his own defence: 'do not husband and wife derive from one stem? Are not both of them united by the flower which gave birth to both, and is not the lily the image of innocence, and is not its union of brother with sister fruitful?' Mignon, it eventually proves, is the Harper's child. Thus Wilhelm is constantly in touch with these two people in whom the whole idea of sex, which differentiates most human beings more sharply than anything else, is indistinct, or tending to revert back to an earlier unity (earlier in the sense that primitive forms of life are sexually undifferentiated).

Wilhelm's own quest is differently directed, and it is significant that both Mignon and the Harper die before the first novel, the *Lehrjahre*, is completed. For Wilhelm, the object of his quest is Natalie, who on her first appearance to him in the forest (where his wound is not meant to be thought of as merely physical) is like a supernatural vision:

Wilhelm, den der heilsame Blick ihrer Augen bisher festgehalten hatte, war nun, als der Überrock fiel, von ihrer schönen Gestalt überrascht. Sie trat näher herzu und legte den Rock sanft über ihn. In diesem Augenblicke, da er den Mund öffnen und einige Worte des Dankes stammeln wollte, wirkte der lebhafte Eindruck ihrer Gegenwart so sonderbar auf seine schon angegriffenen Sinne, daß es ihm auf einmal vorkam, als sei ihr Haupt mit Strahlen umgeben, und über ihr ganzes Bild verbreite sich nach und nach ein glänzendes Licht.*

---

* Wilhelm, who had till this moment been fascinated by the healing look in her eyes, was now, as the cloak fell from her shoulders, astounded at her

She stands for something in Goethe's own life which he expressed at one time by the visionary woman of the poem
'Zueignung', at another by Helen of Troy in *Faust*, and which
he experienced through his encounter with Charlotte von Stein.
Yet Natalie has a quality which distinguishes her from these
and brings her closer to Mignon. She recalls to Wilhelm the
figure of Clorinda, the warrior-woman in Tasso's *Jerusalem
Delivered*, who had also impressed the youthful Goethe, and
Clorinda is described in the novel as the 'Mannweib', the man-
woman, no doubt partly because she dresses as a soldier, partly
because the dual sex was, as Goethe knew from his studies of
occult authors, a symbol of perfection. (There are echoes of
this in the psychology of C. G. Jung.) To bring together
opposite sides of his own nature was always one of Goethe's
aims. He symbolizes this in the vision of Natalie, whom
Wilhelm scarcely ever sees but who leads him onward until
the final pages of the *Lehrjahre*, when she consents to marry him.
At the same time Goethe seems to express something of his
own experience in love by showing Wilhelm repeatedly mistaking some other woman for Natalie, whom he has after all
only glimpsed for an instant, as though hinting that all of
them are reflections of that supreme perfection she possesses.
Of one of them, who actually dresses in male costume, Goethe
allows a character to remark that she is 'a true Amazon, whereas others only walk about in this ambiguous costume as pretty
hermaphrodites'. The implication appears to be that the
'Amazon' is a true fusion of contrasted and complementary
opposites, such as Goethe spoke of frequently in his scientific
writings,[1] whereas others still have less than a seamless unity.

The *Lehrjahre* ends as Wilhelm is about to wed Natalie.
When the *Wanderjahre* begins he has already left her; it is as
though Goethe were unwilling or unable to say what that union
was like: it was ineffable, perhaps, and instantaneous. All the

beautiful form. She approached, and gently laid the coat over him. At this
moment, as he sought to open his mouth and stammer a few words of thanks,
the vivid impression of her presence had so strange an effect on his already
affected senses that it seemed to him all at once as though her head were
surrounded by rays of light, and a gleam spread over her whole person.

same, he does provide a little more indication of his meaning, especially in the references to the 'sick son of a king' and the princess who approaches his bed to heal him, in a picture which Wilhelm remembers from his youth and which turns up again in the final pages. It seems fairly likely that the symbolism of this picture is to be related to the frequent talk in the novel of Hamlet, Wilhelm's favourite character in all Shakespeare (after whom Wilhelm is named). The cure for Hamlet's and Wilhelm's melancholy and despair is to be found through some such woman as Natalie: Wilhelm believes this to be his destiny, already foreshadowed in his fascination with the picture and the figure of Clorinda.

Wilhelm himself is a man of no particular distinction, passive as a rule, and scarcely aware of what he is doing. He is humane, loyal to the theatrical troupe and not ungenerous; he has a tendency to lecture them, but cares for the Harper and Mignon especially; he acquiesces in the love of many women rather than actively sets out to woo them, and is sometimes unaware precisely which of them is sharing his bed. When Goethe says that he wrote the *Lehrjahre* 'as a sleepwalker', one would like to apply the word to Wilhelm also, for he has almost no sense of will or purpose, and even the quest for Natalie is conducted in no vigorous or continuous way. 'Meister', Goethe said in 1814, 'had to be still fermenting, wavering and pliant so that the other characters might develop round him and in contact with him...He was a kind of rod up which the tender ivy could grow.' And indeed, rather as Faust remains in the background of *Part II*, his place being taken by Homunculus, Euphorion, Lynkeus, and sometimes even Mephistopheles, so also Wilhelm seems to exist in and through others rather than in his own right.

The parallel with *Faust* can be taken a little further, for the play was not only the other work which occupied most of Goethe's lifetime; the novel took the same form, having as it were a First and a Second Part in the *Lehrjahre* and the *Wanderjahre*, and even (though less significantly) having an *Urmeister* to correspond to the *Urfaust*. Moreover, there is a sense in

which the love of Wilhelm for Mignon, like that of Faust for
Gretchen (Goethe mentions in his autobiography that the
original of Gretchen in real life used to wear boy's clothing), is
intensified and realized on a higher plane in the love for Natalie
and for Helen. The conclusions of each work are also similar:
both Wilhelm and Faust end by working for the good of the
community, one as a surgeon, the other by reclaiming land
from the sea and establishing a free society.

Again, in rewriting his youthful work, Goethe took towards
it a more detached attitude, just as he did in *Faust*. It required
the encouragement of Schiller in 1794 to make Goethe return
to the *Sendung*; when he did so, the manuscript underwent
many changes. Possibly most important, he changed or developed the ending of the *Sendung*, which had seemed to set
the seal on Wilhelm's career in the theatre. In the *Lehrjahre*,
Wilhelm once again sees a vision of the 'Amazon' as he signs
the contract with the theatre-manager, just as he does at the
end of the *Sendung*, but this time Mignon, as though standing
for his intuition, tries to hinder him, and the episode is merely
one among many more that follow. The triumph on the stage
is no longer the climax of Wilhelm's career, but merely one
step in his progress. In addition, the mysterious strangers who
had occasionally appeared in the *Sendung* with advice and
warnings now prove to be members of a kind of Masonic
society, the Company of the Tower, who watch over Wilhelm's life and to some extent guide it (Goethe was a Free-
mason most of his life). This appears to be a purely human
society, although some of the events apparently caused by it
have a supernatural quality. Thus when Wilhelm plays Hamlet
small flames appear unexpectedly on the stage when the ghost
moves in the 'cellarage'; the ghost itself bears an extraordinary
resemblance to Wilhelm's own father, it sinks into the ground
very realistically, and leaves Wilhelm with a veil inscribed with
the words 'For the first and last time: Flee, young man, flee!'
(These are reminiscent of the message 'Homo fuge' received
by the legendary Faust.) All this suggests that the Company
is taking the part of Fate, and has an unusual control of affairs.

It also shows how Goethe's conception of Wilhelm's destiny had altered since he first conceived the novel. Having been to Italy, and having had there the fantastic sense of penetrating to the heart of Nature, Goethe felt his life to have been guided to this great moment, and no doubt wanted to make this awareness show in his description of Wilhelm. The Company, which he may dimly have intended to draw into the first version, became more and more important in the second, the final books being entirely concerned with it and with Wilhelm's gaining of the 'Lehrbrief' or diploma certifying his initiation into life.

In the rewriting Goethe also altered the style and tone. Where the *Sendung* had told a straightforward narrative of Wilhelm's childhood interest in marionettes and its development into a passion for the live theatre, mirroring Goethe's own childhood, the *Lehrjahre* begins at a point when Wilhelm is already a young man, and makes him tell the story of his youth to the actress Mariane in her dressing-room. The result is a loss in directness and vividness, which Goethe seems candidly to acknowledge when he reports that Mariane almost fell asleep during Wilhelm's narrative. Goethe's intention was very probably to indicate that he did not now share Wilhelm's view of the importance of these early days (seeing that the novel was to take Wilhelm past his purely 'threatrical mission'); all the same, he cannot blame the reader who sympathizes with Mariane and wishes the novel were more entertaining at this point. And when he now makes Wilhelm, aware of his loquacity, turn to the vivacious Mariane with the words 'Now it is for you, Mariane, to tell me of your own youthful pleasures...Tell me, under what circumstances were you educated? What are the first vivid impressions you remember?' he makes his hero appear unnecessarily dull and condescending, thanks to the unskilful use of dialogue to narrate the past.

The later version is certainly ironical up to a point: Goethe speaks of Wilhelm now as 'our friend', and seems as a rule aware of the limited nature of Wilhelm's achievements. So stilted does his language become, however, that the degree and

frequency of his irony must often be in doubt. Thus, after
Wilhelm has overheard the Harper singing one of the most
bitter songs Goethe ever wrote, we find him entering the old
man's room and congratulating him on being able to occupy
himself so agreeably in his solitude.[1] Here one might still just
suppose that Goethe intended to draw attention to the complete insensitivity of Wilhelm. Yet it is very hard indeed to
suppose the same of such a passage as the one following, in
which Mignon gives vent to her grief at the news that Wilhelm had decided to abandon his career in the theatre, and
which is both rhythmically and verbally so bathetic, so clinical
and yet so sentimental, as to come near being only ludicrous:

...Was ist dir, Mignon? rief er aus, was ist dir? Sie richtete ihr
Köpfchen auf und sah ihn an, fuhr auf einmal nach dem Herzen, wie
mit einer Gebärde, welche Schmerzen verbeißt. Er hob sie auf und
sie fiel auf seinen Schoß; er drückte sie an sich und küßte sie. Sie
antwortete durch keinen Händedruck, durch keine Bewegung. Sie
hielt ihr Herz fest, und auf einmal tat sie einen Schrei, der mit
krampfigen Bewegungen des Körpers begleitet war. Sie fuhr auf
und fiel auch sogleich wie an allen Gelenken gebrochen vor ihm
nieder. Es war ein gräßlicher Anblick! — Mein Kind! rief er aus,
indem er sie aufhob und fest umarmte, mein Kind! was ist dir? —
Die Zuckung dauerte fort, die vom Herzen sich den schlotternden
Gliedern mitteilte; sie hing nur in seinen Armen. Er schloß sie an
sein Herz und benetzte sie mit seinen Tränen. Auf einmal schien sie
wieder angespannt, wie eins, das den höchsten körperlichen
Schmerz erträgt; und bald mit einer neuen Heftigkeit wurden alle
ihre Glieder wieder lebendig, und sie warf sich ihm, wie ein
Ressort, das zuschlägt, um den Hals, indem in ihrem Innersten wie
ein gewaltiger Riß geschah, und in dem Augenblick floß ein Strom
von Tränen aus ihren geschlossenen Augen in seinen Busen. Er
hielt sie fest. Sie weinte, und keine Zunge spricht die Gewalt dieser
Tränen aus. Ihre langen Haare waren aufgegangen und hingen vor
der Weinenden nieder, und ihr ganzes Wesen schien in einen Bach
von Tränen unaufhaltsam dahinzuschmelzen. Ihre starren Glieder
wurden gelinde, es ergoß sich ihr Innerstes, und in der Verzweiflung
des Augenblickes fürchtete Wilhelm, sie werde in seinen Armen
zerschmelzen und er nichts von ihr übrig behalten! Er hielt sie nur

fester und fester. — Mein Kind! rief er aus, mein Kind! Du bist ja
mein! wenn dich das Wort trösten kann. Du bist mein! Ich werde
dich behalten, dich nicht verlassen! — Ihre Tränen flossen noch
immer. — Endlich richtete sie sich auf. Eine weiche Heiterkeit
glänzte von ihrem Gesichte. — Mein Vater! rief sie, du willst mich
nicht verlassen! willst mein Vater sein! Ich bin dein Kind!

Sanft fing vor der Türe die Harfe an zu klingen; der Alte brachte
seine herzlichsten Lieder dem Freunde zum Abendopfer, der, sein
Kind immer fester in Armen haltend, des reinsten, unbeschreib-
lichsten Glückes genoß.*¹

Such sentimentality and bathos from an author in the prime
of life, or rather approved by him in the prime of life, for the
original version was almost identical, must have been the kind

---

* 'What is the matter, Mignon', he cried, 'what is the matter?'—She lifted
her little head and looked at him, then clutched at her heart with a gesture
as though she were clenching her teeth at her sufferings. He lifted her up
and she fell onto his lap; he pressed her to him and kissed her. She answered
by never a pressure of the hand, never a word. She clasped her heart and
all at once gave a cry which was accompanied by spasmodic movements of
her body. She started up and fell down again at once at his feet, as though
all her limbs were broken. It was a hideous sight.—'My child!' he cried,
lifting her up and firmly embracing her, 'my child! What is the matter?'—
The trembling continued, communicating itself from her heart to her
shivering limbs; she did no more than hang in his arms. He clasped her to his
heart and bedewed her with his tears. Suddenly she seemed to become taut
again, like one enduring the most intense physical pain; and suddenly,
with renewed violence, all her limbs came to life again, and she threw herself round his neck like a spring snapping shut, while in her innermost being
as it were a mighty rent took place, and at the same moment a flood of
tears flowed from her closed eyes onto his bosom. He held her firmly. She
wept, and no tongue can express the violence of her tears. Her long hair was
loosened and hung down before her weeping form, and her whole being
seemed irresistibly to be melting away in a stream of tears. Her rigid limbs
grew soft; her innermost self poured forth, and in the despair of the
moment Wilhelm feared she might melt away in his arms and he would
have nothing left of her. He held her still more tightly.—'My child!', he
cried, 'my child! You are mine!—if that word can comfort you. You are
mine! I will keep you, I will never leave you!' Her tears continued to flow.
At last she rose. A mild serenity glistened from her face. 'My father!' she
cried. 'You will not leave me! You will be my father! I am your child!'
    Gently the harp began to sound outside the door. It was the old man,
bringing his most heartfelt songs to serenade his friend, who, holding his
child ever more tightly in his arms, enjoyed the purest, most indescribable
happiness.

of thing which made Samuel Butler ask, after reading *Wilhelm Meister* in translation, whether it was a hoax, and whether a man of Goethe's genius could have written it at all. And we cannot reply that Goethe was being ironical here, for there is nothing for him to be ironical about.

The latter parts of the *Lehrjahre* were not rewritten but added to the parts already forming the *Sendung*, which correspond to the first five books of the final work. Here once again the necessity to force the pace, to complete the novel at a time when real inspiration was lacking, is evident. The sixth book, entitled *Confessions of a Beautiful Soul*, has nothing to do with Wilhelm Meister at all, beyond the fact that it is read by a friend of his towards the end of Book 5. In the spirit of the day, which was accustomed to the insertion of separate stories in novels, as in *Tom Jones* and *Pickwick Papers*, Goethe includes the confessions as a tribute to the mentor of his youth, Susanne von Klettenberg, although this lady is not mentioned by name, and the supposed author of the confessions proves later to be an aunt of Natalie's. When, however, the narrative returns to Wilhelm and his doings, it becomes impossible to follow without the most stringent concentration. New characters come and go before they have had time to establish themselves, and leave behind little but the memory of their names. The writing becomes more and more abstract; less and less happens, and banal conversations take up more and more time.

At length, at the end of the Seventh Book, Wilhelm is admitted to a solemn ceremony, where an invisible speaker addresses him from above an altar in a former chapel, and reveals himself as one of the secret guides whom Wilhelm has already encountered on his way through life. The curtains behind the altar open and shut several times to reveal yet more of these mysterious personages, the last of whom forbids him to argue and informs him that he is saved and on the way to his goal. Thereupon the curtains open for the last time to reveal the King of Denmark in complete armour, who tells Wilhelm that he is his father's spirit and bids him enjoy the happiness he has prepared for him. All this portentousness is in preparation for the handing over to Wilhelm of his 'Lehrbrief', a no less portentous and trivial document which begins as follows:

Die Kunst ist lang, das Leben kurz, das Urteil schwierig, die Gelegenheit flüchtig. Handeln ist leicht, denken schwer: nach dem Gedachten handeln unbequem. Aller Anfang ist heiter, die Schwelle ist der Platz der Erwartung. Der Knabe staunt, der Eindruck bestimmt ihn; er lernt spielend, der Ernst überrascht ihn. Die Nachahmung ist uns angeboren, das Nachzuahmende wird nicht leicht erkannt. Selten wird das Treffliche gefunden, seltner geschätzt. Die Höhe reizt uns, nicht die Stufen; den Gipfel im Auge, wandeln wir gern auf der Ebene.*[1]

After some twenty lines of similar content, the awarder of the 'Lehrbrief' himself stops Wilhelm reading further, and the reader may well feel this as a recognition of its jejuneness.

But this is the climax of the novel, reached after some five or six hundred pages; it cannot be thought ironical by any reasonable standard. This, we have to believe, is what the mature Goethe in his mid-forties thought worth communicating to the world as the fruits of his search for wisdom, and we can only stand dismayed at the deterioration of his genius. The plan and intention of the work promises much. Its realization is as flatly disappointing as a work of art could well be.

The sequel to the *Lehrjahre*, the *Wanderjahre*, in which Wilhelm, having passed his apprenticeship, goes out as a journeyman—his 'mastership', in the sense of the medieval guilds, being postponed until the very last pages—was begun within a dozen years of the publication of the earlier part. At first, Goethe wrote separate stories, most of them published in magazines between 1808 and 1818. These then formed the basis of the novel, which appeared in a first edition in 1821, and in a

---

* Art is long, life is short; judgment is difficult, opportunity fleeting. Action is easy, thought is difficult; action in accordance with what has been thought is inconvenient. All beginning is gay, the threshold is the place of expectation. The boy stands astonished; impressions rule him. He learns by playing, seriousness takes him by surprise. Imitation is inborn in us; it is not easy to see what to imitate. It is not often that true excellence is found, still less often is it esteemed. The heights attract us, not the steps; with the summit in view we gladly wander on the plain.

second, enlarged one in 1829. This basis, however, inevitably influenced the novel in its form. The published stories were not themselves about Wilhelm, and in order to incorporate them Goethe adopted the device, already used for the *Confessions of a Beautiful Soul*, of having them mentioned by someone who had read them, whereupon Wilhelm himself in some cases read them also, while in others they were related by some other person. One of Goethe's chief problems here was that, unlike the contemporary novels in which short stories were inserted here and there within the main narrative, his novel consisted to a very large extent of such stories, the narrative linking them together only in a tenuous way. To overcome this, perhaps, he linked stories to narrative by making characters who appeared in the one appear also in the other, but the effect of this was strange, for the characters in the stories inevitably seemed to be fictional people when they appeared in 'real' life, and the artistic unity of the novel could not be sustained. However, as before, Goethe continued to use the novel as a means of writing about the inward landscape which often preoccupied him, and in comparison with the *Lehrjahre* he was sometimes more successful. Certain themes evidently haunt his mind repeatedly: he writes stories of a father and a son who are both in love with the same woman; or of a man who falls in love with a woman, falsely believing her to be someone else; several stories are concerned with mysterious boxes or keys, or with drownings. One of the strange fascinations of the book is the dream-like images which recur everywhere, inexplicable but oddly memorable: the sight of the man skating over frozen flood-water and seeming to be issuing from the low full moon behind his back; the tunnel which leads to a giant castle; the summer-house on a hill-top with its strange arrangement of mirrors which suddenly provide a blinding image of the sun; the path up a mountain by night, on which mysterious flames show the way. The book also contains a Utopia, and a description of the schools there, in which are taught the three forms of reverence which so impressed Carlyle,[1] the mystically inclined Makarie, who is said to move freely in spirit about the solar system, an account of anatomical classes and of Wilhelm's repugnance at cutting up dead bodies of real men and women, an account of the precise operations in use amongst a spinning community in the Alps, plans for developing new land, not without some echoes of Faust's similar project at the end of his life, arguments about the origin of the world and about the proper study of mankind.

As this list may indicate, it is often difficult to perceive any connecting links between one part and another. Goethe himself was content occasionally to speak of the novel as a bouquet, as an 'Aggregat' in which it was pointless to look for any systematic construction,[1] although he also said[2] that 'the connection, aim and purpose lies inside the book itself; though it may not be all of a piece, it is all of a sense, and this was just my problem, to present to the feelings a number of strange external events as a harmony'. Nevertheless, try as one may, it seems impossible to find any such harmony. The expectation of finding one is lessened on hearing from Eckermann[3] how Goethe compiled the novel with the help of a bound volume containing the portions already written, in which the spaces to be filled were indicated by blank sheets of paper, or how, having a large number of aphorisms at his disposal and not knowing how otherwise to fill up the requisite number of volumes expected by his publisher for the collected works, Goethe decided to insert them in the *Wanderjahre*, where they occupied several score of pages, on the pretext that they were taken from certain archives which happened to have been mentioned in the novel.[4] (The aphorisms were withdrawn and printed separately in later editions.) There are too many signs of such disregard of the reader's interest to encourage any serious hope of finding a unifying thread. Characters are referred to before they have been introduced, as though they were already known. Certain words become stock formulae of no distinctive meaning: 'heiter', 'geistreich', 'angenehm', 'behaglich', 'bedeutend' are used frequently without adding much to the sense of the passages where they occur. All the stories are mystifying, not in the sense that they remain in the

mind with the mystery of a poem, but with the irritating sense
of a riddle which does not appear to have any answer. Goethe
intervenes from time to time to pass observations on his own
task as a novelist:

to make clear the importance of this scene, I must report in more
detail on the character and nature of this woman;

in order not to judge our friend falsely, we must direct our attention
to the origins and rise of this worthy personage of advanced years;

here we find ourselves in the position of announcing to the reader
a pause, which is of some years' duration, for which reason we
would gladly have finished off a volume at this point, had this been
possible to combine with the typographical arrangements. However,
the space between two chapters will suffice to bridge over the afore-
said period of time, as we have long been accustomed to allow such
things to happen between the fall and rise of the curtain while we
have been personally present.

Such flaccid, over-explanatory prose becomes wearisome after
only a few repetitions. But apart from all this, Goethe does not
even appear to have completed the book for publication. There
is one story in the *Wanderjahre* which simply breaks off in the
telling, without apology or warning, and its title 'Nicht zu
weit' seems to have no other meaning than that the story is not
intended to go on for too long.

With all these faults it is only reasonable to quote the out-
spoken words of George Henry Lewes, despite the recent
attempts at rehabilitation of this work of Goethe's old age:

It is easy [wrote Lewes in the first full-scale biography of Goethe
ever to be written] for admirers of this work to cite very beautiful
passages; and it is by no means difficult to read under its symbolical
dullness any profound meanings the interpreter wishes to read there.
But for my own part, greatly as I admire Goethe, and profoundly as
his works affect me, I do not recognise in the *Wanderjahre* the old
magic, nor can my love for that writer persuade me that it is well
written, well conceived, or intelligibly executed. I quarrel with no
man who finds delight in the book; but candour compels me to

own that I find in it almost every fault a work can have: it is unintelligible, it is tiresome, it is fragmentary, it is dull, and it is often ill-written.

Or as Henry James more gently but more enigmatically added,

it will be seen that taken as a whole, *Wilhelm Meister* is anything but a novel, as we have grown to understand the word. As a whole, it has, in fact, no very definite character, and, were we not vaguely convinced that its greatness as work of art resides in this very absence of form, we should say that, as a work of art, it is lamentably defective.

Yet this is the novel of which it has been said, in support of the view of so renowned a critic as Friedrich Schlegel, that,

it is a book which 'saves the critic the trouble of judgement'. And why? Because it holds no mystery: 'it judges itself.' And not only does it judge itself, it also represents itself—together with the story it purposes to represent.

To realize the distance between such an observation and the kind of criticism represented by Lewes and James is to understand better the difference between the Romantic theory of self-awareness as self-justification, to which Goethe often subscribed, and to which he gave expression through the irony *Wilhelm Meister* is said to contain, and the contrary belief that self-awareness by itself is rather more likely to lead to tautology and platitude. From one point of view, the fact that Goethe was aware of his limitations, and sought to counterbalance them with irony, worked to his detriment as a novelist. From another, that of no less a man than Schlegel, it was the very thing that made his novel great.

PART IV

1786 TO 1832

10

POEMS OF THE CLASSICAL PERIOD

One surprising thing about the Italian Journey of 1786–8 is the almost complete drying-up of lyric poetry in Goethe, so long as the journey lasted. He did many other things of course; he rewrote or added to several of his best-known plays, he began epics on the Homeric model, he studied enthusiastically a number of topics, he was repeatedly seized with the feeling that he was undergoing a rebirth, and the sexual desires which had almost certainly been stifled at Weimar were now liberated. But his feelings scarcely ever found expression in verse, as they had done in the days before he went to Weimar, and of the poems written in these two years the memorable ones (almost the only ones) are the two sardonic 'Cophtische Lieder', the narration in which Cupid paints a pretty girl who suddenly walks out of the canvas to greet the poet ('Amor als Landschaftsmaler') and the other amusing trifle 'Cupido, loser, eigensinniger Knabe'.

The real fruits of the journey, poetically speaking, came later, after Goethe had returned to Weimar and settled down to live with Christiane Vulpius, for whom and largely about whom he wrote the *Römische Elegien*. With these celebrations of erotic love, modelled on Catullus, Tibullus and Propertius, Goethe struck out a completely new line. He had experimented briefly with classical metres, that is with hexameters and pentameters rather than with the French classicizing alexandrine, as early as 1778. From 1788 onwards, when the *Elegien* were begun, he used this metre in preference to any others for some ten to fifteen years: the great bulk of his poetry immediately after Italy is in this Graeco-Roman form, and Homer became his ideal of the poet. 'Studying Homer again', he writes in an off moment, untypical of him as a whole, 'I feel what unspeakable damage the whole Jewish debauchery has inflicted on us. If we had never heard of these Sodomite practices, these Eyptian and Babylonian fantasies, if Homer had remained our

Bible, what a completely different form mankind would have adopted.' Goethe believed in Homer as a Bible because the excellence of Greek art was based on the excellence of the Greek way of life; and the Greek way of life was based on the principle that every faculty in man should be allowed to develop freely in accordance with its nature. In modern society with its social and religious taboos, such free and natural development was impossible. Goethe was determined to live the natural life, allowing himself also the natural sexual promiscuity of the male, as he believed the Greeks to have done, and thereby he helped to found that myth which ran throughout the nineteenth and into the twentieth century, the myth of the uninhibited Greek, set against that of the hamstrung Christian.

The subject-matter of the *Elegien* is therefore not only sexual love but also the insistence on the male prerogative. As the Third Elegy puts it to a lover whom the poet has rapidly seized and taken to bed,

In the heroic age, when gods and goddesses loved, desire arose at first sight, enjoyment came hard on desire. Do you suppose the goddess of love deliberated long, when once in the grove of Ida Anchises took her fancy? Had Luna been slow to kiss the fair sleeper [Endymion], swiftly Aurora would have waked him in envy. Hero caught sight of Leander at the gay festival, and straight the lover plunged into the midnight flood. Rhea Sylvia, the royal maiden, goes down to the Tiber to draw water, and a god seizes her.

No distinction is drawn between the love of Hero and Leander and the brutal taking of a princess by Mars, and one is reminded of the line from a much later poem, 'Wiederfinden', where this confusion of love and lust is given explicit approval: 'Sei's Ergreifen, sei es Raffen, wenn es nur sich faßt und hält'.*

This is not to say that the whole of the *Elegien* make the same confusion. On the contrary, some of them are, for their time, amazingly and gratifyingly frank in their evocations of love-making, and Goethe's attitude to his mistress is usually softened by a certain humour:

* No matter whether it be seizing or snatching, so long as they hold and clasp one another.

Herbstlich leuchtet die Flamme vom ländlich geselligen Herde,
  Knistert und glänzet, wie rasch! sausend vom Reisig empor.
Diesen Abend erfreut sie mich mehr; denn eh noch zur Kohle
  Sich das Bündel verzehrt, unter die Asche sich neigt,
Kommt mein liebliches Mädchen. Dann flammen Reisig und Scheite,
  Und die erwärmete Nacht wird uns ein glänzendes Fest.
Morgen frühe geschäftig verläßt sie das Lager der Liebe,
  Weckt aus der Asche behend Flammen aufs neue hervor.
Denn vor andern verlieh der Schmeichlerin Amor die Gabe,
  Freude zu wecken, die kaum still wie zu Asche versank.*

He may end one Elegy with the line—'Und der Barbare beherrscht römischen Busen und Leib'†—as though consciously
comparing himself with one of Attila's Huns, but a reader can
only feel that this is being said with a certain self-mockery. As
Friedrich Schlegel wrote, not long after the Elegies first
appeared, there is 'here and there a breath of parody, a gentle
comical touch'; Goethe is aware that he is looking back to
antiquity, and his tongue is very slightly in his cheek, as the
opening words of the first Elegy must make plain:

> Saget, Steine, mir an, o sprecht, ihr hohen Paläste!
> Straßen, redet ein Wort! Genius, regst du dich nicht?‡

There is something of the Strasbourg and Frankfurt Goethe
lurking behind these lines: the man who could tease Friederike
Brion with mock acceptance of classical conventions, and who
still imitates his classical models with a smiling nonchalance.
But there is also something in the *Elegies* of a Goethe who had
scarcely been seen since the anacreontic days of Leipzig, en-

---

* The autumnal flame gleams out from the rustic, companionable hearthplace,
  crackling and shining and leaping so swift from the bundle of twigs. On
  this evening it pleases me more, for before they are burned down, ere they
  sink under ash, my darling maiden is coming. Then will flame twigs and
  whole faggots, and the warming night will be for us one gleaming feast.
  Tomorrow early she'll rise, busily from the bed of love, nimbly awakening
  flames from the ash. For this temptress was granted by Amor the gift, more
  than others, of wakening joys that have scarcely sunk, as though to ash.
† And the barbarian bestrides a Roman body and bosom.
‡ Tell me, you stones, O speak, you lofty palaces; streets, utter a word,
  genius of this place, do you not stir a limb?

joying himself more or less without shame (though there is still here and there a certain awkwardness, a need to declare a justification rather than simply to assert once and for all).

But there was something unnatural in the whole attempt at writing hexameters and elegiac couplets, and this is perhaps the strangest thing about the whole 'rebirth' which the Italian Journey implied. These metres were first used in languages which reckoned by the quantity or length of a syllable, that is, the time it took to speak it, rather than by the accent—this is true at least of Greek, if not of Latin, which was already becoming an accented language in Vergil's time. The foot of the ancient hexameter corresponds to a bar of music in duple-time, composed of two beats of equal length:

Arma vir / umque can / o

When a hexameter is read accentually, as it is in German and other modern languages, it tends to fall into triple time:

Árma vir / úmque can / ó

This Goethe had yet to realize at the time of writing the *Elegies*. As a result his classical lines are often awkward to read: words which are naturally long are crowded together, each into the space, as it were, of a crotchet, when they require a minim, and from time to time the reader needs to reflect and try several arrangements before hitting on the particular one that Goethe seems to have intended.

The hexameter requires six feet, of which the first four may be spondees or dactyls (′ ′ or ′ ˣ ˣ), the fifth must be a dactyl, and the sixth a spondee or trochee. The pentameter, which always follows the hexameter in an elegiac couplet, has four spondees or dactyls (though dactyls are more frequent) and divides its fifth foot between a 'long' syllable in the middle and a 'long' one at the end. Schiller's paradigm gives a reasonably good example, though the stresses are not quite natural, and it must be remembered not only that in most of the feet the second 'long' can be replaced by two 'shorts', but that in accepted German practice a spondee is quite commonly a trochee:

Im Hex | -ameter | steigt ‖ des | Springquells | flüssige | Säule

Im Pent | -ameter | drauf ‖ fällt sie mel | -odisch her | -ab*

Goethe writes in much the same fashion, substituting an occasional dactyl for a spondee as the convention allows, as here:

Laß dich, Ge | -liebte, nicht | reun, ‖ daß | du mir so | schnell dich er | -geben!

Glaub es, ich | denke nicht | frech, ‖ denke nicht | niedrig von | dir†

The stress on 'du' in the first line gives an unneeded emphasis, but otherwise the metre reads perfectly well, so long as you regard it as an accented line in triple time. More difficult to read is a line like this,

Dann versteh ich den Marmor erst recht, ich denk und vergleiche,‡

which, in order to fit the hexameter, must be read

′ ′ | ′ × × | ′ ‖ × × | ′ ′ | ′ | ′ × × | ′ ×

but which in normal speech is likely to be read:

′ × ′ × × ′ ′ ′ ′ × ′ × × ′ ×

The very frequent occurrence of lines like these not only makes for difficult reading; when the ear has grown accustomed to the

* In the hexameter rises the fountain's silvery column;
  In the pentameter aye falling in melody back. (Coleridge's translation)
† Do not repent it, my dear, that you yielded to me so quickly. Believe me, I do not think impudently or cheaply of you.
‡ Then above all I understand marble, I think and compare.

reading which is intended, little is gained. The significance of the poem is not enriched by any counterpoint of stress and metre, words do not acquire added meaning from their position in the line, on the contrary, as in the case of the 'du' just mentioned, stresses often have to be disregarded because they are obviously not meant to be significant but only to maintain the impression that the classical line is still continuing.

Yet Goethe used these metres not only in the *Venezianische Epigramme* of 1790—a collection of Venetian impressions and erotica based on the Latin elegists and Martial—but also in the fragments of epics imitated from Homer, *Nausikaa* (begun 1787), and *Achilleis* (begun 1798), the completed epic *Reineke Fuchs* (1793), the longer poems *Alexis und Dora* (1796), *Euphrosyne* (1797), *Amyntas* (1797), the epigrams written in conjunction with Schiller under the name *Xenien* (1796) and those written after Schiller's death under the title *Zahme Xenien* (1820-7), the 'scientific' poems originally meant for a large-scale work imitating Lucretius, entitled 'Metamorphose der Tiere' (1806) and 'Metamorphose der Pflanzen' (1798), the mysterious, incomprehensible *Weissagungen des Bakis* (1798) and several smaller works.

The most considerable of all these classically inspired poems, apart from the Roman Elegies, remains, however, the completed epic *Hermann und Dorothea* (1796), a deliberate attempt at recreating the Homeric epic in modern terms. Goethe was still hampered here by his choice of classical metre, it is true, and enough must be said to indicate to what extent the 'tyranny of Greece over Germany', as it has been called, was still governing him to his detriment. On the other hand, the purpose of the poem is so completely contrary to that of the *Römische Elegien* as to deserve special comment.

Goethe's use of the hexameter remains as arbitrary as before. Apart from the uncertainty throughout, whether words like 'mit', 'und', 'ihr' and 'mein' are long or short, accented or unaccented, until the whole line has been scanned, there are lines which either could only loosely be reckoned as hexameters, such as 'Von der Erde sich nährend, die weit und breit

sich auftut',* or which demand the impossible in altering
natural stresses, as for instance

> Mit der Kinder roher und übermütiger Unart,†
> (′ ′ ′ ′ ′ x x ′ ′ ′ x x ′ ′)

and

> Heil dem Bürger des kleinen
> Städtchens, welcher ländlich Gewerb mit Bürgergewerb paart!‡
> (‾ ‾ | ‾ ‾ | ‾ x x | ‾ ‾ | ‾ x x | ‾ ‾)

The difficulties of fitting the metre also lead to constructions
which in German look contorted, although in Latin they
would be acceptable:

Und es hörte die Frage, die freundliche, gern in dem Schatten
Hermann des herrlichen Baums,§

or

Alles regt sich, als wollte die Welt, die gestaltete, rückwärts
Lösen in Chaos und Nacht sich auf und neu sich gestalten.‖

Again, while the platitudes of some of the characters are no
doubt meant to indicate their natures, the phrasing of both the
narrator and the characters tends to repetitions and pleonastic
interpolations whose only purpose can be to fill out the line,
as in

> 'Vollendet es selbst; ich gehe zu Bette.'
> Und er wandte sich schnell und eilte, zur Kammer zu gehen,
> Wo ihm das Ehbett stand, und wo er zu ruhen gewohnt war.¶

---

* Nourishing itself on the earth, which opens up far and wide.
† With the rude, exuberant misbehaviour of children.
‡ Praise to the citizen of the small town, who combines country trade and
  town trade.
§ And Hermann gladly heard the friendly question in the shade of the splendid
  tree.
‖ All things are stirring, as though the well-fashioned world were about to
  turn back and dissolve in chaos and night, and be fashioned anew.
¶ 'Complete the matter yourselves, I am going to bed.' And he quickly
  turned and hastened to enter the chamber where his marriage-bed stood,
  where he was accustomed to slumber.

or

> Aber ich wünsche,
> Daß der Herr Pfarrer sich auch in Eurer Gesellschaft befinde.*

or

> Da versetzte der Vater und tat bedeutend den Mund auf.†

Despite the long discussions with Voss (who thought very poorly of Goethe's classical verse) and Schiller and Moritz, all of whom were concerned with recreating the Greek world in Germany, Goethe appears far too often to have written lines which will not scan properly either accentually or quantitatively, and to have allowed himself some latitude in presenting such verses to a public whom he was concerned to educate. It is sometimes suggested that he is ironical in this poem too, as he was in the Elegies, and certainly we may suppose that the lines put into the mouth of the slightly comical apothecary about the pleasingly painted stone dwarves in his garden expressed no view of Goethe's own. On the whole, however, this is a serious poem and in intention a moralizing one, in which irony does not play an obvious part. In any case, if you intend to mock the German 'Bürger', however lightly, by writing about him in the way that Homer wrote about the Achaean heroes, your weapons need to have a sharp edge.

The morality expressed in *Hermann und Dorothea*, and surely intended to all intents and purposes to be taken without reservations, is completely opposed to that of the *Elegies*. There is a patriarchal flavour about the whole story, often Biblical in origin, as in the scene where Hermann meets Dorothea by the well, with its reminiscences of Jacob and Rachel, Isaac and Rebecca. (There is a similar scene in *Werther*.) This in itself serves to show how little store Goethe set by the sneering attack on the Jews already quoted—indeed he was always proudly aware of being 'bibelfest', and was strongly influenced by Biblical language and imagery throughout his life. One of

---

* But I wish that Mr Parson may also find himself in your company.
† Then the father replied, and opened his mouth with solemnity.

Goethe's main purposes in writing the epic was to contrast traditional 'bürgerlich' German values with the violent, new-fangled, rationalistic ideas being propagated by the revolution-aries in France. The story is as simple as it well could be: Hermann, the son of a well-to-do farmer, brings home a refugee from German territory across the Rhine, Dorothea, from a nearby village to which she has come with a party of other refugees. Hermann's father is at first opposed to the match, but yields to the persuasion of the mother, and of the parson and the apothecary, when he sees how well suited to his son Dorothea is. Apart from one or two 'flashbacks', that is the whole of the action, and the greater part of the poem is in the form of discussions about the suitability of the young woman and the justness of the father's opposition. In the course of these dialogues, however, a great deal emerges about the virtues that are most valued: thrift, good husbandry, modesty, charitableness, generosity, cleanliness and orderliness. More than this, these qualities are hypostasized in a way which de-rives in large part from Goethe's admiration for the Greeks. As a young man, before the Italian journey, he had had that liking for certain words, 'gut', 'heilig', 'selig' and so on, which has already been noted.[1] Now this receives a new expression in the Homeric epithet, by which each character is described from time to time by means of the same adjective: Goethe's epic continually speaks of 'der treffliche Pfarrer', 'der edle verständige Pfarrherr', 'die gute, verständige Mutter', 'das herrliche Mädchen', 'das herrliche Paar'.* That four out of the six principal characters are 'trefflich', 'verständig' and 'herr-lich' is indeed an aspect of the idealization, in the philosophical sense of the word, which Goethe intended. These people were not to be seen merely as themselves (though there is some degree of characteristic differentiation between the negligent, miserly apothecary, the benevolent parson, the gruff but good-hearted father and so on). They were meant to have something of that primal quality which Goethe saw in the Greeks, gleaming with

---

* the excellent parson; the noble, understanding parson; the good, under-standing mother; the splendid maiden; the splendid couple.

a real and earthly yet at the same time ideal and almost super-human life. Thus when Hermann describes Dorothea so that she may be recognized by the parson and the apothecary, the effect, partly by virtue of the hexameters, is one of statuesque grandeur, for all that he is describing what we recognize as an ordinary, traditional German peasant costume:

Aber ich geb Euch noch die Zeichen der reinlichen Kleider.
Denn der rote Latz erhebt den gewölbeten Busen,
Schön geschnürt, und es liegt das schwarze Mieder ihr knapp an;
Sauber hat sie den Saum des Hemdes zur Krause gefaltet,
Die ihr das Kinn umgibt, das runde, mit reinlicher Anmut;
Frei und heiter zeigt sich des Kopfes zierliches Eirund;
Stark sind vielmal die Zöpfe um silberne Nadeln gewickelt;
Vielgefaltet und blau fängt unter dem Latze der Rock an
Und umschlägt ihr im Gehn die wohlgebildeten Knöchel.*

And not only people are 'idealized' in this way; the goodness of clear spring water is praised, careful attention is given to the harnessing of the horses, to the 'mächtiges Korn' through which Hermann and Dorothea walk, the great pear-tree at the top of the hill, and the fine 'Römerglas', in which it is still customary today to serve wine from the Rhineland vineyards:

Sorgsam brachte die Mutter des klaren herrlichen Weines,
In geschliffener Flasche auf blankem zinnernem Runde,
Mit den grünlichen Römern, den echten Bechern des Rheinweins —.
Und so sitzend umgaben die drei den glänzend gebohnten,
Runden, braunen Tisch, er stand auf mächtigen Füßen.†

In such descriptions Goethe sought to bring these common objects to life rather as a saucepan and a candle or a leek in a

---

* But I give you this sign too, of the cleanly clothing: for the red waistcoat raises the rounded bosom, finely laced, and the black bodice fits closely; the hem of her blouse is neatly goffered, cupping her round chin with cleanly grace; free and serene is the delicate oval of her face, and her thick tresses are wound many times on silver pins; many-pleated and blue the skirt begins, under the waistcoat, swirling around her well-fashioned ankles as she goes walking.

† Carefully the mother brought the splendid clear wine in a polished flask on a gleaming pewter disc, with the green 'Römer' glasses, the true goblets for Rhine wine—and thus the three sat down around the gleamingly polished, round, brown table, standing on mighty legs.

painting by Chardin are presented, as though nothing in existence could be more of a marvel to see. (Indeed, to gain an impression in perspective of *Hermann und Dorothea*, it is best compared with all that tradition in painting which goes back beyond Chardin into the Netherlands of the seventeenth century, with its discovery of new dignity and splendour in the civilisation of the burgher.) Here was the ideal in the real, just as Goethe hoped to find it in the 'Urpflanze':[1] the Homeric world could still live, at least in poetry. And on these terms Goethe could end the poem on a patriotic note unusual for him:

Dies ist unser! so laß uns sagen und so es behaupten!
Denn es werden noch stets die entschlossenen Völker gepriesen,
Die für Gott und Gesetz, für Eltern, Weiber und Kinder
Stritten und gegen den Feind zusammenstehend erlagen.*

The 'ideals' he had put forward were not only universal and primal, but characteristically German, and thus most suited to oppose the blood-stained rulers across the frontier.

A certain weakness still remains in the thought and content of the poem, it is true. This very patriotic ending is rendered a little suspect by the fact that Hermann, who pronounces it, has already said something very similar earlier on, when his mother found him grieving beneath the pear-tree: he explained his sorrow by his frustrated desire to go out and fight against the revolutionary armies of the French, only to confess at the end of an impassioned speech that he had deliberately assumed the mood in order to deceive his mother.[2] The true cause of his sorrow, he says, was unrequited love. The memory of this is enough to make one doubt just a little his final protestation. Again, the idealization is sometimes carried out in a tactless way, as though mere size were important: thus when the lovers appear in the doorway of the room where the family awaits them it is said that the door looks too small for them to get in, and when Dorothea stumbles on the footpath, leaning her

---

* 'This is ours!' let us say, and let us maintain it so. For it is always determined nations that are praised, who fight for God and the law, for parents, wives and children, and who die together fighting against the foe.

weight on Hermann's shoulder with her cheek against his, Goethe tells us that the young man 'Trug mit Mannesgefühl die Heldengröße des Weibes'* so that the admirable sturdy quality of Dorothea is overdone, and she begins to look like one of those Valkyries who have absurdly come to be thought of as typical of German women. Hermann's weeping on his mother's bosom, by contrast, on account of the father's disregard for his son's affection, seems curiously effeminate in such a hero, and we never see him doing anything remarkable; like Wilhelm Meister and Werther, he is shy and reserved, without much will-power. (It is Dorothea of whom it is related that she snatched a sabre from a French soldier trying to rape her, and cut him down.)

All the same this is a poem which preached goodwill and good works at a time when there was particularly little of these in Europe. It begins with Dorothea helping a woman in labour, and being helped herself by Hermann with a gift of clothes from his own village, and for just such reasons as this it has enjoyed a revival recently in a dramatized form which brought out its relevance to Western Germans in their relations with compatriots fleeing from the East.

The anti-Christian poems which Goethe wrote at just about the same time are at first sight difficult to reconcile with the respect paid to Christian virtues and to the parson in *Hermann und Dorothea*, especially when it is realized that some of them were written as narrative poems for the 'Balladenjahr', in 1797, when together with Schiller Goethe was trying to arouse interest in poetry in a wider audience than that which would read lyrics and elegies. 'Die Braut von Korinth' (1797) is specially striking here, being the story of a Christian bride in the early days of the Church who, after her death, plays the part of a vampire, sucking the life from the living. One understands Goethe's purpose better, here, by remembering that what he opposed was any kind of restrictive belief, such as he believed Christianity to be. Other poems of the same kind (none of them in classical metres) make this clear: 'Der Gott und die Bajadere'

* Bore with manly feeling the heroic size of the woman.

(1797) with its erotic, Indian setting and message that the prostitute is acceptable to the gods when she performs her services out of love; 'Groß ist die Diana der Epheser' (1812) with its contrast between the cerebral god whom St Paul is represented as preaching in Ephesus, and the god of plenitude and rich abundance of life whom the citizens of that city already worshipped. At his best Goethe is trying to cultivate the free acceptance of all generous human qualities, to be affirmative rather than negative, and thus the instinctive prompting of Hermann to help the refugees, and his desire for life-long marriage, is just as acceptable as the equally instinctive promiscuity of the poet in the Elegies. It is only when this all-embracing affirmativeness tends to be literally all-embracing that it contains seeds of catastrophic peril. For some reason Goethe makes the god who is worshipped by the prostitute in the 'Bajadere' poem demand degrading, perhaps masochistic services from her, and these too seem to be part of the totality of human nature which he accepts. Similarly in the *Römische Elegien* violent lust is not distinguished from the tenderest love. On the whole, Goethe's tolerant nature and good humour made no great to-do about such points; but he was aware of them and occasionally gave expression to them as a necessary corollary of what he had come to believe. Some of his later poems bring home the point rather more sharply, as will be seen. In general, however, the period of Goethe's classicizing verse did not produce his best poetry. His generosity was hampered by metres foreign to the genius of his language, and often admirable intentions resulted in laboured or ponderous works through which one has to guess at the intended grandeur, rather than see or hear it from the words on the page.

11

'DIE WAHLVERWANDTSCHAFTEN'

The novel *Die Wahlverwandtschaften* is the only large work of Goethe's, except *Tasso*, in which the ideas of polarity and enhancement, so prominent in his scientific works, form a basis and determine the structure. It is also, however, despite weaknesses in the writing, one of his more moving longer works. Written after his public marriage with Christiane Vulpius, with whom he had lived openly and in defiance of scandalized gossip for nearly twenty years, and at a time when his feelings were aroused by the youthful Minna Herzlieb, it is his most serious attempt at exploring freely and open-mindedly the problem of matrimony and passionate love. He had tried to do this before, but Werther presented a view from outside, by a man who did not know what marriage meant, and Ferdinand in *Stella* had sought to resolve his difficulties by marrying both the women he loved, a solution whose validity for Goethe was shown when, in a later version, he concluded with Ferdinand's suicide. *Die Wahlverwandtschaften* ('The Elective Affinities') treats of Eduard and Charlotte, a wealthy couple approaching middle age and both married for a second time, and the consequences of their love for two guests in their house, 'the Captain', and Ottilie, Charlotte's niece. It comes nearer to a tragic work than anything that Goethe ever wrote, the 'Gretchentragödie' excepted.

The setting is a country estate, the property of Eduard, and a good deal of the novel is taken up with discussions of its management, not without symbolical overtones about man's control of Nature: the construction of paths to reach pleasant viewpoints, the care of the churchyard, the joining up of three lakes (which may well also have some symbolical significance), and landscape gardening in the style newly imported from England. This, with the frequent use of words like * 'angenehm', 'heiter', 'anmutig', 'schön', 'freundlich', 'ruhig', 'ver-

---

* pleasant, serene, graceful, beautiful, friendly, quiet, understanding, splendid.

ständig', 'herrlich', gives an even-tempered atmosphere; the reader is placed in a comfortable world in contrast with the tumult of the inward passions. The practicalities also make it possible to introduce without too much awkwardness the scientific phenomenon which supplies an analogy for the plot, although this device still has an overexplanatory rigidity.

It is in the course of an evening's reading aloud that Eduard comes across the description of certain 'elective affinities' in chemicals, whereby a substance containing two elements will divide, one joining with one outside substance, the other with another, as though the separate parts had actually elected to change partners. Thus, limestone, it is said, is composed of chalk and an acid; if dipped in sulphuric acid the chalk will combine to form plaster and the acid will be given off, to form with water a health-giving drink. In the fashion of Goethe's day, when anthropomorphic 'Naturphilosophen' like Oken and Schelling were constantly on the watch for analogies between the animate and the inanimate world, the characters at once begin to speculate on the possible result of the visits by the Captain and Ottilie, imagining that Eduard will form an association with the Captain, and Charlotte one with Ottilie. They decide that there is no harm in such a temporary regrouping, and after some discussion go ahead with their plans, unaware that Ottilie will fall in love with Eduard, and Charlotte with the Captain.

The scientific analogy, with its overtones of the doctrine of polarity (in so far as it speaks of pairs of 'opposites'), may seem at first glance to be unnecessary, and indeed it plays very little part in the remainder of the story. Its purpose, however, is to bring home the inescapable nature of Eduard's later passion for Ottilie. When the Captain remarks that the chemical substances act as though they had eternal life, and sensibility and reasoning powers, he is preparing the way for the later revelation that neither Eduard nor Ottilie is capable of withstanding the attraction each has for the other. The propriety of speaking of 'elective' affinities is thus doubtful, and is questioned by Charlotte herself: it is rather a question of destiny or providence or a hostile, daemonic force which brings them together or separates them, and at one time or another all these explanations are given. There is even an element of superstition, which is offered apparently quite seriously: the failure of a goblet, inscribed with the letters E and O, to break when thrown in the air, is taken as a good omen; so is the fact that certain plane trees were planted by Eduard on the day that Ottilie was born, and a number of similar coincidences or chance occurrences are ascribed by the narrator to a guiding hand from above. Not all the auguries are of this kind, however, and the novel has been not unjustly described as the first to treat of the workings of the unconscious mind. It is not pure chance that makes Eduard absurdly anxious for the safety of the locket round Ottilie's neck, containing the portrait of her dead father, and when he persuades her to hand it to him, we guess that the request has more significance than he is aware of. An event which hovers between superstition and a theory of the unconscious mind (which was already being prepared in those days, a century before Freud) is that in which Eduard has determined not to see Ottilie but only to leave her a note: as she arrives he hurries back into the room where she will enter, to retrieve his watch, and finds that he has dropped the key outside the door which has now slammed its lock, so that he is trapped into a confrontation against his will. Goethe ascribes this neither to destiny nor to what we might call 'purposeful accident', but may well have been groping his way towards some sense that Eduard unconsciously willed the meeting. Similarly the accidental drowning by Ottilie of Eduard's and Charlotte's baby, just at the moment when it seems that the couple have decided on a divorce, looks like one of those self-prospering actions which people appear to take from time to time without any deliberate intention. Goethe does not explicitly make this point, but in view of the later developments in depth pyschology we may well suppose that he was midway between superstitiousness and a germinating awareness of unconscious motivations.

The uncertainties on such points are due in part to the inadequacies of the novel as a novel. Although *Die Wahlver-*

wandtschaften has much more shape than *Wilhelm Meister*, being by comparison almost classically formed, a certain disregard of the reader is shown, and too often for sustained pleasure. Especially in the early chapters, but also later on, the characters often tell each other of earlier events in which they were both involved, needlessly, since they must already know, and with the evident intention on the author's part of informing the reader. 'We loved one another most dearly, as young people', Charlotte tells Eduard: 'we were separated, you from me, because your father married you, out of avarice, to a rich elderly lady, and I from you, because, not having many prospects, I was obliged to offer my hand to a prosperous man whom I did not love, but respected.'[1] Such a sentence looks like one conceived in the third person by the author, and translated into the first person to give the appearance of dialogue; constant use of this device precludes the indication of character through speech. The dialogue is often stilted quite apart from this feature. It is scarcely credible that Charlotte should reply, when the Captain asks forgiveness immediately after he has kissed her, in such words as these: 'That this moment should be epoch-making in our lives is something we cannot prevent; but that it may be worthy of us lies in our own hands.' Once again, we hear rather Goethe's reflections than any words that Charlotte might utter. At times, he does not overtly make any distinction between himself and his creations, as when the narrator begins a paragraph by describing the actions of the characters in the third person, and then continues to speak of 'my husband' as though Charlotte rather than he were talking.[2] Somewhat similarly, Charlotte refers to herself, in comparison with Ottilie, as 'the elder friend', a description more appropriate coming from the narrator.[3]

The overall structure received more attention: as in *Werther*, there are two parts, with the additional features that they are not only of almost exactly equal length, but that each contains eighteen chapters, showing that the regard for formal symmetry which Goethe had acquired in Italy was still important to him. A certain artificiality is noticeable here too, for the first two-thirds of the second part contribute very little to the story, being largely concerned with the doings of Charlotte's daughter by an earlier marriage; they also contain a short story told by one of the visitors to the house, and several groups of extracts 'from Ottilie's diary', by which one is reminded of a remark made by Goethe himself to his sister, on receiving letters from her, heavily corrected by their father: 'I sometimes have to smile at a good simple-hearted girl making observations that nobody except a perceptive and experienced man could make.'[1] These 'maxims and reflections' are, like those inserted arbitrarily into *Wilhelm Meister* and *Faust*, for the most part unloaded at the most readily available place, and seldom contribute to the understanding of the novel. All the same, the irrelevancies of the second part do serve to indicate the passage of time between the conception and birth of Charlotte's child, as well as to contrast the daughter Luciane with Ottilie; they also, by introducing a description of a Christmastide tableau presented in Eduard's chateau, allow Ottilie to appear dressed as the Mother of God, which is a significant part of the symbolism. (Mignon in *Wilhelm Meister*, with whom Ottilie has much in common, appears similarly at the end of the *Lehrjahre* dressed as an angel,[2] and of course the association of the loved one with divinity, so often found in Goethe, is also reflected.) In connection with this, the unbidden singing of the 'Nunc dimittis' at the baptism of Charlotte's child (though a symbol of spiritual adultery) lends further associations with the Christ-child to the love between Eduard and Ottilie.[3] There is in this part of the novel also a description of the painting of angels on the vault of the chamber where Eduard and Ottilie are eventually interred side by side; questionable though the effectiveness of this may be, it is prepared for by the earlier pages of the second half.

The symbolism in general is less effective than one could wish, chiefly because of its contrived rigidity. No doubt with the doctrine of the complementary opposites in mind, Goethe allows Ottilie to complain of headaches on the left side, and to live in the left wing of the chateau, while Eduard has headaches on the right side and lives in the right wing. Possibly the same doctrine is responsible for the scene in which the priest who baptizes Charlotte's child dies at that precise moment, presenting 'birth and death, coffin and cradle...these mighty opposites' at one single moment,[1] but doing so too appositely for good effect. Rather more credible is the way in which Ottilie shows her love for Eduard when her handwriting increasingly resembles his, and a further sign of her love is her accompaniment of Eduard's erratic flute-playing. Where Charlotte had been accustomed to slowing down and generally accommodating herself to Eduard, who was accustomed to play fast or slow according to the difficulties of the piece, Ottilie, having once heard Eduard play, seems to have no other conception of the music than this: 'she had made his faults so much her own that a kind of living whole emerged from it, which, though not in the proper rhythm, sounded most pleasant and entertaining. The composer himself', Goethe adds, 'would have enjoyed hearing his work distorted in so beautiful a way.' This adaptation by the lover to the beloved is frequently mentioned in Goethe's later work[2] and the conception of love which it implies is clearly his own. The whole conception of the 'apotheosis of the inadequate'[3] is reflected in it.

It is true that, in becoming so closely alike, Eduard and Ottilie do not fulfil the analogy of the 'elective affinities', which produced an entirely new substance after the division of the original elements: in this case, the newcomer has simply taken on the qualities of Eduard, who has yielded nothing of himself. But then the analogy is at most a starting-point from which to develop something of more importance. It establishes the idea of polarity but says nothing of the accompanying idea of 'enhancement,[4] and it is with this that the most interesting parts of the novel are concerned.

After the initial scenes in which the four characters are brought into contact and begin to form their new associations, the first event of special importance takes place when Eduard and Charlotte sleep together, each mentally thinking of the new lover while physically embracing the other. With this

vivid picture of spiritual adultery Goethe sets the stage for the
future development. It becomes clear that the husband and wife
are so possessed with thoughts of infidelity, and so passionately
attached, that their marriage must founder, yet neither is
willing for this to happen. To escape such an end, Eduard
leaves, writing a note to Charlotte in which he both affirms his
intention of giving up Ottilie, and requires that she remain in the
house till he returns, so that it is hard to tell how much he means
to abate his longing for her. He is unsuccessful, and the last
part of the novel is increasingly concerned with ways and
means of uniting either Charlotte or Ottilie with Eduard.
The birth of the child seems temporarily to tilt the scales
towards Charlotte, whose claim on her husband is increased
by it. Then the curious physical resemblance of the child to
both the Captain and Ottilie, its spiritual parents (a further
unhappy instance of Goethe's symbolism), seems to point in
the opposite direction: Eduard and Charlotte have in spirit
if not in body committed adultery, and a divorce is seen by
both of them as the only way out. They have scarcely agreed,
however, when Ottilie accidentally drowns the baby while
crossing the lake in a boat, and at once the issue is in doubt
again. Charlotte sees in the death of her child a sign that her
divorce had providential assent, while Ottilie sees in it a divine
warning against her imprudent intervention in another's
marriage, so that, although the path to the fulfilment of
Eduard's desires is open, he cannot take it. It is again an un-
fortunate feature that the issue should be posed in such terms
of the comparatively superstitious interpretation of ambiguous
portents, rather than of the reasonable consideration of the
interests of the characters, and of the strength of their passions:
this lends a factitious air even to these more gripping parts of
the novel. All the same, the vital point towards which Goethe
was working has not yet been reached.

Eduard and Ottilie both try again to stifle their longings
by leaving the chateau; the accidental slamming of the door,
which forces their confrontation, renders this impossible, and,
although both are intent on renunciation ('Entsagung', a

key word in this and several other works of Goethe's riper years), a daemonic force, contradictory as always,[1] at once demands that they should separate and brings them together again. Returning to the chateau, Ottilie becomes closer than ever to Eduard, yet remains content with his mere presence, without further desires. In this combination of infinite longing and renunciation of all contact, this having and not-having so reminiscent of Rilke in his love-poems, surely lies the point towards which Goethe has been making:

Only the closest proximity could appease them, but then appeasement was complete, and proximity was enough, they needed neither a glance nor a word nor a gesture nor a touch, only the pure being together. Then they were not two people, but only one, in unconscious, perfect ease, content with each other and with the world ...Life was a riddle for them, whose solution they found only in one another's presence.[2]

This paradoxical state combining the greatest passion with the greatest renunciation is one of those fusions which Goethe often spoke of as ideal, or as near to the ideal as men could come in mortal life. It seems to be foreshadowed by one of the remarks in Ottilie's diary, incongruous though it may be there: 'Everything perfect of its kind must transcend its kind and become something different, something incomparable. In some of its notes the nightingale remains a bird, but then it ascends above its species and seems to want to teach its companions what singing is.'[3] The striving for something more than ordinarily human is also suggested by the very remarkable entry in the same 'diary': 'Do what one will, one cannot think of oneself except as a seeing creature. I think men dream only in order not to cease from seeing. It may well happen one day that the inner light in us will move outside of us, so that we no longer have need of any other.'[4] Perhaps this inner light,[5] replacing the outward sun, is already approached in these final moments of Ottilie's life, when the mere presence of the other's love is enough to drive out all sense of the external world and discontent with it. All other attempts at renunciation have failed, success comes only with the determination not to stifle love and yet not to let it govern: it is a hard teaching, not necessarily a universal one, and yet one that commands respect so long as nobody has found any satisfying answer to the conflict of love for one and love for many.

After this, the death of Ottilie by self-starvation is an anti-climax, a regression to the suicide of Werther, though in a different form. One would have admired Goethe's solution for her the more, had she attempted to live on in her love, not desiring requital; as it is, since we know nothing directly of her motives, her end appears just as inconsiderate and as unloving as Werther's. It is even melodramatic: Ottilie's dead body becomes the means of restoring to life a young girl killed by a fall, and crowds of pilgrims begin to make journeys to the grave of the new saint; yet religion has played no notable part in the earlier part of the novel. Goethe's own leanings at this time towards a kind of Catholicism, seldom plainly revealed, need to be remembered in order to make the ending more understandable.

Die Wahlverwandtschaften as a whole is chiefly of interest as an experimental novel, written at a time when Romantic concern with the so-called 'night-side of the soul' was moving towards the psycho-analytical theories at the end of the nineteenth century, and attempting to reach some solution of matrimonial problems through the philosophical scheme of which Goethe became more and more conscious with increasing age. It has the faults of many of his compositions, an easy-going negligence and, curiously enough, an over-rigid formalism to which he pays less than enough respect. Ultimately, its conclusions are rendered ambiguous, not only by Ottilie's virtual suicide but also by the death of Eduard shortly afterwards, after a period during which his fidelity to his wife remains nominal and certainly not spiritual. The novel has been claimed as a defence of matrimony, but since Eduard is buried beside Ottilie, and the narrator ends with the hope that in the resurrection these two rather than the husband and wife may be reunited, it can only be defended on that score with some difficulty. Its most remarkable feature is not so much the attempt at preserving the bond of marriage as its attempt at transcending the situation of Werther by maintaining love at its highest pitch while still offering it no physical satisfaction. One would relinquish a good deal of the superstitions and stilted dialogues had Goethe been able to explore that newer solution more fully and more realistically, even though a more tragic outcome might have been the result.

12

'DER WEST-ÖSTLICHE DIVAN'

In the first decade of the nineteenth century Goethe wrote little poetry that is remembered, apart from the poem 'Dauer im Wechsel' and some sonnets. In 1814, the year which seemed to mark the end of the Napoleonic wars, with the relief which that brought, a variety of circumstances led to a sudden flowering of lyrical inspiration which was to continue for several years. Goethe read Josef von Hammer's (1774–1856) translations of poems by the medieval Persian poet Hafiz and was struck by the resemblance between his own poetic nature and that of his Oriental counterpart. Shortly after, he set out in July 1814 on a journey to his native city of Frankfurt, full of pleasurable expectations, and almost at once began to compose poems in great profusion. Arrived in Frankfurt, he fell in love with Marianne Jung, then aged thirty, just before her marriage with Jakob von Willemer. (The situation had something in common with Goethe's love for Charlotte Buff, also already engaged when he met her, and for Charlotte von Stein, already married.) Out of this love arose a great many more poems, a small number of the finest being by Marianne herself, although this was not generally known at the time, and Goethe began to foresee the possibility of a 'Divan', or collection of poems, emulating that of the Persian but yet remaining essentially German: a kind of synthesis, as the title implies, between East and West, and a bridging across two cultures. He began to write more explicitly in Persian style, with references to Bulbul the nightingale, to attar of roses, houris, and quotations from the Koran, and forming some poems as dialogues between himself, as 'Hatem', and Marianne as 'Suleika'.

One of the attractive features of the *Divan* is the exuberant high spirits in which so much of it is written, all the more remarkable when one reflects that Goethe was nearing seventy at the time. The poem which speaks of him as a snow-capped or in other words white-haired volcano spouting forth his love

is very much in this mood, and so is the one in which the boy
cup-bearer remarks on the drunken state in which his master
the poet retires to bed:

> Perser nennens Bidamag buden,
> Deutsche sagen Katzenjammer.*

Goethe praises Hafiz for his fidelity to Muslim principles, which
forbid the use of alcohol, and at the same time proposes to
follow his 'sacred example' of drinking wine as a way towards
mystical absorption in Allah. (Hugo Wolf's setting of the poem
in question, 'Hans Adam war ein Erdenkloß', is a fine realization of the mood, as are all this composer's settings of poems
from the *Divan*). A genial carefreeness runs through the work:
Goethe changes 'Quell' to 'Quall' so that it will rhyme with
'schal' (but it still does not, as he well knew), and rhymes
'ergötzen' with 'schätzen'; in another place he writes in verses
which rhyme throughout on alternate lines but rhymes on
'Morgenröte' with 'Hatem', leaving the surprised reader with
a void which can only be filled by substituting the poet's own
name.

At one point, he carries this happy fooling into a more serious
context. One of the most often quoted lines from the *Divan*
is that which is thought to run 'Höchstes Glück der Erdenkinder
bleibt doch die Persönlichkeit',† which seems to sum up
Goethe's well-known cult of personality. In point of fact, the
lines are not quite as popular memory would have them, and
read in the original:

> Volk und Knecht und Überwinder,
> Sie gestehn zu jeder Zeit,
> Höchstes Glück der Erdenkinder
> Sei nur die Persönlichkeit.
>
> Jedes Leben sei zu führen,
> Wenn man sich nicht selbst vermißt;
> Alles könne man verlieren,
> Wenn man bliebe, was man ist.‡

---

* Persians call it bidamag buden, Germans say a hangover.
† The highest happiness of earth's children still remains personality.
‡ The crowd, the servant and the conqueror all admit at all times that the

In short, the statement about personality is not in the indicative mood but in the less emphatic subjunctive, being reported speech, 'what people say'. It is also put in the mouth of Suleika, who is at once contradicted by Hatem, although that need not detain us at the moment. More important is the fact that the second verse can be read in two entirely different senses, so that solemn commentary on whether Goethe sided with Suleika's or with Hatem's estimate of the value of personality is beside the point. The first, perhaps more obvious reading of verse 2 is that any life can be led (however bad or difficult) so long as one does not lose one's sense of identity; one can gladly lose everything if only one remains what one is. In making that interpretation, however, we ought to bear in mind the epigram written in Goethe's old age which reads:

> Erkenne dich! — Was soll das heißen?
> Es heißt: Sei nur! und sei auch nicht!
> Es ist eben ein Spruch der lieben Weisen,
> Der sich in der Kürze widerspricht.*

Thus a second reading of verse two may justifiably be made along these lines: Any life can be led (you can be anyone you choose, adopt whatever mask you like) so long as you don't become overweening about yourself ('sich vermißt' as a part of the verb 'sich vermessen', instead of 'sich vermissen'); you may very well lose everything if you remain stubbornly what you are. In short the chameleon Goethe, the Faust in him who could adopt so many guises, underlies the second reading, while the permanent self, the 'Mittelpunkt' of 'Wandrers Sturmlied', the self who was 'free from fear, too great for envy'[1] underlies the first. His whole conception of 'Dauer im Wechsel'† is neatly conveyed in the punning sequence, and Goethe's laughing disregard of over-serious interpreters is im-

---

highest happiness of earth's children is naught but personality. Any life can be led, if one does not lack self-esteem; one could lose everything if one remained what one is.

* Know thyself!—Well, what does that mean? It means 'Be!' and again 'Be not at all!' It is just a saying of our friends the sages, which, when put briefly, contradicts itself.

† 'Enduringness in Change.'

plied by the very fact that he wrote as he did. (The thought of this poem echoes in Hegel's doctrine of the negation of Self.)

It was just such a duality-in-unity, though not expressed in just this way, that Goethe admired in Hafiz. Hafiz could write in praise of women and wine, and apparently run counter to all the highest precepts of Islam, and yet be blessed and blissful: this, as 'Offenbar Geheimnis'* declares, is the unforgivable sin in the eyes of the people, who call Hafiz a mystic without understanding what they are saying:

> Du aber bist mystisch rein,
> Weil sie dich nicht verstehn,
> Der du, ohne fromm zu sein, selig bist!
> Das wollen sie dir nicht zugestehn.†

Goethe had much the same sense that, although not 'fromm', not pious or orthodox in his beliefs, he was saved, and had always felt that his love of particular women was not merely individual, but a reflection of some lover beyond them all, so that his love was both earthly and heavenly at one and the same time. As quite a young man he had translated into German the Song of Solomon, the most sensuous of all books in the Bible, and was no doubt well aware that it is a book often interpreted in a mystical sense, concerning the love between the creature and the creator. This mixture or fusion of the sexual with the spiritual was to be a not infrequent theme of Goethe's later poetry, and is nowhere more openly stated than in the poem 'Selige Sehnsucht',‡ one of the first of the *Divan* poems to be written. Here, in the tripping, insouciant metre, which Goethe used very often in this collection, he describes the poet awake in bed, his wife or mistress asleep beside him, and feeling the attraction of the candle-flame alongside in just the same way as the moth desires to fly in and be burned to ashes. In this longing he sees a desire to move out of the cycle

---

* 'Open Secret.'
† But you are mystically pure, while they do not understand you; you who, without being devout, are blissful—they won't grant you that.
‡ 'Blessed Longing.'

of mere procreation and further procreation to a union which he can still only describe in sexual terms as a 'höhere Begattung', a higher consummation. To 'die' in the arms of a greater beloved than a mortal wife would be truly to live, and so Goethe concludes, in words now famous for the last three words of the second line:

> Und so lang du das nicht hast,
> Dieses: Stirb und werde!
> Bist du nur ein trüber Gast
> Auf der dunklen Erde.*

Only a man who has died in this way can 'werden'—and here a possible misconstruction must be observed. The phrase 'Stirb und werde' is so close to the idea of death and rebirth that the special meaning of 'werden' is easily overlooked. It means of course 'to become', but has the further sense, common in German but strange in English, of 'growing', 'developing', 'becoming something else', so that the real sense here is probably that the self must 'die' in order to be at one with the world-soul ('Come, world-soul, fill us through and through' is a line from another part of the *Divan*) and to grow in time and space along with it. In the end, 'Selige Sehnsucht' proves to be not a poem about entry into a higher existence in the sense of a supernatural one, but about re-entry into the natural order in a more intense ('gesteigert') form.

The *Divan* is a varied work, not only in themes and forms but also in quality. It contains some of Goethe's most subtly phrased love-lyrics, including 'Vollmondnacht' and 'An vollen Büschelzweigen', as well as some which were not written by him at all, in the normal sense, although whether Marianne von Willemer would ever, without having loved Goethe, have written poems as distinctive as 'Hochbeglückt in deiner Liebe' and 'Ach, um deine feuchten Schwingen' is not so much as open to question. The collection also contains metaphysical poems and drinking-songs, lovers' dialogues and

---

* And as long as you have not that 'Die, and become!' you are but a dismal guest on the dark earth.

moral apophthegms, epigrams, a legend, versified translations from the Koran, and a large number of the day-to-day trivia which Goethe often wrote in autograph albums and the like. There is no special pattern, except that the poems in most of the Books are grouped round a central theme, and the last of all is, appropriately, the 'Book of Paradise', although the other Books have not led towards it in the way that the earlier sections of the *Divine Comedy* lead towards their conclusion. What binds most of the *Divan* poems together is the underlying idea and mood they express. Goethe writes now rather in the spirit of the laughing saint whom he admired in the *Italienische Reise*, Filippo Neri, whose motto, borrowed from St Bernard, ran thus: 'Spernere mundum, spernere neminem, spernere se ipsum, spernere se sperni.'* To despise himself and despise being despised was the keynote of Goethe's ideas now, and the paradox it expresses is the one he had always tended towards. It accounts for the carefree and sometimes careless way in which he writes, for half the point of his wisdom is that it looks like the folly of a clown (calling to mind the Chinese sage who was last seen walking out beyond the Great Wall into the wilderness, with his left sandal balanced on his head). It also accounts for the taunting, ironical note which Hugo Wolf's settings bring out so well. There is perhaps no better way of indicating this mood than by referring to the first few poems of the 'Buch Hafis', in which a bewildering kaleidoscope of attitudes flits before the reader. In the first, 'Beiname',† the Poet (in whom we are very possibly invited to see Goethe himself) asks of Hafiz whence his name comes, and is told that it is one given to those who have a profound knowledge of the Koran. To this the Poet replies that he resembles Hafiz to perfection, since he knows the Holy Writ of his own land with equal thoroughness—and we know that Goethe prided himself on being 'bibelfest'. Thus both the poets are established first of all as thoroughly respectable adherents of their respective religions. The second poem, 'Anklage',‡ at once sounds a

---

* Despise the world, despise nobody, despise yourself, despise being despised.
† 'Cognomen.'   ‡ 'Accusation.'

contradictory note. For the greater part, it is a rhymed translation from the Koran, warning the faithful against poets because
they are close to liars and rogues, and denouncing their madness
and irresponsibility. (Shades of *Tasso* hover in the background
here.) Goethe then adds to the quotation from the Koran an
appeal to loyal Muslims to confound the poets, among whom
Hafiz is named first, so that a decidedly ambiguous attitude
towards him is conveyed. The third poem, 'Fetwa' continues
in the same vein, being a verse-translation based on an extant
pronouncement (or 'fetwa') on Hafiz by a famous mufti of
Constantinople, Ebusuud, and declaring that, while there is a
great deal of truth in the poet's writings, there are also some
unorthodoxies: those who wish to avoid eternal torment should
learn to distinguish poison from its antidote. But the sequence
of thought does not end with this cautious pronouncement. It
is followed at once by 'Der Deutsche dankt',* in which Goethe
(presumably) greets the mufti with a jovial mock-approval.
The little unorthodoxies which Ebusuud detects are precisely
where the true poet is at home in his exuberant living: for the
poet, whether his name be Hafiz or Goethe, poison and cure
are one and the same:

> Schlangengift und Theriak muß
> Ihm das eine wie das andre scheinen.
> Töten wird nicht jenes, dies nicht heilen.
> Denn das wahre Leben ist des Handelns
> Ewige Unschuld, die sich so erweiset,
> Daß sie niemand schadet als sich selber.†[1]

The poet lives in a world without distinctions, where ortho-
doxy and unorthodoxy, piety and impiety, earthly and
heavenly love are all one. He can praise Hafiz in one poem and
have him condemned in another, while attaching himself
neither to the praise nor to the condemnation, but only to the
flow of activity in and around him, 'the eternal innocence of

---

* The German gives thanks.

† Poison and antidote must to him seem both alike. The former will not kill,
nor will the latter heal, for true life is the eternal innocence of action, which
reveals itself by harming no one but itself.

action', Goethe's continual theme. He is 'werdend', in the sense of the verse from 'Selige Sehnsucht', progressing through and along with history in all its inevitable contradictoriness. The fusion which *Tasso* had only barely suggested is stated and developed here.

In some ways, this philosophy or sagacity has attractions, especially in so far as it leads to tolerance and the enjoyment of other existences, and to the opposite of bigotry, although the poems suggestive of homosexual love between the Poet and his boy cup-bearer in the 'Schenkenbuch' show how wide the tolerance was. A more seriously troubling, even a repellent aspect, is shown in the 'Buch Timur', where Goethe does not shrink from drawing the consequences of what he said in the 'Buch Hafis'. In the first poem of this Book, 'Der Winter und Timur',* Goethe created one of the most ferocious poems he had ever written, for all that he modelled it closely on the Latin translation of an Arabic poem. Timur, or Tamburlaine, the brutal and ruthless Mongol conqueror, on whom Goethe projects some of his feelings about Napoleon, is made the subject of a withering philippic, as the personified Winter gathers all its forces of frost and snow to hurl in elemental fury at the man who has presumed to take up elemental power for himself. All Goethe's belief in the daemonic[1] goes into this poem, and above all his sense that the daemon could only be opposed by the daemon. He might well have written as a motto to this poem the phrase he used as motto for the twentieth book of his autobiography, 'Nemo contra deum nisi deus ipse'.[2] The pendant to it, however, and the only other poem in this particular book, strikes a completely different note: it might well be called its complementary or polar opposite. 'An Suleika' ('Dir mit Wohlgeruch zu kosen')† is another poem in the light-hearted, tripping trochees of many other poems in the *Divan*, and describes for the first three verses how thousands of roses must be destroyed by fire in order to make a thimbleful of the scent which heightens the lovers'

---

* 'Winter and Tamburlaine.'

† To cherish you with sweet perfume.

pleasure in one another. Only in the last verse is this simple thought related to that of the preceding poem, and then in a way which applies the ideas of polarity and duality-in-unity in a way almost incredible.

Sollte jene Qual uns quälen,
Da sie unsre Lust vermehrt?
Hat nicht Myriaden Seelen
Timurs Herrschaft aufgezehrt?*

The thought that the lovers might be tormented by the torment of the roses seems over-scrupulous: we can scarcely guess why it should occur in the normal way to anyone's mind. The justification which is then offered, however, is at once inappropriate and hideous. The lovers need not concern themselves, since after all so great a man as Tamburlaine destroyed, for the heightening of his own form of enjoyment, not thousands of roses but myriads of souls. Nowhere in the whole of Goethe's writing is there any quite so bold a suggestion that sheer evil is a part of the acceptable cosmic order, and one which the really all-embracing man can not only tolerate but actively welcome. At this point, midway through the *Divan*, its ideas momentarily take a turn which seems to portend the far greater callousness which Germany was to witness a century later. After the concentration camps, one reads 'An Suleika' with at worst a sense of dismay that Goethe of all people could have written it, at best a recognition that it represents an instructive *reductio ad absurdum*.

The idea of polarity always contains potentially the idea that evil as well as good is part of a divinely ordained or fatal order of things, and therefore in some sense to be accepted and possibly even practised. Goethe was chary of emphasizing this or of allowing it to enter his consciousness with all its implications: we have seen it hovering in the background of his poem 'Harzreise im Winter' and of the *Römische Elegien*, as well as in *Faust*, but it is nowhere as developed in his thought as it is in

---

* Should that torment torment us, since it increases our pleasure? Did not Tamburlaine's rule consume myriads of souls?

that of Nietzsche, of whose debt to Goethe there is no doubt. At the root, however, Goethe's doctrine, like Nietzsche's, is not so much an illumination of the usual as an apotheosis of the actual, or perhaps it is more accurate to say that it is often rather a diminution of the ideal in order that it may be represented by the real. This is most apparent in the 'Buch des Paradieses', in which the Muslim Paradise, though presented with a certain irony, still seems meant to be accorded a certain regard. Even the Mahomet of the first poem in this Book ('Berechtigte Männer')* seems not to think too highly of the joys he promises, when he suggests that men should resign themselves ('sich schicken') to the heavenly peace he offers—as though it is all they are likely to get, poor though it is. And in the dialogue between the Poet and the houri, 'Deine Liebe, dein Kuß mich entzückt',† the reason for this becomes clear. The houri, one of those maidens whose duty it is to attend in paradise on the warriors who have died fighting for Islam, seems to the poet to resemble closely the woman Suleika, whom he loved on earth. She replies to his question about this, that when she and her fellows were first created they were perfect in every way, 'scharmant', and 'reizend, geistig, munter',‡ beyond anything that even the angels had known. The trouble was that the Muslim warriors had left girls of their own on earth whom they preferred to these heavenly beings, and wanted to get back to them in ordinary life. The Prophet therefore ordained that the houris should no longer attempt to please with heavenly beauty, but conform to the expectations of the faithful by resembling their former sweethearts in every respect. For this reason the present houri seems to the poet to be Suleika, and, seeing that he is a German, she has condescended to speak in 'Knittelreime', as being the form most likely to please him.

All this forms an amusing exchange, but like *Faust* it is meant as a 'serious joke':[1] Goethe is not merely satirizing what he may take to be the Muslim idea of heaven, but ironically putting forward ideas of his own. The idea of Heaven in *Faust* is of a

---

* 'Men with rights.'
† 'Your love, your kiss delights me.' ‡ charming, witty, gay.

place where the 'inadequate' becomes an event,[1] and that is precisely what is happening here in the *Divan*. The inadequacy of the poet's conception of perfect beauty is met by the houri's transforming herself into the form of the woman he loved, and so far as he is concerned, as he declares, it is of no consequence to him whether this really is Suleika or a spiritual being who has assumed her form. The issue of truth and illusion does not concern him: the inadequate is perfect enough.

But behind this serious joke one cannot help feeling a certain bitterness. Is the German Poet really as delighted as he makes out, one wonders, at being addressed in the roughest and crudest of metres, not far from doggerel, when he is capable of almost any metre in the book of European prosody? And is he really persuaded that this houri, who appears to do nothing with him but speak of kissing and let him count her fingers, is the exact image of the Suleika whom we have encountered in other poems of the *Divan*, impulsive, delighted and gay, treating her lover as an equal, yet affectionate and witty, gently yielding but not submissive, self-contained yet generously open? 'Scharmant'—the Germanized 'Fremdwort'—seems a proper word to describe the houri, but not one that will fit Suleika-Marianne. The poem seems to illustrate what the houri says, that 'in eternal life you have to put up with everything': a not unattractive paradox in itself, but one which in this case results in both poet and houri, in their mutual adaptation, levelling themselves down to a point below the real expectations of either.

A proper understanding of Goethe's later poetry can nevertheless be gained more easily from reflecting on this poem than on most others. His own carefreeness or carelessness in rhyming, and in observance of metrical rules and conventions, is characteristic of this same broadly confident feeling that, as he says in another poem, if God had wanted him to be different, he would have made him different. So long as he is in this mood he is no longer striving, as Wilhelm Meister strove, after some ideal perfection, and for the greater part this is the mood of the *Divan*. He will, of course, return to the quest for the ideal when he comes to write about Faust's quest for Helen in a few years' time, and when Faust goes to heaven it will not be to meet any houri-maiden but to be received by Gretchen and to be enriched by her beyond measure. Faust is still only at the stage of the pupa ('im Puppenstand') at the end of the play, and has still to develop the wings of his future condition. Yet even in *Faust* something of the *Divan* mood operates: it is perhaps because of a certain lack of urgent expectation in Goethe that the encounter between Faust and Helen fails to be as wonderful as we suppose it is going to be.

The same consideration affects the quality of the *Divan* as poetry. A very great deal of it is in the trochaic tetrameters of which several examples have already been quoted, and these usually have a steady regularity in the stress and fall, a lack of distinctiveness, a metronomic rigidity in the beat which suggests some over-confident laxity: one can be lulled to inattention by this kind of writing, which may well arise from the poet's relaxed sense that since all things are welcome all poetic inspiration is welcome, no matter what its quality. On the other hand, poems which remain memorable have an intensity which transforms this usual metre into something of greater intensity. There is no chance of remaining inattentive after such a beginning as that of the poem 'Wiederfinden':

> Ist es möglich! Stern der Sterne,
> Drück' ich wieder dich ans Herz!
> Ach, was ist die Nacht der Ferne
> Für ein Abgrund, für ein Schmerz!
> Ja, du bist es! meiner Freuden
> Süßer, lieber Widerpart;
> Eingedenk vergangner Leiden,
> Schaudr' ich vor der Gegenwart.*

This has just the same metre as the majority of the *Divan* poems. Yet the passion, and the complexity of the thought, give it a

---

* Is it possible? Star of stars! Is it you I press to my heart again? Ah, what an abyss of pain there is in the dark night of separation. Yes, it is you, dear, sweet counterpart of my joys; remembering past sufferings, I shudder at the present moment.

distinctive rhythmical life, moving from delighted exclamation
to relief and thence to a surprisingly quiet, awe-struck conclusion. It is surely because Goethe is not content with illusion,
as the poet who confronts the houri is, because it matters to
him that he has lost the 'beloved woman' and found her again
(in Marianne: the poem was written soon after meeting her for
the first time), and because he knows what elemental dis-
turbance love causes, that his verse here becomes more alive.

Similarly, another of the distinctive poems in the *Divan* is so
because of the careful attention to detail, the respect for and
love of the object outside, rather than the attempt at adaptation
or assimilation to it. The famous poem on the chestnuts of the
Castle Terrace at Heidelberg shows just such a concern for the
particular nature of the tree, and is expressed accordingly in
rhythms of constantly varied kinds: indeed the rhythms themselves are part of the means whereby that nature is expressed:

> An vollen Büschelzweigen,
> Geliebte, sieh nur hin!
> Laß dir die Früchte zeigen,
> Umschalet stachlig grün.
>
> Sie hängen längst geballet,
> Still, unbekannt mit sich,
> Ein Ast, der schaukelnd wallet,
> Wiegt sie geduldiglich.*

'Unbekannt mit sich': was this perhaps the point towards
which the sophistication and self-awareness of the *Divan* was
really tending, that ultimately Goethe's poetry (of which these
chestnuts are later in the poem seen to be a symbol) should
become as he had often wanted it to be, un-self-conscious, rich,
and swaying with a movement not its own? Given the conditions of his writing it is not surprising if he achieved that only
rarely: he would include in his published works almost anything he wrote, without distinction, and often without correc-

---

* On full, clustering twigs, beloved, look there, let me show you the fruits,
in their green, prickly shells. For long now they have hung there, rounded
and concentrated, silent, unknown to themselves. A branch, lolling and
swinging, patiently cradles them.

tion, and it would be a marvel if in his normal day-to-day existence he achieved such a free state of mind, not letting his right hand know what his left hand was doing, for more than a short while from time to time. Still, that was the way he chose to write, and we owe to it some twenty poems of great distinction, among a mass of trivia, light-hearted banter, an occasional descent into perversion, and some attempts at realizing the nature of non-European culture such as few men of Goethe's day were concerned enough to make. In many ways, the *Divan* is rather like the pattern of any everyday existence, with its heights and its depths thrown into sharper relief, and in most of his moods Goethe would probably have been content to let it be regarded in that light, as the record of 'ein Werden'.

13

POEMS OF HIS OLD AGE

To speak of an optical illusion, Goethe wrote on one occasion, was blasphemy. If a stick in water appeared to be crooked, he apparently implied, there was no illusion about that: you were meant to see it as crooked (and it was just as much a part of the divine plan, he might have added, that the crookedness of the world should be regarded not as illusion but as truth). Whether he meant that the unpleasant facts were not to be blinked away, or whether he meant that they were to be accepted, however unpalatable, as part of the divine scheme of things, is not obvious from this brief remark. It is not completely clear from the poem 'Epirrhema', which says that in considering Nature one must always consider each individual thing as though it were all things, and which concludes:

> Freuet euch des wahren Scheins,
> Euch des ernsten Spieles:
> Kein Lebendiges ist ein Eins,
> Immer ist's ein Vieles.*

There are overtones here of the 'seriously intended jokes' of *Faust Part II*[1] and perhaps intimations of Nietzsche's teaching about Apollo as the 'Gott des schönen Scheins'† (using 'Schein' here in a double sense, both of 'shine' and of 'illusion'). The root of Goethe's thought seems to be that, while the individual nature of Man precludes him from having any true knowledge of or identity with the Godhead, the very 'illusion' in which he lives his life is true all the same. As Hegel wrote, 'the realisation of the infinite End consists solely in the overcoming of the illusion by reason of which it seems unaccomplished'. No living person is as alone as he imagines himself to be; he is always a manifold being in whom the deity is always present. Life is

---

* Rejoice in the true illusion, the serious sport: no living creature is a single unit, it is always manifold.
† God of fair illusion.

'ein Tand, und wird so durchgetändelt',* as Goethe put it at another time: it is a fatuous dream that one has to live through, and yet a serious matter at the same time, since to mope over life's tragedies is to miss the whole point of existence, which is to delight in all that happens with an insouciant gaiety. Something of the mood Goethe has in view can be guessed from the poetic nature of the verse just quoted: the rhythm is jaunty, the rhyme on 'Scheins' (which is genitive) and 'Eins' (which is not) has a slightly comical note, and the very odd noun 'ein Vieles' ('a many') is equally light-hearted. Goethe is not particularly solemn in conveying the essence of a lifetime's wisdom: if he puts on the beard of a prophet he leaves the elastic showing.

As always, the vital thing for Goethe in his old age is that the purely negative attitude of a Mephistopheles should be discarded though not disregarded. Men are not cut off by their individuality from praising and enjoying and knowing truly the works of their Creator (as Kant and Schiller sometimes implied); the 'open secret' of the world is always open for anyone who has eyes to see and ears to hear. In just such a spirit Goethe wrote the poem 'Allerdings',† quoting words from an early eighteenth-century Swiss poet to the effect that no man could penetrate the secrets of Nature. With a humorous impatience very typical of the poetry of his old age, Goethe retorts that this is all nonsense: with Schopenhauer, his younger contemporary, he might have said 'We *are* the thing-in-itself':

> '*Ins Innre der Natur*' —
> O du Philister! —
> '*Dringt kein erschaffener Geist!*'
> Mich und Geschwister
> Mögt ihr an solches Wort
> Nur nicht erinnern!
> Wir denken: Ort für Ort
> Sind wir im Innern.‡

---

* a trifle that you trifle away.　　　　　† 'By all means.'

‡ '*Into the heart of Nature*'—You old Philistine!—'*no created mind can penetrate!*'. I and my friends would rather you didn't remind us of such talk. To our way of thinking, we are in her wherever we go.

The interpolated 'O du Philister! is just as much a part of Goethe's meaning as his subsequent explanation, that is, his humour is part of his acceptance of what happens in the world. The essential meaning of the poem is revealed, however, in the final lines, when Goethe declares that Nature has no external and internal aspects anyhow: we are not, as individuals, divided into an external and an internal self, but are, in an inexplicable way, both at once:

> Natur hat weder Kern
> Noch Schale,
> Alles ist sie mit einemmale.
> Dich prüfe du nur allermeist,
> Ob du Kern oder Schale seist.*

(Note again the odd rhyme on '-meist' and 'seist'.)

Goethe has in mind here that anybody who reflects is aware both of his surface appearance, and of the complex, unexpressed motives which accompany or cause every action: he knows how his apparent altruism can very well be egoistic at the same time, though the people he lives with may not be immediately aware of this. In the same way, Nature has two aspects, one which appears to us benevolent (or hostile, according to circumstances) and another which appears the contrary. The duality in man is a counterpart of the duality in Nature, and thus demonstrates not only the unity between Man and Nature but also the unity-in-duality of each individual, for I remain myself, one and indivisible, however complex my internal awareness becomes. And since this is how all things are, the essential thing in living is, while not remaining unaware of the 'negative' pole of existence, to live thankfully in the knowledge that one's own self reflects the unity-in-duality divinely ordained for everything that exists at all.

The whole basis of Goethe's philosophy remains, however, paradoxical. If it is essential to praise and 'affirm' existence, it is also essential to strive not to exist in any separation and

---

* Nature has neither kernel or shell, she is all things at once. Test yourself above all—are you a kernel or are you a shell?

individuality. This is the burden of the poem 'Urworte. Orphisch',* which proceeds verse by verse to outline the diametrically opposed forces which rule men's lives, now 'contracting' them into compliance and communion, now 'expanding' them into self-assertion and isolation. First the 'Daemon' leads a man into a certain channel from which he cannot escape, then 'Tyche' or Chance gives some opportunity for variety, and 'Eros' seems to promise complete liberty, till it leads to obligation and the requirement of faithfulness, where-upon 'Anangke' or Necessity reasserts itself once again, and he finds himself only more confined than ever. This alternation seems to be typical of the doctrine of polarity, and at other times Goethe welcomes it; there is no such thing as being 'scheinfrei',† as the fourth verse of this poem puts it, for 'Schein' (seeming) is truth, the opposites are identified. With the fifth 'Urwort', however, 'Elpis' or Hope, the alternation between extreme poles is seen as not inescapable. There is always the chance of rising beyond them, and thus the hope of transcend-ing polarity:

> Ein Flügelschlag — und hinter uns Äonen !‡

To be beyond all the aeons of Time, in a timeless world where individuation does not exist, is the alternative which Goethe is always ready to put forward, as he does in the *Divan*:

> Bis im Anschaun ewiger Liebe
> Wir verschweben, wir verschwinden.§

For him, as he put it in the epigram already quoted,[1] to know oneself is both to be and not to be: that is, perhaps, to recognize the contending opposites within oneself, whether of good and evil, truth and falsehood, and so on, but to realize also that there is a part of one's self which observes this conflict and does not exist within it; also, more importantly, that this self is capable both of rejoicing in existence and of willingly giving up its existence.

---

* 'Primal Words. Orphic.'   † seemingly free.
‡ One beat of our wings—and we place aeons behind us.
§ Till in gazing on divine love we hover away and vanish.

Thus it is that Goethe could write two poems, 'Eins und Alles' (1821) and 'Vermächtnis' (1829),* the first of which ends:

> Denn alles muß in Nichts zerfallen,
> Wenn es im Sein beharren will†

—with an apparent insistence on the need to give up one's being—while the second begins:

> Kein Wesen kann zu nichts zerfallen!
> Das Ew'ge regt sich fort in allen,
> Am Sein erhalte dich beglückt!‡

For to give up one's being is in his terms to become one with all Being: it is to 'die' in order to 'become'.[1] Activity, movement incorporating the polar opposites, deeds and not words or thoughts remain the essentially divine characteristic. Indeed, the thought of such a poem as 'Vermächtnis' is hard to follow, not merely in that it is illogical, but rather that it makes so many unaccountable leaps from one thought to another. Thus the first two verses advise the seeker after truth to realize how the moon and earth revolve around the sun, and continues in the third verse to use the sun as an analogy for the conscience which shines on the circling deeds of the individual as they pass round day by day; but the analogy seems inapt, in that conscience is normally thought of, not as merely illuminating, but as offering the possibility (which may be rejected) of changing one's course of action. Similarly the sixth verse says that once one has come to feel that what is fruitful is true, one will test the governance of all things—which, Goethe adds, will go on behaving as it always has done; one will then join the 'smallest band' (of wise men? of saints?). Such a verse as this seems impossible to follow except as a string of disconnected remarks thrown off almost at random:

> Und war es endlich dir gelungen,
> Und bist du vom Gefühl durchdrungen:

---

* 'One and All.' 'Testament.'

† For everything must splinter into nothing, if it seeks to persist in being.

‡ No being can splinter into nothing. The Eternal constantly stirs in all things. Hold fast to Being and rejoice!

Was fruchtbar ist, allein ist wahr —
Du prüfst das allgemeine Walten,
Es wird nach seiner Weise schalten,
Geselle dich zur kleinsten Schar.*

What is true of many of Goethe's plays, that their structure is 'discrete', and their sequence of scenes inconsequential, is also true of such a verse as this.

The 'wisdom' poems of Goethe's old age are valuable because the paradoxes they usually express do correspond to facets of experience, when they remain stated in the abstract. We are aware of the odd sense of permanency and impermanency in ordinary life, and of the strange way in which the 'self' who scrutinizes the actions of the 'self' and sometimes seems so distinct, yet remains part of the same self and dare not detach itself wholly without risk of insanity or evildoing. This Goethe's epigrams and 'Sprüche' illuminate and make memorable, while the unportentous rhythms he uses make them the more acceptable and even the more amusing and entertaining. The chief shortcomings arise from the attempt at extending the concise, epigrammatic utterance into something more detailed, which often has such results as that just noted in the sixth verse of 'Vermächtnis'.

The really impressive poems of Goethe's old age are thus not his more philosophical ones but those in which he makes no attempt at defining the indefinable or expressing the inexpressible, relying on suggestion to convey the mysterious quality of which he was aware. Perhaps the most moving of them is the 'Elegie' which he wrote in 1823 after the catastrophic realization at Marienbad that his love for the young Ulrike von Levetzow could not end in marriage. Written in a regular stanza form which is all the more remarkable in that Goethe was never more profoundly moved, and so never more prone to let his feelings pour forth as they had done in his

* And when you have finally succeeded, and when you are permeated with the feeling that only what is fruitful is true—then test the general governance of things, it will behave in its usual manner, and join yourself to the smallest group.

youth, this poem advances all Goethe's own wisdom to comfort him in this desperate situation, but places the phrases in the mouth of Ulrike, so that it is the poet himself who replies:

> Du hast gut reden, dacht' ich: zum Geleite
> Gab dir ein Gott die Gunst des Augenblickes
> Und jeder fühlt an deiner holden Seite
> Sich augenblicks den Günstling des Geschickes;
> Mich schreckt der Wink, von dir mich zu entfernen,
> Was hilft es mir, so hohe Weisheit lernen!*

Goethe was still as capable as Romeo of 'hanging up' philosophy, unless philosophy could make a Juliet.

The 'Marienbader Elegie' owes much of its movingness to this complete freedom and unattachment to ideas which at other times Goethe took at least half seriously. Other poems of his last decade do not so much as refer to his 'Weltanschauung', but achieve their success through their use of the 'body' of the language to express what the abstract sense only partly conveys. One of the most notable of all is the poem written in the Chinese manner, which contrasts well with a very early poem in exactly the same verse-form, metre, and rhyme-scheme, and yet surpasses it completely in subtlety both of rhythm and meaning. The earlier poem 'Gern verlass ich diese Hütte'† (1768) is in the trochaic tetrameters already encountered in 'Mahomets-Gesang' and as the principal metre of the *Divan*, but with a tone more akin to the lightly tripping measure of many of the *Divan* poems than the triumphant march of the 'Gesang'. Goethe says here how gladly he leaves the cottage where his 'Schöne' is staying (the word, suggesting a mere flirtation, was changed later to 'Liebe'), in order to walk among the dead branches of a forest in the moonlight; he is about to go on to make something more of the incompre-

---

* It's all very well for you to talk, I thought. Some God gave you as your companion the favour of every moment, and at your sweet side everyone feels instantly he is fortune's favourite. I am fearful at this sign that I must leave you. What help is it to me, to learn such lofty wisdom!
† 'Gladly do I leave this hut.'

hensible joy which seizes him in this desolate landscape, when the anacreontic mood makes him feel a fool, and as Heine might have done he ends with a modest joke, saying that all the same he would give a thousand such nights if only his girl would grant him a single one. This is all very well, but we know he has gone against a different and probably better intention, since in the first line he was declaring how glad he was to leave the cottage. Something more was burgeoning, and Goethe was not then prepared, possibly not bold enough, possibly just too young to be over-troubled anyway, to discover what it was. In the later poem, written nearly sixty years later, the exploration has been made, and with what looks like a conscious reminiscence, Goethe returns to the former theme with 'Dämmrung senkte sich von oben'.

> Dämmrung senkte sich von oben,
> Schon ist alle Nähe fern;
> Doch zuerst emporgehoben
> Holden Lichts der Abendstern!
> Alles schwankt ins Ungewisse,
> Nebel schleichen in die Höh;
> Schwarzvertiefte Finsternisse
> Widerspiegelnd ruht der See.
>
> Nun am östlichen Bereiche
> Ahn ich Mondenglanz und -Glut,
> Schlanker Weiden Haargezweige
> Scherzen auf der nächsten Flut.
> Durch bewegter Schatten Spiele
> Zittert Lunas Zauberschein,
> Und durchs Auge schleicht die Kühle
> Sänftigend ins Herz hinein.*

---

* Twilight descended from above, already all that was near is afar; yet first, on high, with its pure light, the evening star! All things sway into uncertainty, mists steal upwards; black-deepened darknesses reflected in it, the lake reposes.

Now in the eastern region I sense a gleaming, glowing moon, hair-fine twigs of slender willows jest upon the nearby stream. Through the play of moving shadows trembles Luna's magic light, and through the eye the coolness steals calmingly into my heart.

The theme is almost the same: darkness has fallen, and there is something disturbing in the black waters of the lake, yet even within this slightly menacing scene there is the reassurance of the presence of the evening star. The rhythm has numerous slight alterations of pace (where the earlier poem had few), the most significant, in the first verse, being that of the last two lines, with the variety of sounds in 'Schwarzvertiefte Finsternisse'* itself providing a sense of threat, while the 'Widerspiegelnd ruht der See',† with its ritardando in the last syllables, spreads a more peaceful mood.

The second verse supplies the contrast. In the poem of 1768 the moon had been present, in an unusually powerful phrase too: 'Luna bricht die Nacht der Eichen'‡ suggested a particularly strong sense of walled-in oppression that needed to be penetrated. In the later poem, the intensity of the moon's light increases with the line:

> Nun im östlichen Bereiche
> Ahn ich Mondenglanz und -Glut.§

The 'gleam', which is at first suggested, becomes a 'glow', perhaps almost a glare: certainly 'Monden-Glut' suggests a very powerful light indeed. In this new day, the menacing shadows of 'Schwarzvertiefte Finsternisse' receive their reply, in sound, in 'Schlanker Weiden Haargezweige', ‖ and this criss-cross of willow-branches is understandably an image of laughter, as the next line runs on 'Scherzen auf der nächsten Flut'.¶ The feeling of menace has been grasped, and in the presence of the moon it is turning into something new.

In the last four lines the new sense suggests itself more definitely, though still without sharp outlines. Goethe still uses the Latin name which had been the mark of anacreontics in his youth:

* Black-deepened darknesses.
† Reflecting lies the lake.
‡ Luna breaks the oak-trees' night.
§ Now in the Eastern zone I sense the gleam and glowing of the Moon.
‖ The hair-twigs of slender willows.
¶ Jest upon the nearby waters.

> Durch bewegter Schatten Spiele
> Zittert Lunas Zauberschein,*

But he adds a last couplet which has nothing in common with the 'throwaway' wish to spend a night with his girl-friend:

> Und durchs Auge schleicht die Kühle
> Sänftigend ins Herz hinein.†

It is a strange thing to find Goethe concluding that the coolness of the evening *steals* ('schleicht') into his spirit through the eye, and that by doing so it brings him peace, yet that is precisely what he does say, and precisely how he suggests that the menace of the scene, perhaps of the thought of death, is not so much overcome as calmly taken in and accepted.

Here the moon is one of Goethe's chief aids in coming to peace with himself; it was so all his life, and always had a curious fascination for him. One of the strangest events in the *Wanderjahre* is the one in the story 'Der Mann von 50 Jahren', in which a man is seen skating over the ice, apparently advancing swiftly out of the low-lying moon on the horizon; there are fears in Act II of *Faust Part II* that the moon will descend and crush the celebrants of the Classical Walpurgis Night; Galatea at the end of the same Act descends out of the moon, which presides over the whole love-feast in the Aegean Sea. Iphigenie addresses her prayer to Diana with a vivid awareness that the goddess is in some sense the moon, and the esoteric sense of the last two verses of 'An den Mond' (i.e. 'Füllest wieder Busch und Tal') appears to be that true bliss is to know the courses of the moon within oneself. Similarly in the poems of Goethe's old age the moon continues to stand for something particularly close to him, and not only to stand for it, but to be the most direct and realizable form of it. The moon in Goethe's poetry is not a symbol or an allegory but an image, one of the comparatively few in his store. Since this is so, one cannot interpret it, but only point to the kind of poem in which it appears, and the way in which it is effective. One

---

* Through the play of moving shadows trembles Luna's magic beam.
† And through the eye the coolness steals calmingly into my heart.

particularly good example from the poems of Goethe's last decade is the poem beginning 'Um Mitternacht ging ich, klein, kleiner Knabe',* in which, as in 'Dämmrung senkte sich', there is first of all a sense of disquiet: the small boy of the first verse has no liking for the dark night in which he finds himself, and yet is comforted by the sight of the stars. In the second verse, this light becomes greater: planets and Northern lights play above the lover's head, and as he advances through life so this light becomes more intense, until at last the moon itself appears in full glory:

> Bis dann zuletzt des vollen Mondes Helle
> So klar und deutlich mir ins Finstere drang,
> Auch der Gedanke willig, sinnig, schnelle,
> Sich ums Vergangne wie ums Künftige schlang,
> Um Mitternacht.†

The full sense of this short poem is evidently that the three verses cover a lifetime, whose end is crowned with the fullest possible realisation, conveyed not least by the full roundedness of the opening vowels in 'vollen Mondes Helle'. The darkness thus illuminated is evidently not merely physical, as is shown also by the thought which instantaneously embraces past and future in one. With the ambiguous 'Um Mitternacht' recurring at the end of each verse like a burden, suggesting both a doom and a solemn moment of release into a new day, Goethe makes this poem 'tell' in a way that his philosophical poems cannot do.[1]

Less subtle in effect, but more passionate in its declaration is the poem 'Dem aufgehenden Vollmonde', with the subtitle 'Dornburg, 25 August 1828'. The opening verses of this are of an extreme simplicity, though Goethe's distress at the thought of the moon's distancing itself from him is a reminder of how intensely he felt its 'approach' in the stories and poems

---

* At midnight I went, a small, small boy.'
† Until at last the full moon in all its brightness pierced down so clear and plain into my dark, and my thought, willing, sensual, and swift, wrapped itself round both the past and the future, at midnight.

already mentioned, and how he longed in a sense to be identified with it:

> Willst du mich sogleich verlassen?
> Warst im Augenblick so nah!
> Dich umfinstern Wolkenmassen,
> Und nun bist du gar nicht da.
>
> Doch du fühlst, wie ich betrübt bin,
> Blickt dein Rand herauf als Stern!
> Zeugest mir, daß ich geliebt bin,
> Sei das Liebchen noch so fern.*

Yet the third and last verse accepts the increasing distance
between moon and earth, and breaks rhythmically into an impassioned welcome to its dominant glory radiating over the
night. Here is the poetic expression, in contrast with the
abstract or philosophical one, of Goethe's conviction that the
world exists to be illumined and praised. He himself is separated
both from the moon and his beloved—this separateness is an
essential part of his meaning—and yet he writes in these terms:

> So hinan denn! hell und heller,
> Reiner Bahn, in voller Pracht!
> Schlägt mein Herz auch schmerzlich schneller,
> Überselig ist die Nacht.†

This is a glimpse, dated almost as though to vouch for its
authenticity, of the exultation which Goethe believed to be the
proper human condition, or at any rate the condition for which
men were created, though they might not realize it ever within
their lifetimes. Almost all his work had been directed in one
way or another to achieving this end—it is as though he had
always borne in mind that demand which Yahweh made of
Job, to know where Job had been when the earth was created,

---

* Will you leave me so suddenly? A moment ago you were so close. Masses
of cloud darken round you, and now you are gone. Yet you feel how sad
I am, and your rim peeps out like a star, witnessing I am beloved, however
far away my love.

† So go on then, brighter, brighter, on a pure path, in full resplendence.
Though my heart may beat more painfully and faster, this night is blessed
beyond compare.

and all the sons of God shouted for joy. Nothing else had mattered to Goethe so much as the regaining of the power to join in that shout again, and as a consequence he had from time to time been led either into dullness and inconsequentiality, or into a disregard of tragedy and evil, for he was prone to take the short cut. Still, of all his work such poems as the one written at Dornburg show most clearly what he would most have liked to achieve, and what, from time to time, he was able to achieve in the course of eighty-two years.

14

CONCLUSION

Eighty-two years, over sixty of them devoted chiefly to writing
—there is no other man of genius whose working life covers so
long a span, or who so continually applied himself to the task
in hand. 'Keep a firm hold on the present', was Goethe's advice
to Eckermann; 'every mood and condition, every moment is
of infinite value, for it is the representative of a whole eternity'
(3 November 1823). And Goethe surely believed that, even
though it runs clean against the condition of Faust's pact, according to which any attachment to the passing moment spelled
damnation. Or it would be truer to say that he believed it at
the moment of speaking the words, but was ready to contradict
them at another time had he been in the mood to do so.
Eckermann himself draws attention to the numerous self-
contradictions recorded in his *Conversations*, defending them
on the grounds that they are all 'individual aspects of truth,
collectively indicating the essence and leading towards an
approach to the truth itself'. The multiplicity of facets was,
however, at once Goethe's strength and his weakness. His
attachment to the mood and condition of the moment liberated
him from the desolations of his youth (and of his old age) and
enabled him to go on writing in the awareness of his inadequacies. His belief—no matter how fitfully he held it—that such
an attachment was self-justifying, or, to use Eckermann's terms,
that his vicissitudes might indicate the essence of truth, seems
to have led him into more inadequacies than he need have had.
The astonishing variety of his life and of his works was enough
to tempt any man to claim for them more comprehensiveness
than was possible, as though the sheer accumulation of moods
and conditions warranted the title which Carlyle gave, of the
'Universal Man'. Yet the idea that each moment is the representative of a 'whole eternity' (the phrasing, if Eckermann has
it right, suggests an eternal backing for every instant, and may
foreshadow Nietzsche's 'Eternal Recurrence') does not imply

any value in the moment. Some other backing than mere eternity is needed, if there is to be talk of value—a sense, as it might be, that the mood or moment, whether good or bad, flat or triumphant, can be offered towards a personal purpose, perceptible or even imperceptible. In speaking to Eckermann on this occasion, Goethe seems to associate value with the very fact of being, and one recalls here again that exclamation of his in Italy, 'How true, how existent!'

Since Goethe was able to say this, though, he was also able to speak, inconsistently but unconcernedly, of value as depending on a personal and purposive relationship. Faust would not be saved without the intercession of Gretchen and the 'love from on high' of which the angels sing, and several poems in the *Divan* make a similar affirmation. So once again we find duality. There is nothing to which Goethe will let himself be pinned down, and the best of his work results from his Protean life which was able to go on providing fresh impulses through to his final years. But if that account of him is accepted, it does mean that sustained excellence is scarcely to be thought of. None of Goethe's longer works is successful as a whole, and he excels most, as Coleridge observed, in his ballads and lyrics, to which we can add his epigrams and gnomic sayings, his maxims and conversations, such a ballad-like work as the 'Gretchen-tragedy', especially as it is in the *Urfaust* version, in his diaries, especially those written before and during his journey to Italy, and in his letters for the same period. It is for this reason that one of the most exhilarating collections is the work entitled *Der junge Goethe*, edited by Max Morris, which reprints almost every scrap of paper Goethe wrote on in his early days.

Characterization is seldom within his reach or purpose, since that requires a continued observation over a long period, together with an ultimately definable point of view. Goethe's characters more often surprise by their unaccountable volte-faces than by clarity of delineation, and almost all his central characters are passive, fluid, unpurposive. His plots are either quite simple or do not exist, so that the usual impression from a play or a novel—*Iphigenie* and *Tasso* excepted—is of a winding stream which turns aside almost as chance dictates. His object is less to entertain or to move the reader than to reveal himself as he is, or to project his problems, conflicts and beliefs into various personalities who interact: very rarely, in his major works, is one likely to experience laughter or tears. But if this is all part of his belief in self-justifying existence, the daemonic in him which either cannot or will not take a view wider than the present, his deliberate adoption of formal techniques does not necessarily lead to happier results. His use of classical metres and of the Italian stanza led him into padding out his lines, and into doing violence (as it must be called) to the natural stresses of German, so that where the subject-matter concerns freedom from constriction, as it does in the *Römische Elegien*, the writing itself tends to convey the opposite sensation.

Noticeable in the very texture of Goethe's writing, on the other hand, is the kind of thing that must have come to him in a flash, or in a moment of musing relaxation. The new words which he coined in his youth in such profusion are a case in point: his mind could produce such fresh combinations of sense and sound because, perhaps, it was alive to new possibilities in a way that none of Goethe's immediate contemporaries were. Or again, one is struck by the occasional *trouvaille* or *aperçu*, the sudden startling image, seldom developed or ramified, which seems to come out of depths beyond normal consciousness. Sometimes, a particular image haunts Goethe throughout his life, and goes on acquiring meaning from year to year, as does the image of the moon, and then it seems as though he were reverting without any special intention to a theme which he knows concerns him, though he can do no more than make of it the poem which he happens to write. In such an event, one can understand his objection to the criticism of Madame de Staël, that she made the mistake of treating the works separately, without seeing their inner connection. To follow the imagery of the moon, or the sun, the centre, the circumference, or of any of the four elements, from poem to poem or from poems into novels and plays as well, is to gain an appreciation of a certain essential self that persists through all the chameleon changes. Equally revealing—though equally hard to provide with a name—are Goethe's melodies and rhythms. Encased in hexameters, these become inaudible: given free play they do not automatically take life as the 'Stürmer und Dränger' thought they would; on the contrary, they can be as heavy or as light as any passing moment. Goethe's advantage was that he was not only willing to let the rhythms shape themselves as they would, but that he had the kind of personality which would now and again let forth something that really sang. Then there would be a hesitant grace, or a lilt of melancholy or a wholehearted acceptance that belongs to music rather than to literal meaning and words, and which is inaccessible outside the language in which it exists. And at its happiest moments Goethe's invention would combine these qualities and features —melodiousness, imagery and so on—with a form that apparently came into existence with them. 'Über allen Gipfeln' has a form—it has rhyme and symmetry and a climax, a pause and a dying fall. 'Kennst du das Land' is unlike any other poem that was ever written, but it has its individual pattern, consistently maintained, and enriching the total sense by echoes from one refrain to another. And the poem which Goethe seems to have prized more than any other, the 'Marienbader Elegie' which he wrote on vellum and kept in a box like a jewel, is not only his most deeply felt, and a purely 'occasional' poem, but also one in which he uses an unusual and consistent verse-pattern to varied effect.

Where, perhaps, we go wrong, is in expecting Goethe to achieve such combinations more often than he does. A certain kind of criticism tends to encourage us in this, by suggesting that the faults we may be aware of are negligible, and that nothing can affect our total estimate of his work. Such criticism starts from suppositions very close to Goethe's own, if not identical with them. It supposes that to yield oneself to 'natural processes', not merely acting on impulse but adapting to the life and times in which one is born, so that one is 'rooted in the soil' of those times, and flourishes in them by fruitful conformity with their climate, is to ensure something much greater than mere survival. 'Wherever he went', writes Barker Fairley, 'we can be sure that Goethe took his belief in natural law, whether in the form of polarity or some other form, along with him. Provided he did this, he could go as far abroad as he liked, *there could be no loss of coherence or of unity either in his work or in his person.*' (The italics are mine.) In such a passage there is an abdication from criticism comparable to that of the political philosopher who will admit no validity to any argument against the State as the expression of the general will of the people, or to that of the theologian who will admit none to any argument against divine perfection. The theologian may have some justification, since he is speaking of a quality of which no man has any knowledge. The political philosopher and the literary critic can have none, for they are writing of men and institutions whose qualities can be seen and whose value can be appreciated. We know, and we can see for ourselves, that Goethe's work did lose in coherence and unity, sometimes severely. To argue that it could not, or that even a great loss of unity can be ignored within the whole, is to use language that can be used properly, if it can be used at all, only of a god.

More acceptable is the idea that Goethe's affirmativeness was essential if he was to survive in the flood of irrationalism, and against the day-to-day discouragements, in which he found himself. Professor Fairley yields too much when he argues that in Goethe's case 'the question of how to live and how to make life controllable' had to take priority over 'the question of being wise and the question of being creative', if he means that in Goethe's life the questions are properly separable. But one can agree that if Goethe had stopped to assess all he was doing he might well have ceased writing, or, like several of his contemporaries, gone out of his mind: there were times when he felt himself not far from it. He had, after all, very little on which he could build. The masterpieces of German literature before his own day were five hundred years old, and only beginning to be newly appreciated. Since the time of the great epics and the Minnesingers not one German work of literature had achieved international fame, until *Werther* took Europe by

he was also prepared to say 'It is indispensable to have such a companion to whom questions can be put, who has words of enlightenment for every situation in life, someone by whom to orientate ourselves, who indicates standards and teaches us to give shape to our own day, not to waste the time granted to us, and to introduce sequence into our inward activity.' So long as such a companion does remain indispensable—and Jaspers brought down a storm of denunciation on his head in 1949 for being as derogatory as he was, in the address he gave in that bicentenary year—Goethe will retain his position as the wise elder counsellor. If, on the other hand, the time for a more critical reading of him has arrived, his achievement will be seen in a more varied light; he will be less revered and more esteemed. In either event, the enigma of his ambitions and his achievements will go on fascinating readers for a good many generations to come; the last word is still a long way off.

NOTES

PAGE 17

  1 *Faust*, ll. 1770–5.

PAGE 21

  1 *Faust*, ll. 4715–28.

PAGE 38

  1 See p. 143 below.

PAGE 39

  1 See further my *Introduction to German Poetry*, pp. 65–6.
  2 See further my *Poems of Goethe*, p. 45.
  3 See *Poems of Goethe*, pp. 85–6.

PAGE 41

  1 See *Poems of Goethe*, p. 58, also *German Life and Letters*, XVIII (July 1965), pp. 279–290.

PAGE 43

  1 See p. 74 below.

PAGE 44

  1 See p. 82 below.   2 See *Poems of Goethe*, p. 70.

PAGE 49

  1 See Thackeray's 'Sorrows of Werther' in the volume of his *Works* (1900) entitled 'Ballads'.

PAGE 53

  1 'Letter' of 10 May.

PAGE 54

  1 A surviving fragment shows that Goethe did at one time propose to tell the story of Werther's reception of the pistols through Werther himself, not by the narrator. The same events are told by the narrator in the published versions.

PAGE 59

1 Letter of 25 March 1776.

PAGE 61

1   *Götz*, I, iii.

2   *Goethe's Major Plays*, p. 21.

PAGE 62

1   *Götz*, III, xix.
3   *Götz*, v, v.
5   *Götz*, IV, ii.

2   See pp. 172–3 below.
4   *Götz*, v, iv.

PAGE 64

1   *Egmont*, II, ii.

PAGE 65

1   *Egmont*, II, ii.

PAGE 66

1   See pp. 111–12 below.

PAGE 67

1   *Egmont*, II, ii.

2   *Egmont*, v, ii.

PAGE 68

1   *Egmont*, II, ii.

PAGE 69

1   See p. 137 below.

PAGE 70

1   See p. 117 below.

2   *Poetics*, ch. XVI.

PAGE 71

1   Record no. LPMS 43015-7.

PAGE 72

1   *Iphigenie*, IV, v.

PAGE 73

1   *Iphigenie*, I, v.

PAGE 74

1 *Iphigenie*, III, i.
3 See p. 160 below.

2 *Iphigenie*, III, ii.
4 *Iphigenie*, III, ii.

PAGE 75

1 *Iphigenie*, III, iii.

2 See p. 143 below.

PAGE 76

1 *Iphigenie*, I, ii.

PAGE 77

1 *Iphigenie*, IV, i.

PAGE 78

1 Cp. also the situation in *Die Wahlverwandtschaften*, pp. 222–3 below.
2 *Iphigenie*, IV, v.

PAGE 80

1 *Iphigenie*, IV, iv.

PAGE 82

1 See p. 117 below.

2 *Tasso*, III, 2.

PAGE 83

1 *Tasso*, I, 4.
3 *Tasso*, II, 4.

2 *Tasso*, II, 3.
4 *Tasso*, IV, 4.

PAGE 84

1 *Tasso*, I, 4.
3 *Tasso*, V, 1.

2 *Tasso*, III, 4.

PAGE 85

1 *Tasso*, I, 2.

2 *Ibid.*

PAGE 86

1 *Tasso*, V, 2.
3 See p. 149 below.

2 *Tasso*, II, 1.
4 *Tasso*, III, 2.

PAGE 87

1 *Tasso*, II, 1.

PAGE 88

1 *Tasso*, II, 3.   2 *Tasso*, V, 3.

PAGE 89

1 *Tasso*, V, 4.

PAGE 90

1 *Faust*, ll. 746–8.

PAGE 100

1 Diary, July 1779.

PAGE 101

1 Letter, 29 October 1780.   2 Letter, 6 July 1781.

PAGE 102

1   Letter, 13 February 1781.

PAGE 103

1 *Dichtung und Wahrheit*, Book 16.   2 *Ibid.* Book 8.
3 Letter, 9(?) April 1781.

PAGE 104

1 Letter, 7 May 1781.   2 See pp. 41, 117–20.

PAGE 105

1 Letter, September 1786.   2 Diary, 27 September 1786.

PAGE 106

1 See p. 65 above.   2 Diary, 5 October 1786.
3 Diary, 10 October 1786.   4 Letter, 24 November 1786.
5 Letter, 1 November 1786.

PAGE 107

1 *Italienische Reise*, 26 March 1787.
2 C. H. Trevelyan, *Goethe and the Greeks*, p. 148.

PAGE 108

1 Letter of Schiller, 23 August 1794.

PAGE 109

1 Letter of Schiller, 31 August 1794.
2 Letter of Schiller, 23 August 1794.

PAGE 110

1 Letter of Jacobi, 27 August 1774.   2 *Italienische Reise*, 22 March 1787.
3 Letter, 26 July 1782.   4 Diary, 13 May 1780.

PAGE 111

1 *Dichtung und Wahrheit*, Book 20.   2 Eckermann, 24 March 1829.

PAGE 112

1 Eckermann, 18 February 1831.   2 Eckermann, 28 February 1831.
3 Eckermann, 29 March 1831.   4 Eckermann, 8 March 1831.
5 Eckermann, 18 March 1831.   6 Eckermann, 11 March 1828.

PAGE 113

1 Letter, 8 February 1796 and see p. 4 above.

PAGE 115

1 Letter of July 1786.

PAGE 116

1 *Die Italienische Reise*, 17 April 1787.

PAGE 117

1 *Zur Farbenlehre*, para. 242.

PAGE 118

1 *Faust*, lines 1766–7.

PAGE 119

1 Cp. p. 105 above.   2 *Zur Farbenlehre*.

PAGE 122

1 See my *Goethe the Alchemist*, p. 77.
2 See p. 229 below.

PAGE 123

1 See p. 106 above.
2 See *Goethe the Alchemist*, p. 87.

PAGE 127

1 Lessing, Literaturbrief no. 17.

PAGE 134

1 *Faust*, l. 790.
3 *Faust*, ll. 4695–703.

2 *Faust*, ll. 501–9.
4 *Faust*, ll. 1070–99.

PAGE 135

1 *Faust*, l. 324.
3 Eckermann.

2 *Faust*, ll. 328–9.
4 *Faust*, ll. 11936–7.

PAGE 136

1 *Faust*, l. 345.
3 *Faust*, ll. 1770–5.
5 *Faust*, l. 1765.

2 *Faust*, l. 346.
4 *Faust*, l. 1802.

PAGE 137

1 *Faust*, ll. 1754–5.
3 *Faust*, ll. 1692–706.

2 *Faust*, l. 1759.
4 *Faust*, l. 1775.

PAGE 138

1 *Faust*, ll. 1860–7.

PAGE 139

1 *Faust*, ll. 3217–50.

2 *Faust*, l. 9419.

PAGE 141

1 *Faust*, ll. 3117–39.

PAGE 142

1 *Faust*, l. 1748.
3 *Faust*, l. 1775.

2 *Faust*, l. 1758.
4 *Faust*, ll. 1761–3.

PAGE 143

1 See p. 38 above.
3 See p. 21 above.

2 *Faust*, ll. 1224–37.
4 *Faust*, ll. 1379–80.

PAGE 144

1 *Faust*, l. 620.
3 *Faust*, ll. 1797–800.

2 *Faust*, ll. 1339–44.
4 *Faust*, ll. 2038–9.

PAGE 145

1 *Faust*, ll. 2296–301.

PAGE 146

1 *Faust*, l. 3536.
3 *Faust*, l. 3022.

2 *Faust*, l. 3008.
4 *Faust*, ll. 2805–10.

PAGE 147

1 *Faust*, ll. 1336–7.

2 *Faust*, ll. 1112–17.

PAGE 148

1 *Faust*, ll. 3431–58.

2 *Faust*, l. 3456.

PAGE 149

1 *Faust*, l. 2738.
3 *Faust*, ll. 3071–2.

2 *Faust*, ll. 1591–1606.
4 *Faust*, ll. 3217–39.

PAGE 152

1 *Faust*, l. 4406.
3 *Faust*, l. 4596.

2 *Faust*, l. 4441.

PAGE 153

1 *Faust*, l. 4518–9.
3 *Faust*, l. 4606.

2 *Faust*, l. 4604.

PAGE 156

1 Eckermann, 6 May 1827.

PAGE 157

1 See p. 136 above.
3 *Faust*, l. 455.
5 *Faust*, l. 620.
7 *Faust*, ll. 1566–71.
9 *Faust*, l. 2439.

2 *Faust*, ll. 382–3.
4 *Faust*, ll. 460–81.
6 *Faust*, ll. 1110–17.
8 *Faust*, l. 1815.

PAGE 158

1 *Poetics*, VIII.

2 *Faust*, ll. 1782–5.

PAGE 159

1 *Faust*, ll. 1766–7.
3 See p. 117 above.

2 *Faust*, l. 4040.

PAGE 162

1 See p. 143 above.   2 *Faust*, l. 6555.

PAGE 163

1 *Faust*, ll. 1766–7.

PAGE 164

1 *Faust*, ll. 10055–66.   2 *Faust*, l. 3207 and l. 9419.
3 *Faust*, l. 7003.

PAGE 165

1 *Faust*, l. 11639.   2 *Faust*, ll. 6687–8.
3 *Faust*, l. 12105.   4 *Faust*, ll. 5357–80.

PAGE 166

1 *Faust*, ll. 5793–4.   2 *Faust*, ll. 5305–44.

PAGE 168

1 *Faust*, ll. 9192–212.   2 *Faust*, ll. 9258–63.

PAGE 169

1 *Faust*, l. 9334.   2 *Faust*, ll. 9365–84.
3 *Faust*, ll. 9411–18.

PAGE 170

1 *Faust*, ll. 8999–9009.   2 *Faust*, ll. 9482–505.

PAGE 171

1 See letter to Iken, 23 September 1827.
2 *Faust*, l. 10219.   3 *Faust*, l. 11242.

PAGE 172

1 *Faust*, l. 11248.   2 *Faust*, l. 11563.
3 *Faust*, ll. 11153 and 11345.   4 *Faust*, l. 11242.
5 *Faust*, ll. 11255–8.   6 *Faust*, ll. 11271–2.

PAGE 173

1 *Faust*, l. 11348.   2 *Faust*, l. 11371.

PAGE 174

1 *Faust*, ll. 11497–8.   2 *Faust*, l. 11500.

PAGE 175

1 *Faust*, ll. 11404–5.
3 *Faust*, ll. 11127–8.

2 *Faust*, l. 11423.
4 *Faust*, ll. 11559–86.

PAGE 176

1 *Faust*, ll. 11574–6.
3 *Faust*, l. 11540.

2 *Faust*, l. 11502.
4 *Faust*, l. 11554.

PAGE 177

1 *Faust*, ll. 11583–4.

PAGE 178

1 *Faust*, l. 11681.

2 *Faust*, l. 11762.

PAGE 179

1 ll. 11802–6.
3 *Faust*, ll. 11838–9.

2 *Faust*, ll. 11809–16.

PAGE 180

1 *Faust*, ll. 11817–24.
3 *Faust*, ll. 11807–8.

2 See p. 204 above.

PAGE 181

1 *Faust*, ll. 11936–41.
3 *Faust*, ll. 11997–12000.

2 Eckermann, 6 June 1831.

PAGE 182

1 *War and Peace*, III, xvi.
3 *Faust*, ll. 12096–100.

2 See p. 21 above.

PAGE 184

1 See p. 235 below.

2 *Faust*, ll. 12107–8.

PAGE 187

1 *Lehrjahre*, IV, vi.

2 See p. 147 above.

PAGE 188

1 But see p. 56.

PAGE 189

1 See p. 117 above.

PAGE 193

1 *Lehrjahre*, II, xiii.

PAGE 194

1 *Lehrjahre*, II, xiv.

PAGE 196

1 *Lehrjahre*, VII, ix.

PAGE 197

1 *Wanderjahre*, II, i.

PAGE 198

1 18 February 1830, to Fr. v. Müller.
2 7 September 1821, to Zauper.   3 Eckermann, 11 September 1828.
4 Eckermann, 15 May 1831.

PAGE 211

1 See p. 36 above.

PAGE 213

1 See p. 115 above.
2 Cp. the duplicity of Tasso, p. 88 above.

PAGE 219

1 *Die Wahlverwandtschaften*, I, i.   2 *Die Wahlverwandtschaften*, I, iii.
3 *Die Wahlverwandtschaften*, I, ii.

PAGE 220

1 Letter, 12 September 1767.   2 See my *Poems of Goethe*, p. 121.
3 Cp. p. 101 above.

PAGE 221

1 *Die Wahlverwandtschaften*, II, viii.   2 Cp. p. 235 below.
3 See p. 184 above.   4 See p. 118 above.

PAGE 223

1 See p. 111 above.   2 *Die Wahlverwandtschaften*, II, xvii.
3 *Die Wahlverwandtschaften*, II, ix.   4 *Die Wahlverwandtschaften*, II, iii.
5 Cp. p. 174 above.

PAGE 228

1 See p. 33 above.

PAGE 232

1 Note the curious last line.

PAGE 233

1 See p. 111 above.   2 See p. 19 above.

PAGE 235

1 See p. 165 above.

PAGE 236

1 See p. 184 above.

PAGE 240

1 See p. 184 above.

PAGE 243

1 See p. 228 above.

PAGE 244

1 See p. 230 above.

PAGE 250

1 See my *Introduction to German Poetry*, pp. xvii–xx, for a fuller account of this poem.

SELECT BIBLIOGRAPHY

BIBLIOGRAPHICAL WORKS

Körner, J. *Bibliographisches Handbuch des deutschen Schrifttums.* Berne 1949.
Especially pp. 243–62 and 287–92.
Nicolai, H., Burkhardt, G. and Schröter, K. *Goethe-Bibliographie.* Heidelberg, 1955–65. Founder H. Pyritz.
Complete up to 1954; bibliographies for later years in progress. See also:
Carré, J.-M. *Goethe en Angleterre.* Paris, 1920.
Leppmann, W. *The German Image of Goethe.* Oxford, 1961.

EDITIONS

Weimarer (or *Sophien-*) *Ausgabe.* 143 vols., 1887–1918.
Standard edition with very full critical apparatus. A revision based on the Weimar archives is under way.
Hamburger Ausgabe. 14 vols., begun 1948. Text edited by E. Trunz.
Contains a large proportion of Goethe's works with extensive notes and bibliographies.

REFERENCE WORKS

Gräf, H. G. *Goethe über seine Dichtungen. Versuch einer Sammlung aller Aussagen des Dichters über seine poetischen Werke.* 9 vols., Frankfurt 1901–14.
von Biedermann, W. and von Biedermann, F. *Goethes Gespräche.* 5 vols., 2nd ed., Leipzig 1909–11.
Zeitler, J. *Goethe-Handbuch.* 3 vols. Stuttgart, 1916–18.
Revised edition in progress, ed. A. Zastrau, Stuttgart, begun 1961.
Fischer, P. *Goethe-Wortschatz. Ein sprachgeschichtliches Wörterbuch zu Goethes sämtlichen Werken.* Leipzig, 1929.

PERIODICALS

Jahrbuch der Goethe-Gesellschaft: the periodical of the Society has appeared since 1880 under several titles.
Publications of the English Goethe Society, first series 1886–1912; new series since 1920.

LIFE AND TIMES

Lewes, G. H. *The Life of Goethe*. 2nd ed., partly rewritten, London, 1864. (Now in Everymans Library.)

Bielschowsky, A. *Goethe. Sein Leben und seine Werke*, 2 vols., 2nd ed., rev. W. Linden, Munich, 1928. Eng. trans. of 1st ed., New York and London, 1905.

Müller, G. *Kleine Goethe-Biographie*. 3rd ed., Bonn, 1955.

Mann, Thomas. *Lotte in Weimar* (a novel). Stockholm, 1939. Eng. trans. London, 1940.

Bruford, W. H. *Theatre, Drama and Audience in Goethe's Germany*. London, 1950.

Boerner, P. *Goethe in Selbstzeugnissen und Bilddokumenten*. Hamburg, 1964.
   Small paperback, profusely illustrated.

GENERAL STUDIES

Scherer, Edmond. 'Goethe', *Études sur la littérature contemporaine*, vol. VI. Paris, 1882.

Croce, Benedetto. *Goethe*. Bari, 1919. Eng. trans. London, 1923.

Brandes, Georg. *Goethe*. Berlin, 1921.

Lukács, Georg. *Goethe und seine Zeit*. Berne, 1947.

Schweitzer, Albert. *Goethe*. London, 1949.

Jaspers, Karl. *Unsere Zukunft und Goethe*. Bremen, 1949.

Viëtor, Karl. *Goethe the Poet* and *Goethe the Thinker*. Cambridge, Massachusetts, 1949.

Staiger, Emil. *Goethe*. 3 vols., Zürich, 1957–9.

GOETHE AND THE ENGLISH-SPEAKING WORLD

Carré, J.-M. *Goethe en Angleterre*. Paris, 1920.
   There are essays in the *Collected Works* of Carlyle, Hazlitt, De Quincey and Emerson. The principal general studies have been by G. H. Lewes (2nd ed., 1864), J. Sime (1888) J. R. Seeley (1894), P. Hume Brown (1920), H. W. Nevinson (1931), J. M. Robertson (2nd ed., 1932), Barker Fairley (1932, 1947). E. M. Wilkinson and L. A. Willoughby, 1962.

See also:

Arnold, Matthew. 'A French Critic on Goethe', *Mixed Essays*. 2nd ed., London, 1880.

Santayana, George. 'Goethe's Faust', *Three Philosophical Poets*. Cambridge, Massachusetts, 1910 (since reprinted in paperback form).

Eliot, T. S. 'Goethe as the Sage', *On Poetry and Poets*. London, 1957.

Eliot, George. 'The Morality of Wilhelm Meister', *Essays*, ed. Thomas Pinney. London, 1963.

SPECIAL TOPICS

Arber, Agnes. 'Goethe's Botany', *Chronica Botanica*, vol. x, no. 2. Waltham, Massachusetts, 1946.

Beutler, E. 'Der Streit um die Faustdichtung', *Essays um Goethe*, vol. i. Wiesbaden, 1946.

Heller, Erich. 'Goethe and the Avoidance of Tragedy', *The Disinherited Mind*. Cambridge, 1952.

Palmer, P. M. and More, R. P. *The Sources of the Faust Tradition*, New York, 1936.

TRANSLATIONS

Bayard Taylor's Victorian translation of *Faust* remains the most poetic and accurate; Philip Wayne's is a good 'modern English' version; Louis MacNeice's was well conceived for radio performance, but is abridged. For most other works the Bohn Edition (14 vols., London, 1848–90) must be used. Recent translations include, however, H. M. Waidson's *Kindred by Choice* (*Die Wahlverwandtschaften*), E. Wilkins and E. Kaiser's *Truth and Fantasy* (abridged from *Dichtung und Wahrheit*), W. H. Auden's *The Italian Journey*, John Arden's *Ironhand* (adapted from *Götz*), and the prose translations by D. Luke in his selection of Goethe's poems in the 'Penguin Poets' series.

GOETHE'S LIFE AND WORKS*

Year and Goethe's age	Works	Life	Contemporary events
1749	—	Goethe born 28 Aug., Frankfurt am Main	Johnson: *Vanity of Human Wishes*
1755(6)	—	—	First ten cantos of Klopstock's *Messias*. Lisbon earthquake (ground of religious dispute)
1756(7)	—	—	Beginning of Seven Years' War
1759(10)	—	Thought to have seen puppet *Faust* by now. Frankfurt occupied by French troops	Voltaire: *Candide*
1760(11)	—	Saw French plays at Frankfurt	Sterne: *Tristram Shandy*
1762(13)	—	—	Rousseau: *Émile*. Macpherson: *Ossian*
1763(14)	—	Heard Mozart perform. Met 'Gretchen'	End of Seven Years' War
1765(16)	—	At Leipzig University; taught by Gottsched, Gellert, etc.	Johnson: Edition of Shakespeare
1766(17)	—	Love affair with Käthchen Schönkopf. Met Friederike Oeser	Goldsmith: *The Vicar of Wakefield*

* The dates of Goethe's works are the dates of writing; publication followed in a year or two except in the case of lyric poems and of works for which publication is specially mentioned. Dates of works not by Goethe refer to publication or performance.

	Goethe's works	Biographical	Contemporary works
1767(18)	Poems: Buch Annette Play: *Die Laune des Verliebten*	Still at Leipzig. Read Shakespeare at about this time	Lessing: *Minna von Barnhelm* and *Hamburgische Dramaturgie* Herder: *Fragmente* —
1768(19)	Play: *Die Mitschuldigen* (begun)	Returned home. Influenced by Pietists, especially Susanna von Klettenberg. Severe illness. Read alchemists, Swedenborg, Paracelsus	—
1770(21)	Poems: Willkommen und Abschied; Mailied; Heidenröslein Plays for *Götz, Faust, Cäsar* (last never completed)	At Strasbourg University. In love with Friederike Brion at Sesenheim. Met Herder. Influenced by him, Hamann, 'Ossian', Rousseau, Shakespeare	Klopstock: *Oden* Smollett: *Humphry Clinker*
1771(22)	Plays: First version of *Götz* (= 'Urgötz') Translations: 'Ossian', Aesop	Allowed to practise as advocate in Frankfurt. Friendship with 'Mephistopheles' Merck	Lessing: *Emilia Galotti*
1772(23)	Poems: Wandrers Sturmlied; Der Wanderer Essays: Von deutscher Baukunst; Zum Schäkespears Tag	Summer at Wetzlar (Imperial Chancelry). Met Charlotte Buff (later Kestner), the model for Werther's Lotte	
1773(24)	Plays: GÖTZ VON BERLICHINGEN; *Mahomet; Prometheus* (both unfinished); *Satyros; Pater Brey; Das Jahrmarktsfest zu Plundersweilern; Götter, Helden und Wieland*	At Frankfurt. Met theologian Lavater, philosopher Jacobi, poets Klopstock and Stolberg. Passion for portrait-drawing. Goethe's sister (Cornelia) married. Read Spinoza, the Koran	Herder (and Goethe etc.): *Von deutscher Art und Kunst* Goldsmith: *She Stoops to Conquer*
1774(25)	Poems: Ganymed; Prometheus; An Schwager Kronos; Der König in Thule Play: *Clavigo* Novel: DIE LEIDEN DES JUNGEN WERTHER	Travelled with Lavater. Met novelists Jung-Stilling, Heinse, also Carl August, Duke of Weimar. Very great popular success of *Werther*	Wieland: *Die Abderiten* Chesterfield: *Letters to his Natural Son*

Year and Goethe's age	Works	Life	Contemporary events
1775(26)	Poems: Lilis Park; Lieder an Lili. Plays: EGMONT begun; Erwin und Elmire; Claudine von Villa Bella. Novel: Wilhelm Meisters Theatralische Sendung (= 'Urmeister') begun. Essays: Contributions to Lavater's physiognomical work	In love with Lili Schönemann. Travelled to Switzerland, had distant view of Italy. Invited to Weimar by Duke Carl August. Met novelist Wieland, also Charlotte von Stein	American War of Independence. Beaumarchais: Le Barbier de Séville. Sheridan: The Rivals
1776(27)	Poems: Der du von dem Himmel bist; Warum gabst du uns die tiefen Blicke; Hans Sachsens poetische Sendung; Rastlose Liebe; An den Geist des Johannes Secundus. Plays: Die Geschwister; Stella	Settled down in Weimar, took over 'Gartenhaus' in park, began official duties, studied mineralogy, geology, botany. Deeper relationship with Frau von Stein, continuing for next ten years	American Declaration of Independence. Klinger: Sturm und Drang. Lenz: Die Soldaten. H. Wagner: Die Kindermörderin. Gibbon: Decline and Fall of the Roman Empire (vol. I)
1777(28)	Poem: Harzreise im Winter. Plays: Lila; Der Triumph der Empfindsamkeit	Journey to Harz Mountains	—
1778(29)	Poems: An den Mond (Füllest wieder...); Der Fischer. Play: IPHIGENIE AUF TAURIS begun (prose-version)	Journey to Berlin	War of the Bavarian Succession. Voltaire and Rousseau died
1779(30)	Poem: Grenzen der Menschheit. Play: Jery und Bätely	Appointed 'Geheimrat' (Privy Counsellor). Journey to Switzerland	Lessing: Nathan der Weise. Hume: Natural Religion (posthumous)
1780(31)	Poems: Über allen Gipfeln; Meine Göttin	Read part of Faust to Duke of Weimar. Increasingly occupied with duties and	Wieland: Oberon. Joseph II's social reforms in Austria

276

Year			
	Play: TORQUATO TASSO begun (prose-version)	scientific studies	
1781(32)	Poem: An Lida Plays: Die Fischerin; Elpenor	In Weimar most of the year	Rousseau: Confessions Schiller: Die Räuber Kant: Kritik der reinen Vernunft
1782(33)	Poems: Erlkönig; Wer sich der Einsamkeit ergibt	Received patent of nobility. Estranged from Herder	Cowper: John Gilpin Laclos: Les Liaisons Dangereuses
1783(34)	Poems: Ilmenau; Das Göttliche; Wer nie sein Brot mit Tränen aß	Began teaching Frau von Stein's son Fritz. Reconciled with Herder	Pitt's first ministry began
1784(35)	Poems: Zueignung (Der Morgen kam); Kennst du das Land Play: Scherz, List und Rache Epic poem: Die Geheimnisse (never completed) Essay: Über den Granit	Discovered that intermaxillary bone exists in human jaw as well as that of animals	Schiller: Kabale und Liebe Beaumarchais: Le Mariage de Figaro Herder: Ideen zu einer Philosophie der Geschichte der Menschheit
1785(36)	Poem: Nur wer die Sehnsucht kennt	Letters to Jacobi on Spinoza. Mozart set 'Das Veilchen' to music	Moritz: Anton Reiser begun
1786(37)	Play: IPHIGENIE AUF TAURIS completed	Estranged from Lavater. Left for Italy from Karlsbad via Munich, Brenner Pass, Verona, Venice, Florence, Rome. Met Tischbein and Angelika Kaufmann (painters) and Moritz (writer)	Frederick the Great died. Mozart: Le Nozze di Figaro Burns: Poems, chiefly in Scottish Dialect Beckford: Vathek
1787(38)	Play: EGMONT completed Epic poem: Nausikaa (never completed)	Carnival in Rome. Naples, Vesuvius, Pompeii, Sicily; back in Rome by June. Studies of ancient art and architecture	Schiller: Don Carlos Bernardin de St Pierre: Paul et Virginie Mozart: Don Giovanni

Year and Goethe's age	Works	Life	Contemporary events
1788(39)	Poems: Cophtische Lieder; Amor als Landschaftsmaler. RÖMISCHE ELEGIEN begun. Plays: Earlier plays revised. Additions to Faust. TORQUATO TASSO completed	Decided against a career as a painter. Back in Weimar by June. Lived with Christiane Vulpius. Estranged from Charlotte von Stein	Kant: *Die Kritik der praktischen Vernunft*
1789(40)	—	Journey to Harz Mountains. Met Wilhelm von Humboldt (statesman). Son August born	Storming of the Bastille. Blake: *Songs of Innocence*.
1790(41)	Poems: Venezianische Epigramme. Play: *Der Groß-Cophta*; FAUST, EIN FRAGMENT published. Science: *Versuch, die Metamorphose der Pflanzen zu erklären*	Journeys to Venice and Silesia. Conversation with Schiller about Kant	Kant: *Die Kritik der Urteilskraft*. Burke: *Reflections on the French Revolution*
1791(42)	Science: *Beiträge zur Optik I*	In charge of Weimar Theatre (till 1817)	Franklin: *Autobiography*. Paine: *Rights of Man*. Boswell: *Life of Johnson*
1792(43)	Autobiography: *Die Kampagne in Frankreich*. Science: *Beiträge zur Optik II*	Accompanied Duke of Weimar on campaign in France against the revolutionaries	Wollstonecraft: *Rights of Woman*
1793(44)	Play: *Der Bürgergeneral*. Epic poem: *Reineke Fuchs*. Autobiography: *Die Belagerung von Mainz*	At siege of Mainz	Execution of Louis XVI and Reign of Terror in France. Schiller: *Über Anmut und Würde*. Wordsworth: *Descriptive Sketches*

1794(45)	Play: *Die Aufgeregten* Stories: *Unterhaltungen deutscher Ausgewanderten* (incl. *Märchen*) Novel: *Wilhelm Meister* largely rewritten	Beginning of friendship with Schiller (till Schiller's death in 1805)	Fichte: *Wissenschaftslehre* Blake: *Europe* Radcliffe: *Mysteries of Udolpho*
1795(46)	Poems: Meeres Stille; Glückliche Fahrt; An die Türen will ich schleichen Novel: WILHELM MEISTERS LEHRJAHRE published (1795–6)	Met Alexander von Humboldt (explorer)	Schiller: *Briefe über die ästhetische Erziehung*
1796(47)	Poems: *Xenien*; So laßt mich scheinen; Alexis und Dora Epic poem: HERMANN UND DOROTHEA Translation: Cellini's *Autobiography*	A. W. von Schlegel, translator of Shakespeare, settled in Jena near Weimar. Goethe and Schiller collaborated in writing *Xenien* (epigrams)	Napoleon's campaigns in Italy. Hölderlin's principal poems written 1796–1802 Lewis: *The Monk*
1797(48)	Poems: Der Schatzgräber; Die Braut von Korinth; Der Gott und die Bajadere; Legende; Der Zauberlehrling; Zueignung (Ihr naht euch wieder); Euphrosyne; Amyntas	Collaborated with Schiller in writing ballads ('Das Balladenjahr'). Experiments with caterpillars and metamorphosis of insects. Burned all letters kept hitherto. Journey to Switzerland. F. von Schlegel, critic, settled in Jena	Schiller: *Wallenstein* trilogy begun A. von Schlegel: translations of Shakespeare begun Hölderlin: *Hyperion* begun
1798(49)	Poems: *Die Weissagungen des Bakis*; Die Metamorphose der Pflanzen Plays: parts of *Faust*; *Die Zauberflöte, zweiter Teil* begun Epic poem: *Achilleis* (never completed)	Edited journal *Die Propyläen* (1798–1800). Schelling (philosopher) settled in Jena	Wordsworth and Coleridge: *Lyrical Ballads* Schlegel: *Das Athenäum* Haydn: *Die Schöpfung*
1799(50)	Play: *Die natürliche Tochter* (only a part completed) Translation: Voltaire's *Mahomet*	Schiller settled in Weimar	F. von Schlegel: *Lucinde*

Year and Goethe's age	Works	Life	Contemporary events
1800 (51)	Play: *Palüophron und Neoterpe*; parts of *Faust*, including scene for *Part II*. Translation: Voltaire's *Tancred*	Experiments with magnets	Schiller: *Maria Stuart* Novalis: *Hymnen an die Nacht*
1801 (52)	Poem: Dauer im Wechsel Play: parts of *Faust*	Studied history of chromatics. Met Hegel, the philosopher, now settled in Jena	Schiller: *Die Jungfrau von Orleans* Chateaubriand: *Atala*
1802 (53)	Poems: Schäfers Klagelied; Weltseele; Ritter Kurts Brautfahrt	Founded training-school for actors. Planned reorganization of libraries at Weimar and Jena	Novalis: *Heinrich von Ofterdingen*
1803 (54)	Poems: various sonnets	Period of withdrawal and depression. Founded *Jenaische Allgemeine Literatur-Zeitung*	Schiller: *Die Braut von Messina*
1804 (55)	Essays: *Winckelmann und sein Jahrhundert*; *Rameaus Neffe*	Met Madame de Staël, propagator of German literature in France	Napoleon crowned Emperor Schiller: *Wilhelm Tell*
1805 (56)	Poem: Epilog zu Schillers Glocke	Unwell for several months	Death of Schiller. Battle of Trafalgar Beethoven: *Fidelio*
1806 (57)	Poem: Die Metamorphose der Tiere Plays: FAUST ERSTER TEIL completed (published 1808) *Pandora* begun	Again unwell. Goethe saved from French troops plundering in Weimar by Christiane, whom he married officially four days later	Dissolution of Holy Roman Empire. Battle of Jena: humiliation of Prussia and Austria
1807 (58)	Poems: various sonnets. Wirkung in die Ferne Novels: DIE WAHLVERWANDTSCHAFTEN begun; WILHELM MEISTERS WANDERJAHRE begun	Frequented circle of Johanna von Schopenhauer. Spent summer as usual at Karlsbad (Bohemia)	Vom Stein's reforms in Prussia. Beginning of patriotic German movement against Napoleon

Year	Goethe's works	Goethe's life	Contemporary events
1808(59)	Novel: *Wanderjahre* continued sporadically for many years	Death of Goethe's mother. Met Napoleon at Erfurt	Kleist: *Penthesilea*
1809(60)	Autobiography: DICHTUNG UND WAHRHEIT begun (publ. 1811–31)	—	A. von Schlegel: *Dramatische Kunst*
1810(61)	Poem: *Das Tagebuch*; Science: *Zur Farbenlehre*	—	Kleist: *Prinz Friedrich von Homburg*
1811(62)	—	—	Jane Austen: *Sense and Sensibility*
1812(63)	Poems: Groß ist die Diana der Epheser; Was wär ein Gott...	Met Beethoven	Napoleon's retreat from Moscow; Hegel: *Logik* begun
1813(64)	Poems: Der Totentanz; Die Wandelnde Glocke; Gefunden	Met Schopenhauer	Byron: *The Giaour*; Shelley: *Queen Mab*
1814(65)	Poems: DER WEST-ÖSTLICHE DIVAN begun; Play: *Des Epimenides Erwachen*; Autobiography: DIE ITALIENISCHE REISE begun	In love with Marianne von Willemer. Journey to rivers Rhine and Main	Scott: *Waverley*; Wordsworth: *The Excursion*
1815(66)	Poems: *Divan* continued	Journey to Rhineland. Became 'Staatsminister'. Studied meteorology	Napoleon's escape from Elba and defeat at Waterloo
1816(67)	Poems: *Divan* continued; Play: work on *Faust Part II*	Death of Goethe's wife. His son engaged to Ottilie von Pogwisch	Coleridge: *Kubla Khan*
1817(68)	Poems: *Divan* continued; Urworte. Orphisch; Science: *Zur Morphologie*	Arrangements for a botanical museum and veterinary school	Period of political reaction began; Keats: *Poems*; Beethoven: *Mass in D*; Mary Shelley: *Frankenstein*
1818(69)	Poems: *Divan* continued; Um Mitternacht ging ich...	—	—
1819(70)	Poem: *Epirrhema*	Met Prince Metternich	Schopenhauer: *Die Welt als Wille und Vorstellung*
1820(71)	Poems: Allerdings; Zahme Xenien begun	—	—

Year and Goethe's age	Works	Life	Contemporary events
1821 (72)	Poems: Paria; Eins und Alles; Novel: WILHELM MEISTERS WANDERJAHRE published (2nd ed. 1829)	—	Grillparzer: Das goldene Vließ; De Quincey: Opium Eater; Weber: Der Freischütz
1822 (73)	—	Visited by Mendelssohn	Heine: Gedichte
1823 (74)	Poems: 'Marienbader' Elegie; Aussöhnung	In love with Ulrike von Levetzow. Began conversations with Eckermann	Carlyle: Life of Schiller; Lamb: Essays of Elia
1824 (75)	Poem: An Werther	First letter to Thomas Carlyle	Carlyle: Wilhelm Meister (translation)
1825 (76)	Play: FAUST ZWEITER TEIL taken up again; work continued till 1831; Science: Versuch einer Witterungslehre	Visited by Carl Maria von Weber	Grillparzer: König Ottokar
1826 (77)	Poem: Schillers Reliquien; Story: Novelle	Visited by Grillparzer	Eichendorff: Taugenichts; Fenimore Cooper: The Last of the Mohicans
1827 (78)	—	Death of Charlotte von Stein	Hugo: Préface de 'Cromwell'
1828 (79)	Poems: Chinesisch-deutsche Tages- und Jahreszeiten; Der Bräutigam; Dem aufgehenden Vollmonde	Death of Carl August, Duke of Weimar	Taylor: Historic Survey of German Poetry begun
1829 (80)	Poem: Vermächtnis	Berlioz sent settings of Faust	Balzac: La Comédie Humaine begun
1830 (81)	—	Nerval sent translation of Faust. Visited by Thackeray	July Revolution in France; Tennyson: Poems
1831 (82)	Play: FAUST ZWEITER TEIL completed (published posthumously, 1832)	Homage from Carlyle and other British friends	Stendhal: Le Rouge et le Noir; Poe: Poems
1832 (82)	—	Died on 22 March	—

INDEX

Aesop, 275
alchemists, alchemy, 98, 104, 114, 115, 117, 119, 122, 140, 275
alexandrine, 10, 27, 29, 38, 39, 43, 203
alliteration, 35
anacreontic verse, 13 (*see also* 8), 248
anatomy, 114, 117
Anton Reiser, 28–9
Arber, A., 124
Arden, J., 61
Ariosto, 84
Aristotle, 70, 158
Arnold, M., vii

Bach, J. S., 8, 183–4
Bacon, Francis, 122
Bailey, P. J., 128
'Balladenjahr', 214
Baudelaire, 6
Baumgart, H., 155
Beaumarchais, 276, 277
Becker, Maria, 71
Beethoven, 3, 18, 69, 280, 281
Berlioz, 18, 128, 282
Beutler, E., 155
Bible, The, 3, 99, 144, 210, 229, 231
Bielschowsky, A., 98, 154
'Bildungsroman', 15
Blücher, 18, 19
Bodmer, 29
Boehme, 118, 122, 124
Boito, 128
botany, 114, 117, 120–2, 123, 276
Brahma, 179
Brandes, G., 155
Brecht, 58 (Brechtian theatre), 65
Breitinger, 29
Brentano, Maximiliane, 48
Brion, Friederike, 9, 30, 33, 34, 56, 129, 163, 205, 275
Bruford, W. H., 50
Buff, Charlotte, 9, 48, 226
Burckhardt, J., 128
Burdach, K., 155, 156, 157
Busoni, 128
Butler, Samuel, 195
Byron, 18, 111, 112, 128, 171, 281

Carl August, duke of Weimar, 8, 9, 43, 59, 112, 275, 276, 282
Carlyle, 3, 18, 197, 253, 280
Catullus, 3, 13, 203
Cellini, 279
Chamisso, 128
Chardin, Jean-Baptiste, 213
Chardin, Teilhard de, 124
Chinese poetry, 246
Christ, Christian, Christianity, 18, 28, 71, 81 (Jesus), 90, 98, 100, 101, 102, 110, 112, 119, 172, 181, 204, 214–15, 220
chromatics, 116, 117–19, 123
classicism, 10, 27, 64, 70, 99
Coleridge, S. T., 128, 138, 207 (n.), 254, 279, 281
Communist Manifesto, 5
Cooper, Fenimore, 18, 280
Croce, B., 155, 160
Curran, J. P., 176

'daemonic', the, 16, 19, 66, 110–13, 223, 233, 243, 255
Dampier, W., 124
Delacroix, 18, 151
Dickens, 186 (*David Copperfield*)
Die Propyläen, 279
Disraeli, 186
Ducis, J. F., 58
Düntzer, H., 98
Dürer, 8

Eckermann, J. P., 97, 98, 111, 125, 135, 156, 181, 198, 253, 282
Eichendorff, 280
elegiac couplet, 13, 29, 206
Eliot, George, 7, 23
Eliot, T. S., vii, 39, 165
Emrich, W., 155
'Entsagung', 18, 223–4
Epictetus, 100
Euripides, 3, 70–71, 99

Fabricius, Katharina, 113
Fairley, B., 257
Faust-books, 127
Fichte, 154, 186, 277
Flaubert, 186

Foscolo, Ugo, 55
France, French, 8, 10, 15, 16, 56, 58, 64, 70, 99, 127, 211, 213
Frankfurt am Main, 8, 9, 33, 99, 226, 274, 275
Frederick II of Prussia, 100, 127, 277
Freemasonry, 191
free rhythms, 11, 29
French Revolution, 14, 15, 16, 213, 278
Freud, 7, 171, 218

Gellert, 27, 28, 38, 274
geology, 114, 117, 276
Gide, André, 4, 55, 165
Goethe, August von (Goethe's son), 278
Goethe, Christiane von (Goethe's wife, née Vulpius), 13, 203, 216, 278, 280, 281
Goethe, Cornelia (Goethe's sister), 56, 275
Goethe, Johann Kaspar (Goethe's father), 8
Goethe, Johann Wolfgang von
  'Ach, um deine feuchten Schwingen', 230
  Achilleis, 208, 279
  'Adler und Taube', 38
  Alexis und Dora, 208, 279
  'Allerdings', 241, 281
  'Amor als Landschaftsmaler', 203, 278
  'Amyntas', 208, 279
  'An den Geist des Johannes Secundus', 276
  'An den Mond', 36, 43, 45, 249, 276
  'An die Türen...', 279
  'Anklage', 231
  'An Lida', 277
  Annalen, 97, 98
  'An Schwager Kronos', 30, 40, 275
  'An Suleika', 233
  'An vollen Büschelzweigen', 230, 238
  'An Werther', 282
  'Auf Christiane R.', 34
  'Aussöhnung', 282
  autobiography, see *Dichtung und Wahrheit*
  'Beiname', 231
  Beiträge zur Optik, 116, 278
  Briefe aus der Schweiz, 98
  Buch Annette, 275
  Cäsar, 275
  Cellini's autobiography, 279
  Chinesisch-deutsche Tages- und Jahreszeiten, 282
  Claudine von Villa Bella, 276

Clavigo, 56, 57, 151, 275
  'Cophtische Lieder', 203, 278
  'Dämmrung senkte sich von oben', 247
  'Das Göttliche', 42, 277
  Das Jahrmarktsfest zu Plundersweilern, 56, 275
  'Das Tagebuch', 281
  'Das Veilchen', 38, 277
  'Dauer im Wechsel', 226, 228, 280
  'Deine Liebe, dein Kuß mich entzückt', 235
  'Dem aufgehenden Vollmonde', 250, 282
  'Der Bräutigam', 282
  Der Bürgergeneral, 14, 278
  'Der du von dem Himmel bist', 38, 276
  'Der Fischer', 276
  'Der Gott und die Bajadere', 214–15, 279
  Der Groß-Cophta, 278
  'Der König in Thule', 40, 275
  'Der Schatzgräber', 279
  'Der Totentanz', 281
  Der wandernde Jude, 102, 106
  'Der Wandrer', 275
  Der West-Östliche Divan, 17, 20, 184, 226–39, 246, 254, 281
  'Der Winter und Timur', 233
  'Der Zauberlehrling', 279
  Des Epimenides Erwachen, 281
  Dichtung und Wahrheit, 16, 97, 98–101, 102, 103, 112, 281
  Die Aufgeregten, 14, 279
  Die Belagerung von Mainz, 98, 278
  'Die Braut von Korinth', 214, 279
  Die Fischerin, 56, 277
  Die Geheimnisse, 277
  Die Geschwister, 56, 276
  Die Kampagne in Frankreich, 98, 278
  Die Laune des Verliebten, 56
  Die Leiden des jungen Werther, see *Werthers Leiden*
  'Die Metamorphose der Pflanzen', 118, 208, 279
  'Die Metamorphose der Tiere', 208, 280
  Die Mitschuldigen, 56, 275
  Die natürliche Tochter, 14, 57, 279
  Die Wahlverwandtschaften, 15, 118, 122, 140, 216–25, 280
  'Die wandelnde Glocke', 281
  Die Weissagungen des Bakis, 208, 279
  Die Zauberflöte, zweiter Teil, 279

Goethe Johann Wolfgang von (*cont.*)
Egmont, 5, 10, 13, 57, 64–70, 71, 75, 81,
98, 106, 173, 183, 276, 277
'Ein zärtlich jugendlicher Kummer',
36
'Eins und Alles', 244, 282
'Elegie', 22, 245–6, 256, 282
Elpenor, 279
'Epilog zu Schillers Glocke', 282
'Epirrhema', 240, 281
'Erkenne dich...', 228
'Erlkönig', 11, 45, 277
Erwin und Elmire, 46, 276
Euphrosyne, 208, 279
Faust, 3, 5, 6, 7, 8, 12, 15, 17, 18, 19, 20,
21, 43 (pt. II), 53, 56, 62 (pt. II), 66,
69, 74 (pt. II), 75, 77, 86, 90, 97, 98,
102, 112, 113, 114, 115, 117, 118,
121, 125, 126–85, 187, 188, 190–91,
182, 221, 228, 234, 235, 237, 240,
249, 253, 258, 275, 276, 278, 279,
280, 281, 282
Faust, ein Fragment, 141, 278
'Fetter grüne, du Laub', 46
'Ganymed', 35, 40, 117, 275
'Gefunden', 281
'Gern verlass ich diese Hütte', 246
'Gesang der Geister...', 42
Geschichte Gottfriedens von Berlichingen
mit der eisernen Hand, 57
'Glück der Entfernung', 33
'Glückliche Fahrt', 279
Götter, Helden und Wieland, 56, 275
Götz von Berlichingen, 8, 15, 57–65, 69,
70, 98, 275
'Grenzen der Menschheit', 42–3, 276
'Groß ist die Diana der Epheser', 215,
281
'Hans Sachsens Poetische Sendung',
276
'Harzreise im Winter', 40, 41, 42, 104,
234, 276
'Heidenröslein', 275
Hermann und Dorothea, 14, 15, 208–15,
279
'Hochbeglückt in deiner Liebe', 230
'Ilmenau', 39, 43, 47, 277
'In tausend Formen magst du dich
verstecken', 121
Iphigenie auf Tauris, 7, 10, 13, 22, 43,
57, 70–81, 89, 107, 254, 276, 277
Italienische Reise, Die, 97, 98, 231
Jery und Bätely, 278
'Katechisation', 39

'Kennst du das Land', 46–7, 277,
'Legende', 278
'Liebhaber in allen Gestalten', 35
Lila, 276
'Lilis Park', 34, 38, 276
Mahomet, 275 (*see also* 279)
'Mahomets-Gesang', 39, 40, 41–2, 246
'Mailied', 31–2, 37, 275
'Märchen', 278
'Marienbader Elegie', *see* 'Elegie'
'Meeres Stille', 279
'Meine Göttin', 276
'Meine Ruh ist hin', 46
Nausikaa, 208, 277
'Novelle', 282
'Nur wer die Sehnsucht kennt', 45, 277
'offenbar Geheimnis', 229
Paläophron und Neoterpe, 282
Pandora, 56, 280
'Paria', 179, 282
'Parzenlied', 72, 78–9
Pater Brey, 275
'Poetische Gedanken über die Höllen-
fahrt Jesu Christi', 28
Prometheus, 275
'Prometheus', 40, 117, 273
Rameaus Neffe, 280
'Rastlose Liebe', 276
Reineke Fuchs, 208, 278
'Ritter Kurts Brautfahrt', 280
Römische Elegien, 13, 203–8, 234, 255,
278
Satyros, 275
'Schäfers Klagelied', 280
Scherz, List und Rache, 277
'Schillers Reliquien', 282
scientific writings, 3, 11, 18, 114–25,
281, 282
'Selige Sehnsucht', 122, 229
'Sesenheimer Lyrik', 30–1
'So laßt mich scheinen', 279
Sonnets, 280
Stella, 56, 216, 276
Tancred, 280
Theory of Colours, *see* Zur Farbenlehre
Torquato Tasso, 7, 10, 13, 22, 44, 57, 81–
93, 117–18, 233, 254, 277, 278
Triumph der Empfindsamkeit, Der, 274
'Über allen Gipfeln', 45, 276
'Über den Granit', 277
'Um Mitternacht ging ich...' 250,
281
Unterhaltungen deutscher Ausgewander-
ten, 279

Goethe Johann Wolfgang von (*cont.*)
  Urfaust, 129–33, 136, 138, 151, 152, 153
  'Urworte. Orphisch', 111, 120, 243, 254, 281
  Venezianische Epigramme, 208, 278
  'Vermächtnis', 174, 244–5, 282
  Versuch, die Metamorphose der Pflanzen zu erklären, 116, 278
  Versuch einer Witterungslehre, 282
  'Vollmondnacht', 230
  'Von deutscher Baukunst', 275
  'Wandrers Sturmlied', 35, 40, 228, 275
  'Warum gabst du uns...', 276
  'Was wär ein Gott...', 281
  'Weltseele', 280
  'Wer nie sein Brot...', 277
  'Wer sich der Einsamkeit ergibt', 277
  Werthers Leiden, 6, 8, 9, 15, 20, 23, 48–55, 82, 90, 101, 117, 210, 216, 219, 224, 257, 275
  'Wiederfinden', 122, 180, 204, 237
  Wilhelm Meister, 5, 6, 7, 11, 15, 19, 45, 56, 90, 97, 98, 101, 121, 140, 162, 175, 186–200, 219, 220, 249, 279, 280, 281, 282
  Wilhelm Meisters Theatralische Sendung, 186–7, 195, 276
  'Willkommen und Abschied', 36, 37, 275
  Winckelmann und sein Jahrhundert, 99, 280
  'Wirkung in die Ferne', 280
  Xenien, 208, 279
  Zahme Xenien, 208, 281
  'Zueignung' ('Der Morgen kam'), 40, 43–4, 46, 90, 189, 277
  'Zueignung' ('Ihr naht euch...'), 279
  'Zum Shäckespears Tag', 275
  Zur Farbenlehre, 15, 16, 281
  Zur Morphologie, 281
  'Zwischen Lavater und Basedow', 38
Goethe, Katharina Elisabeth (Goethe's mother), 29
Goethe, Ottilie von, *see* Pogwisch, Ottilie von
Gogol, 6
Gottsched, 274
Gounod, 128
Grabbe, 128
Greece, 12, 99, 107–8, 166, 204, 208, 210

Grillparzer, 18, 282
Grimm, Herman, 154
Gryphius, Andreas, 27, 59
Gundolf, F., 21, 24, 155
Gwinner, W., 154

Hafiz, 17, 226 ff.
Hamann, 98, 100, 275
Hammer, J. von, 17, 226
Haydn, 8, 279
Hebbel, 165
Hegel, Hegelian, 16, 125, 134, 139, 154, 229, 240, 280, 281
Heine, 18, 128, 247, 282
Heinse, 275
Heller, E., 124
Hemingway, 4
Herder, 5, 17, 40, 58, 98, 100, 111, 127, 275, 277
'Herrnhuter', 98
Herzlieb, Minna, 216
Hesiod, 100
hexameter, 13, 29, 203, 208–10, 212
Hoffmann, E. T. A., 6
Holy Roman Empire, 99, 280
Homer, 12, 99, 203, 208
Hugo, Victor, 18, 111, 282
Humboldt, A. von, 18, 279
Humboldt, W. von, 278
Hume, 275

iambic pentameters, 71
iambic trimeters, 27
Ibsen, 128
Ilm, river, 11
imagery, 36, 249, 255
intermaxillary bone, 114, 121, 277
Islam, 17, 18, 226 ff.
Italian stanza, 10, 40, 44, 255
Italy, Italian journeys, 43, 47, 48, 56, 99, 102, 103, 105–8, 141, 162, 163, 192, 203, 206, 219, 276, 277

Jacobi, F., 110, 275, 277
James, Henry, 186, 200
Jaspers, K., 258–9
Jena, 16, 18, 99, 280
Jenaische Allgemeine Literatur-Zeitung, 280
Jerusalem, K., 48
Jews, 203, 210
Job, Book of, 3, 100, 133, 251–2
Johnson, Samuel, vii–ix, 274
Joseph II, Emperor of Austria, 6, 276
Joyce, James, 4, 103

Jung, C. G., 189
Jung, Marianne, *see* Willemer, Marianne von
Jung-Stilling, 275

Kafka, 6
Kant, 134, 139, 241, 277, 278
Karlsbad, 280
Kaufmann, A., 277
Keats, 35, 281
Keller, Gottfried, 165, 186
Kestner, J. C., 48
Kierkegaard, 154
Kleist, 281
Klettenberg, Susanna von, 129, 114, 117, 195, 275
Klinger, 128, 276
Klopstock, 29–31, 37, 274, 275
'Knittelvers', 37, 126–7, 235–6
Koran, The, 3, 226, 231, 232, 275

La Roche, M. von, *see* Brentano, Maximiliane
Lavater, 98, 100, 103, 114, 275, 276, 277
Leibniz, 28, 101, 136, 156, 183
Leipzig, 30, 59–60, 63, 274, 275
Lenau, 128
Lenin, 6
Lenz, R. M. J., 276
Lessing, 111, 127, 275, 276
Levetzow, Ulrike von, 19, 245, 282
Lewes, G. H., 199–200
'Lida' *see also* Charlotte von Stein, 10
Linnaeus (Linné), 3, 98, 114
Liszt, 128
Lucretius, 208
Lunacharsky, 128
Luther, 61, 127, 135, 143, 185

Madach, Imre, 128
Mahler, Gustav, 128
Mann, Thomas, 5, 104, 128, 186
Manzoni, 111
Marlowe, 127, 136, 148, 168
Martial, 208
Marx, Karl, 6
Mendelssohn, Felix, 18, 128, 282
Menzel, Wolfgang, 154
Merck, J. H., 275
Merian-Genast, E., 49
Metternich, 18, 281
Meyer, C. F., 165
Meyer, J. H., 113

Mieckiewicz, 18
Mignon, 45
mineralogy, 276
Minor, J., 155
Molière, 99, 111
Montgomery, M., 155
Mörike, 165
Moritz, K. P., 28–9, 107, 210, 277
Morris, Max, 254
Mozart, 8, 19, 111, 274, 277
Müller, G., 98
Müller, 'Maler', 128
Mussorgsky, 128
mysticism, mystics, 98, 103, 122, 229

naïve and reflective poets, 109
Napoleon, 3, 16, 17, 19, 20, 55, 99, 111, 233, 279, 280, 281
Nature, 36, 52, 82, 109, 115, 116, 117, 118, 122, 150
neo-Platonists, 117, 119, 122, 140
Neri, Filippo, 231
Nerval, Gérard de, 18, 128, 282
Neumann, Balthasar, 183
Newton, 125
Nietzsche, 4, 57, 182, 235, 240, 253
Novalis, 186, 280
Nuremberg, 60

Oeser, Friederike, 274
Oken, Lorenz, 217
optics, 116
Orphic songs, 100
Ossian, Ossianic, 54, 58, 275
ottava rima, *see* Italian stanza

Panama canal, 18
Paracelsus, 275
Pasternak, B., 128
Peacock, R., 61, 89, 90
Peter the Great, 112
Petsch, R., 155
Pfizer, 127
Philosophers' Stone, 104, 117, 119
physiognomy, 114
Pietism, Pietists, 29, 57, 98, 114, 117, 275
Pindar, 37, 99
Piranesi, 11
Plato, Platonic, 12, 121
Poe, 6, 282
Pogwisch, Ottilie von, 281
polarity, 20, 40, 47, 70, 82–1, 117, 118, 120, 135, 136, 137, 158–9, 161, 164,

polarity (*cont.*)
167, 178, 188, 189, 216, 217, 221, 233, 234, 242–5
Propertius, 3, 13, 203
puppets, 99
Pushkin, 18
Pyritz, H., viii

Racine, 99, 130
Rickert, H., 155
Rilke, 4, 6, 35, 55, 223
Roman Catholicism, 48, 224
Romantic, Romanticism, 6, 15, 97
Rossini, 111
Rousseau, Jean-Jacques, 4, 55, 57, 99, 186, 274, 275, 276, 277
Ruskin, 131

Sachs, Hans, 37, 126
St John's Gospel, 20, 143
Sanskrit literature, 18
Santayana, G., 155, 185
Sartre, J.-P., 4
Schelling, 128, 139, 154, 217, 279
Scherer, Edmond, 55
Schiller, J. C. F., 15, 16, 17, 64, 65, 66, 67, 68, 98, 108–10, 111, 116, 191, 207, 208, 210, 214, 241, 277, 278, 279, 280
Schlegel, A. W. von, 279, 281
Schlegel, F. von, 13, 15, 186, 200, 205, 279
Schmidt, Erich, 155
Schönemann, Lili, 9, 33, 34, 38, 276
Schönkopf, Katharina, 274
Schopenhauer, Arthur, 241, 281
Schopenhauer, Johanna, 280
Schumann, Robert, 128
Schweitzer, A., 258
Scott, Sir Walter, 7, 18, 111, 281
Shakespeare, viii, 3, 8, 17, 53 (*Hamlet*), 56, 58, 59, 60, 63 (*Henry V*), 64, 70, 98, 100, 111, 131, 151, 179 (*All's Well* and *Troilus*), 190, 191 (*Hamlet*), 275
Shelley, 128, 281
Sherrington, C., 125
Sicily, 106–7, 116
Socrates, 112
Song of Solomon, 100
Sophocles, 111, 130
Spengler, O., 124
Spies, Johann, 127
Spinoza, 3, 98, 100, 102–3, 275, 277
Spohr, 128
Staël, Mme de, 255, 280

Staiger, E., vii, 22, 49, 155
'Steigerung' (synthesis, enhancement), 82, 118, 119, 159, 162, 167, 221–4, 226, 230
Stein, Charlotte von, 3, 9, 10, 34–5, 101, 102, 104, 106, 110, 115, 163, 189, 226, 276, 277, 278, 282
Stein, 'Fritz' von, 277
Steiner, Rudolf, 124
Stendhal, 18, 282
Sterne, Laurence, 111, 274
Stifter, 186
'Stillen im Lande, die', 98
Stoics, 100
Stolberg, C. and F. L., 275
Strasbourg, 275
'Sturm und Drang', 9, 10, 38, 44, 123, 143, 152, 162, 256
Suez canal, 18
Swedenborg, Swedenborgians, 98, 114, 117, 124, 275
Switzerland, 47, 276
synthesis, *see* 'Steigerung'

Tamburlaine, 19, 233–4
Tasso, 189
Thackeray, 18, 282
Tibullus, 3, 13, 203
Tischbein, W., 277
Toynbee, A., 124
Toynbee, P., 50
transmigration of souls, 102
Traumann, 155
Trendelenburg, A., 155
Trevelyan, C. H., 107
trochaic tetrameter, 39, 237, 246
Troll, W., 124
Turgenev, 131

'Urlandschaft', 'Urmensch', 'Urpflanze', 12, 110, 115–16, 213

Valéry, Paul, 128
Viëtor, K., 155
Voltaire, 3, 99, 274, 276, 279, 280
Von deutscher Art und Kunst, 58
Voss, 210
Vulpius, Christiane, 13, 203, 216, 278, 280, 281

Wagner, Heinrich, 276
Wagner, Richard, 128
War and Peace, 181–2
Weber, Carl Maria von, 18, 282

Webern, Anton, 124
Weidman, 128
Weimar, 7–11, 15, 18, 43, 45, 70, 81, 87, 102, 114, 163, 203, 276, 277, 278, 280
Weimar edition, 114
Wetzlar, 9, 275
Whyte, L. L., 124

Widman, 127
Wieland, 43, 59, 102, 275, 276
Wiese, B. von, 177
Willemer, Jakob von, 226
Willemer, Marianne von, 17, 226, 230, 236, 238, 281
Winckelmann, 99
Wolf, Hugo, 227, 231